IMPEACHMENT OF A PRESIDENT

Andrew Johnson, the Blacks, and Reconstruction

IMPEACHMENT

Andrew Johnson

OF A

the Blacks, and Reconstruction

PRESIDENT

by Hans L. Trefousse

FORDHAM UNIVERSITY PRESS • 1999

First edition published by The University of Tennessee Press, 1975.

ISBN 0-8232-1922-4 (hardcover)
ISBN 0-8232-1923-2 (paperback)
ISSN 1523-4606

Reconstructing America, no. 1

03   02   01   00   99   5   4   3   2   1

Printed in the United States of America

For Shellie

Contents

Introduction

Since the first publication of this book in 1975, no additional studies specifically dealing with the impeachment of Andrew Johnson have appeared, except Chief Justice William H. Rehnquist's *Grand Inquests: The Historical Impeachments of Justice Samuel Chase and President Andrew Johnson*, which treats it in part. But the general trend of the previous works on the subject and on Reconstruction has continued, especially with the appearance in 1988 of Eric Foner's now-standard work on Reconstruction, *Reconstruction: America's Unfinished Revolution 1863–1877*. Johnson is no longer seen as the hero who, according to previous generations, defended the Constitution, but rather as a racist resisting the reasonable attempts of Republican congressmen to safeguard the gains of the Civil War. The two biographies of Chief Justice Salmon P. Chase— John Niven's *Salmon P. Chase: A Biography* and Frederick J. Blue's *Salmon P. Chase: A Life in Politics*—also follow the modern trend, as does Brooks Simpson's study, *The Reconstruction Presidents*. For these scholars, the impeachment was simply an incident in the general Reconstruction struggle, which is now generally seen as an effort to facilitate the integration of the freed people into Southern society, a difficult task hampered by racism and Andrew Johnson.

Impeachment itself, however, has been very much in the news. At the time this book was written, it was generally believed that never again would a President be impeached for purely political reasons. The resignation of President Richard M. Nixon seemed to prove the point, as the charges against him were not of a political but of a constitutional nature. In 1998, however, this prediction was proven to have been erroneous. The impeachment of President William J. Clinton, ostensibly for perjury and obstruction of justice, but, as was widely believed, in reality for his political differences with the right wing of the Republican Party, show that impeachment for political reasons is not a discarded notion, though its effectiveness remains to be seen.

Comparisons of the Johnson and Clinton impeachments have become most instructive. In both cases, tremendous party pressure brought about the indictment; in both cases, the real cause of the impeachment did not seem to be the ostensible one, the violation of the Tenure of Office Act in 1868, perjury and obstruction of justice in 1998; and in both cases, the President's bitter opponents, Thaddeus Stevens, Benjamin F. Butler, and others in 1868, and particularly Kenneth W. Starr and his supporters in 1998, had been pursuing the President for a long time. In 1868 as in 1999, the facts of the case were pretty clear; the real question was whether the offenses charged rose to the constitutional standard of "high crimes and misdemeanors." And race was a factor then as later; Republican insistence on civil rights for African Americans clashed with Johnson's ideas of keeping the South a "white man's country," a conflict of interests leading to the trial. In 1998 Clinton enjoyed the overwhelming support of the African American community, while many of his opponents have been accused of racist ties. Then as 130 years later, the impeachment trial was a great social affair; tickets were equally sought in both instances, although modern observers can watch the trial on television.

The differences are equally clear. Andrew Johnson never committed an indictable crime; William J. Clinton has been charged with perjury. Johnson was unpopular, especially in the North, while Clinton has enjoyed widespread popular approval. In view of the impeaching party's control of two-thirds of the Senate, a great number of people were certain that Johnson would be convicted, but as the party favoring the conviction of Clinton lacks that majority, he is generally expected to be acquitted. Moreover, the position of the two Chief Justices is different. While in 1868 Salmon P. Chase was opposed to the process and threatened to end the trial if he were not given the rights of a presiding officer, William H. Rehnquist, who himself has written on impeachment, has no such problems. Nor was the public as indifferent to the process in 1868 as in 1998–99.

What the long-range effects of the latest impeachment will be is not yet clear. But it is likely that the Presidency will be weakened much as it was in 1868 and that, in case of an acquittal, the tradition of not impeaching a President for political reasons will be strengthened.

Because the terms "African American" or "black" had not yet been generally accepted when the original edition went to press, this volume contains many references to the older term, "Negro." It must be understood that this is merely due to the lapse of time, and no secondary meaning is intended.

It is to be hoped that this second Presidential impeachment— during which, in spite of the racial divide concerning approval and disapproval, both sides profess to be opposed to racism—will lead to better, not worse, relations between blacks and whites and that the resilience of American institutions even during moments of crisis will once more be affirmed.

Staten Island, New York
1999

ADDITIONAL LITERATURE

Blue, Frederick J. *Salmon P. Chase: A Life in Politics*. Kent, Ohio: Kent State University Press, 1987.

Bushnell, Eleanore. *Crimes, Follies, and Misfortunes: The Federal Impeachment Trials*. Urbana, Ill.: University of Illinois Press, 1992.

Foner, Eric. *Reconstruction: America's Unfinished Revolution 1863– 1877*. New York: Harper & Row, 1988.

Niven, John. *Salmon P. Chase: A Biography*. New York: Oxford, 1995.

Rehnquist, William H. *Grand Inquests: The Historic Impeachments of Justice Samuel Chase and President Andrew Johnson.* New York: Morrow, 1992.

Simpson, Brooks. *The Reconstruction Presidents.* Lawrence, Kans.: University Press of Kansas, 1998.

Preface

There are few Presidents of the United States whose historical image has changed more frequently than that of Andrew Johnson. In the immediate aftermath of the Civil War and Reconstruction, he was considered inept and stubborn. After some time, however, Reconstruction was no longer seen as a holy crusade, and his reputation began to improve. The emphasis was on reconciliation between North and South. The Negroes' rights were forgotten, and even the Ku Klux Klan seemed romantic in retrospect. Thus the determined opponent of black suffrage came into his own. By the 1920s, Johnson had become a great hero who had courageously defended the Constitution against unprincipled radicals. But as circumstances changed again and racial problems were once more weighing upon America's conscience, the seventeenth President's achievements began to appear more questionable. Perhaps he had not been so admirable after all; perhaps his stubborn resistance to radical demands for black suffrage merited disapprobation rather than praise. His portrait was tarnished a second time. Not only was he now labeled a racist, but an inept politician as well.

In the various assessments of the controversial Unionist from Tennessee, his dramatic impeachment and trial have generally been considered of great significance. One of the best-known works to rehabilitate the President was David Miller DeWitt's *The Impeachment and Trial of Andrew Johnson*, published in 1903. Fifty-seven years later Milton Lomask entitled his sympathetic study *Andrew Johnson: President on Trial*. Articles in learned and popular magazines have dealt so exhaustively with the subject that Eric L. McKitrick has called it "one of the best ventilated episodes in history."

Because of the renewed interest in removing public officials from office in the 1970s, impeachment has once more attracted the attention of scholars. In a book dealing with all the cases under the Constitution, Irving Brant has argued that, in general, conviction could only be obtained for indictable offenses. Raoul Berger, in his *Impeachment: The Constitutional Problems*, has taken the exact opposite view. And Michael Les Benedict, in a new treatment of the Johnson case, has sought to show that the President merited his fate and should have been convicted.

The meticulous accounts which have been written about the great inquest have generally concentrated on the mechanics of the process—the preparations, the trial, and the acquittal. Benedict's work is an exception, but its unique approach to the trial makes additional research inevitable. What remains to be investigated further is the relationship of the impeachment to the failure of Reconstruction, the causes of the failure to convict, and the consequences of the acquittal. Why was Andrew Johnson impeached in the first place? Was it not true that he had been shackled successfully by a powerful majority, that his term had only one more year to run, and that he seemed thoroughly discredited? Was he not believed to be so stubborn and ineffective that the Republican party might well have carried out its program without him and disregarded his efforts at obstruction?

Considering the answers to these and related questions, it must be remembered that Johnson was a Southerner, born in poverty and reared with most of the prejudices of his class and section. Like many of his neighbors in Tennessee, he was a Unionist. Anxious to preserve "the Constitution as it is and the Union as it was," in 1861 he was one of the sponsors of the Johnson-Crittenden resolutions strictly limiting national war aims. The domestic institutions of the states were not to be disturbed. Wartime developments brought about the abolition of slavery, but he did not consider emancipation a reason to change his fundamental views of the

Constitution and Union. When it is recalled that he remained determined to preserve the traditional social order of his section with its insistence on white supremacy, his actions become more readily intelligible.

Honest, stubborn, and certain of the justice of his cause, Johnson was not the man to flinch from the implications of decisions which might interfere temporarily with his long-range aims. Often alienating potential allies, he probably could have achieved more had he cooperated with moderate Republicans. In part, he might even have realized his white supremacist aims. But once he had made his decision, once he had refused to come to terms with the moderates, his subsequent actions were not illogical. His policy may not have been the most intelligent—he was no political genius—but it was not wholly unsuccessful.

Johnson's character, too, bears reexamination. Was he, after all, really so rash? Did he, in fact, speak without thinking beforehand? To be sure, he often delivered ill-advised harangues, and he frequently made mistakes. He failed to win renomination in 1868 and could not prevent radical Reconstruction. Nevertheless, he was also capable of careful planning, and the subsequent failure of the effort to reform the South casts serious doubts on at least some of these suppositions. In addition, the deposition of the diary of Benjamin B. French, the commissioner of public buildings in Washington, at the Library of Congress, sheds some new light on the President's habits and motives. It is possible that Andrew Johnson, in retarding radical Reconstruction, played a more fateful role in Amerian history than has generally been realized. This study is an attempt to discover that role.

ACKNOWLEDGMENTS

My thanks are due first to my colleagues, Professors Robert A. East and Ari Hoogenboom, who freely gave of their time and made valuable suggestions. Harold M. Hyman of Rice University also read the entire manuscript and offered constructive criticism. Professors John H. and LaWanda Cox of the City University of New York and John Niven of the Claremont Graduate School were always helpful, while Dr. Robert Horowitz and Dr. Lawrence Grossman of the Graduate Center of City University of New York, as well as Mrs. Francene Moskowitz of the same institution, pointed out some important material I might otherwise have missed. In addition, I should like to express my gratitude to the librarians of the various depositories I visited, especially at Brooklyn College, the Graduate Center of the City University of New York, the Manuscript Division of the Library of Congress, Harvard, Princeton, Columbia, Duke, and the University of North Carolina, as well as at the New York Historical Society and the Historical Society of Pennsylvania. Finally, my wife and my son not only helped with the editing, but kept me from many errors. They know how grateful I am for their patience.

IMPEACHMENT OF A PRESIDENT

Andrew Johnson, the Blacks, and Reconstruction

One.

Andrew Johnson and Reconstruction

Andrew Johnson inherited problems of staggering proportions when he became President of the United States. Four
years of Civil War had left vast areas of the South physically dev-
astated. Railroads had been torn up, cities leveled, villages destroyed, and farms desolated. In most Southern states, government
had come to a standstill after the dispersal of the Confederate legislatures. With Southern leaders in exile or disgrace, courts and
other governmental functions were in abeyance.

But the most pressing problem was that of the freed slaves. Almost four million human beings had been liberated—men, women,
and children who in some manner had to be given a new place in
society. Emancipation was the most striking result of the war, but it
had also created a host of new difficulties. What was to be the
position of the freedmen in America? Were they to be free in fact
as well as in name; were they to enjoy the rights of citizens; or
were they to be released from slavery merely to become serfs of
their former masters?

The key to many of these problems was the question of suffrage.
If the Southern states were to be readmitted to their former prerogatives within the Union without far-reaching changes, the old
ruling classes—the great planters and their allies—would soon be
back in control. Politically they would make common cause with
the Northern Democrats, and, because of the lapse of the three-
fifths compromise, after 1870 the South would have greater strength
in Congress than ever before. The Negroes' place under such circumstances would be a strictly subordinate one. Only if suffrage

were to be extended to the blacks was there a chance that freedmen's civil rights would also be protected. Negroes themselves would then be able to safeguard their privileges, and a viable Republican organization might be established in the South. However, despite the evident advantage of impartial suffrage to themselves, many Northerners, even those favoring civil rights for the emancipated slaves, were reluctant to permit them to vote.

Abraham Lincoln had struggled with most of these problems before his assassination. He had sought to reanimate governments in various Southern states, and he had signed a Freedmen's Bureau Bill to help freedmen and refugees in the desolated region. In his last public speech he had even called for limited Negro suffrage. But when Lincoln died, hostilities had not yet completely ended, so that most of his measures must be regarded as wartime expedients.[1] It is impossible to say what he might have done in times of peace.

Andrew Johnson thought he knew the answer. Had not the martyred President, like himself, been a man of the people? Had he not believed in a speedy restoration of state governments? Had he not repeatedly stated that no state could legally secede, so that all the states were still in the Union? Johnson believed he understood his predecessor. If Congress objected to presidential policies, Johnson knew that Lincoln, too, had had trouble with the radicals.[2] Unlike the Great Emancipator, however, Johnson was not really in sympathy with any of the radicals' aims. He overlooked the fact that Lincoln's measures had been wartime improvisations.

Johnson's misreading of Lincoln's intentions was to cause many of his troubles as President, for unlike Lincoln, Johnson had always been a Jacksonian Democrat: "The Last Jacksonian," as Kenneth M. Stampp has called him.[3] And Andrew Johnson, like Andrew Jackson, conceived of an America ruled by whites. Democracy was to him a precious good, a good to be protected, preserved, and extended under the Constitution. But as the Constitution had been written by white men, he believed that its benefits were reserved for whites.

Before the war Johnson himself had owned slaves. He had defended the peculiar institution in Congress, was convinced of the inferiority of the black race, and in 1860 had voted for John C. Breckinridge and a Federal Slave Code for the territories. Even when he broke with his associates on the question of secession, he had been careful to state, "In most I shall say on this occasion . . . , I shall not differ very markedly from my southern friends."[4] During the war, it is true, he had promised to become a Moses to lead the Negroes out of bondage,[5] but his fundamental convictions never changed. As late as 1865 he told Senator John Conness of California that he had never been opposed to slavery for the blacks, that Negroes were happiest in that condition—or a similar one— and that white men alone must manage the South.[6] In 1866 he remarked to Benjamin B. French, the commissioner of public buildings, that everyone had to admit that the white race was superior to the black. Conceding that the whites must do their best to bring the blacks up to their present level, he still thought that his own race would, in the meantime, make such progress that the relative position of the two races would remain the same in the end.[7]

Unlike many large plantation owners' views, his notions of racial superiority were tinged with animosity. According to Colonel William G. Moore, his private secretary, the President at times "exhibited a morbid distress and feeling against negroes." In the summer of 1865 he became incensed at the presence of black troops in Tennessee.[8] In February 1867 he denounced the Reconstruction Bill as a measure to tread the suffering people of the South under foot "to protect niggers,"[9] and in early 1868 he expressed annoyance at seeing black instead of white laborers on the White House grounds.[10] Frederick Douglass was not mistaken when, on Inauguration Day in 1865, he thought he detected in Johnson a real aversion to the Negro race.[11]

This biased attitude of the President of the United States made it impossible for Johnson to sympathize in any way with policies furthering racial equality. Whether some of the Republicans favored Negro suffrage merely for political reasons, or whether they really believed in integrating the blacks into American political life, made very little difference at the time. The radicals were the chief proponents of progress for the freed blacks. Had Lincoln been alive, they might have been able to realize some of their plans because he had not really been opposed to many of their final aims. Not only had Lincoln detested slavery—"if slavery is not wrong, nothing is wrong," he said—but he had gradually been able to overcome his confining upbringing and background so that he could, toward the end of his life, advocate at least limited enfranchisement of the blacks.[12] During the war, speaking of the radicals' war aims, Lincoln declared that, in the end, he would have to side with them. They were "utterly lawless—the unhandiest devils to deal with," he remarked, but their faces were "set Zionwards."[13]

Johnson agreed that the radicals were devils, but he did not think they were facing Zionwards. As time went on he believed them devils, pure and simple. As he saw it, they were destroying the Constitution by seeking to impose Negro suffrage upon the South. Did not the Constitution leave the power to determine suffrage qualifications to the states? The basic law was in danger, and he thought it was the task of the President to save it. Whatever temporary vicissitudes he might encounter, he was certain that history and his country would ultimately recognize the purity of his intentions.[14]

For the cause of racial justice, it was a great misfortune that the President of the United States should have felt this way just at that time. Immediately after the war, because of the eclipse of the Southern ruling class, it would have been comparatively simple to enfranchise at least some of the Negroes in the former Confederacy. But if steps were to be taken to give the vote even to selected freedmen, rapid action was necessary. Once the "rebels" had recovered their right to vote, it would be increasingly difficult to advance the blacks. Speed was of the essence: ". . . a *little* vigor now would be worth more than *much* hereafter," the Virginia Unionist John C. Underwood pointed out on April 28, 1865.[15] But the President had different ideas.

To achieve his aims of maintaining the traditional subordination of the blacks, Johnson might have compromised with the moderate Republicans in Congress and continued within the party organization. He might thus have neutralized the radicals and prevented full integration of the Negroes by endorsing mere half measures. Conceivably, he might thus have secured his own renomination and retained his influence in national councils.

Working within the regular organization, however, whether Democratic or Republican, was not Johnson's way. In 1860 he had broken with his associates on the secession question; he was ready to do so again on Reconstruction. In view of the fact that the moderates were not at all hostile to him, this determination may not have been the most judicious. It probably brought about greater cooperation between them and the radicals and led to some of the very measures he wanted to avoid. Nevertheless, not believing in even the minimum concessions to black equality advocated by the moderates, he could not yield—at least not in the beginning. Once his decision had been made, the methods he used were not unreasonable, and to a surprising extent, whether consciously planned or not, they were not wholly unsuccessful.

In attempting to impose his views on a reluctant Congress, the President at first acted with great circumspection. On the day after his accession to the presidency, some of his former colleagues on the radical Joint Committee on the Conduct of the War came to call on him. He was affable. Benjamin F. Wade, the chairman, told him that the committee had faith in him; there would be "no trouble now in running the government." Johnson expressed his thanks. "You can judge my policy by the past . . . ," he told his visitors. "I hold this: Robbery is a crime, rape is a crime; murder is a crime, and *crime* must be punished. . . . Treason must be made infamous and traitors must be impoverished." The statesmen left, more enthusiastic than ever about their host.[16] Their good opinion of the President did not change even during subsequent interviews, when he seemed more determined to exact retribution from leading Confederates than they were themselves.[17]

The question of punishing leading Confederates, however, was not really a crucial matter. Who was going to govern the South, and what was going to be done with the freedmen—these were the issues confronting the nation. If the blacks were not given the vote, Democrats would undoubtedly capture every single Southern state. By combining with their counterparts in the North, they would soon regain the majority they had lost in 1861.

It was not expected that the Republican party would willingly permit this development. Not only the radicals, but also the moderates would hesitate before committing political suicide. Johnson, who must have been aware of this difficulty, was at first careful not to reveal his plans in full. On April 18, addressing a group of visitors from Illinois, he delivered a speech of considerable length. He committed himself to nothing specific, but, as the conservative Orville H. Browning put it, "indicated a radical policy." When he heard that General William T. Sherman had granted easy terms of surrender to the beaten Confederates, the President delighted the radicals by vehemently denouncing and countermanding the convention. A group of Indianians heard him agree with Governor Oliver P. Morton's views on the necessity of relying upon Southern loyalists. "May God bless you for your noble utterances to the Delegations which have waited upon you. They came to Missouri Radicals as a new life to the almost dying," Charles D. Drake, the border state's radical leader, wrote to him.[18]

Other leading radicals were equally misled. After talking to Johnson, Henry Winter Davis, the Maryland unconditional Unionist, was certain that the new President was more amenable to radical ideas than Lincoln. Charles Sumner, who had come to see Johnson in order to demonstrate the necessity of black suffrage, left perfectly satisfied. The President had been so astute as to lead him to believe he favored the measure. And the chief justice, who was about to take a trip to the South, after an interview "almost hoped" Johnson would be favorably disposed to the enfranchisement of the freedmen. Carl Schurz shared these misconceptions.[19]

It has often been stated that Johnson soon experienced a change of mind. In reality, there is no evidence that he had ever sympathized with the radicals' view of Reconstruction. He agreed with them about the necessity to punish the leading insurgents, and he wanted the governing power kept in the hands of loyalists, but he never for a moment doubted the proposition that the states had not seceded. And he never favored Negro suffrage on a large scale.

From the President's point of view, his moves were not unreasonable. By not offending potential critics upon his accession, he averted a demand for an immediate recall of Congress. The radicals themselves had advised him against a special session,[20] and he was in no hurry to disabuse them of their notions. They would be demanding the opposite course soon enough.

When Johnson finally proceeded to implement his own plan of Reconstruction, the radicals were utterly confounded. To be sure, they had had a warning when the administration recognized the Restored Government of Virginia although it was based on white suffrage. But it was not until May 29, when he issued his Proclamation of Amnesty and appointed a provisional governor for North Carolina, that Johnson's intentions became obvious. By urging the white electorate to call a convention, he had disregarded demands for black suffrage. "Is it possible to devise any plan to arrest the government in its ruinous career?" Thaddeus Stevens asked Sumner, and Benjamin Loan of Missouri characterized the North Carolina proclamation as being "in direct opposition to the views of the radical Union party."[21] Something had evidently gone wrong.

Nevertheless, Johnson's opponents were still hoping that he might change his mind. "I would entreat you to go to Washington as soon as you conveniently can," Carl Schurz wrote to Sumner. "The President's opinions are quite unsettled on the most vital points." To Johnson himself, Schurz sent a letter suggesting that the President solve the Negro suffrage issue in South Carolina by ruling that all male inhabitants had the right to vote because the old state constitution contained property qualifications. George S. Boutwell also still thought the North Carolina proclamation might prove an exception.[22] Johnson might yet realize the implications of his policy.

Johnson had no intention whatever of reconsidering his policies of white Reconstruction. Proclamations similar to those issued for

North Carolina followed in short order for other states, and some of the radicals were beginning to lose patience.[23] But the administration still held out hope. James Harlan, secretary of the interior, first assured Congressman Elihu B. Washburne of Illinois that Johnson was "as inflexibly right on all the main points in the great struggle as the most ardent could desire." Then, in a letter to Sumner, Harlan asserted that he did not think the President would make an issue with Congress about Negro suffrage.[24] Attorney General James Speed insisted that he himself favored enfranchising the freedmen,[25] and Secretary of the Navy Gideon Welles also sought to dispel Sumner's fears. "Our friends," he wrote, "entertain widely differing views of the question of suffrage in the rebel States." Admitting that he did not know whether these differences could be reconciled, Welles nevertheless sought to protect his chief. "I do not think there is on the part of the President or of his advisers any opposition to the most liberal extension of the election franchise," he asserted. Sumner politely thanked Welles, but warned that the administration's policy would surely lead to disaster. Could not the cabinet "save" Johnson and thus "save the country?"[25]

The President's own efforts to make his policies palatable to the North are well known. In an oft-quoted letter to Governor William Sharkey of Mississippi, on August 15 he suggested that the state extend the franchise to "all persons of color" who owned real estate valued at not less than two hundred and fifty dollars. Such a measure "would completely disarm the adversary," he explained. Moreover, it could be "done with perfect safety." "And as a consequence," he concluded, "the radicals, who are wild upon negro franchise, will be completely foiled in their attempts to keep the Southern States from renewing their relations to the Union. . . ."[26]

The governor failed to carry out Johnson's suggestions, but the President repeated the idea, this time for public consumption, in an interview with a New Orleans journalist. Advising Louisiana to emulate Massachusetts, he suggested literacy qualifications for blacks and whites alike. If a Negro can read the Constitution, give him the vote, he said. "There are not 500 in Louisiana who can answer that test; but it will be doing justice to all and stop this Northern clamor." Reports were circulated that the President had expressed himself in favor of Negro suffrage, at least of a limited type, but had expressed doubts about his powers to implement it.[27] And as late as October 1865 he still addressed a black regiment in such friendly terms that the Chicago *Tribune* concluded he had completely disproved Copperhead claims that he considered the United States a white man's country.[28]

While avoiding a final break with members of the Republican party, the President did not sacrifice any essentials in his plan to restore the Union almost to what it had been before the war. In the first place, despite all talk of punishing traitors, he inaugurated an extremely liberal policy of pardoning leading ex-Confederates. In accordance with his Proclamation of Amnesty, there were fourteen exempted classes—high Confederate officials, those who had violated their oath of allegiance, and all those owning property worth more than twenty thousand dollars, among others. But he had reserved his right of issuing individual pardons, and there were few applicants to whom he refused them.[29]

There has been much speculation about the motives for Johnson's leniency. His Southern origins and his desire to win fame in the section of his birth, his secret admiration for the Southern aristocracy that had always treated him with condescension, if not contempt, and the exhilaration of proving to those who looked down upon him that he was a high-minded person—all these may well have influenced his thinking. Nevertheless, it is also possible he knew that the help of former Confederates was sorely needed if the South was to be restored in such a way as to preserve the Union "as it was." Only experienced Southern leaders could successfully counter radical plans for the freedmen's elevation. As a result, the old elite in the Southern states, the men who had previously resigned themselves to a life of retirement, reappeared in politics.

The Southerners were delighted. Although they had originally regarded Johnson's accession with apprehension, his policies soon reassured them,[30] and in various areas of the former Confederacy they once more ruled supreme. Even *The New York Times*, generally friendly to the President, deplored this situation. "This misplaced leniency is making the leading rebels . . . , who are daily receiving pardons, still more disloyal than before," it reported.[31] It was therefore not surprising that radical members of Congress received bitter accounts from Southern correspondents. "To leave the negro to be dealt with by those whose prejudices are of the most bitter character against him, will be barbarous," wrote one of Stevens' informants. "Whatever genuine Union sentiment was forming and would in time have grown up, has been checked by Mr. Johnson's course. . . . He is now the favorite of all the disaffected elements here."[32] But the President was determined and thus persisted.

Johnson did not confine himself to inaugurating new governments based on white suffrage. The basic problem of reconstructing the South was one of landholding. Were the freedmen to be allowed a modicum of personal and real property? Would some sort of independent farming class be established in place of the former slaves? Leading Northern radicals believed this solution to be just and equitable; conservatives, on the other hand, regarded it with horror. Because of the vicissitudes of war, de facto black landholding had been established in such areas as the Sea Islands off South Carolina and the coastal strip of abandoned plantations set aside by General Sherman for the exclusive occupancy of the freedmen. Both areas were nuclei which could serve as models for future black landownership.[33] The Freedmen's Bureau, established to assist the former slaves, lent its support to the idea. General O. O. Howard, the commissioner in charge of the bureau, in July had prepared a circular directing that land be set aside for refugees and freedmen.[34]

But such policies directly conflicted with the President's views of Reconstruction. If he wanted to maintain the dominance of the white race, Johnson could not permit the transfer of land to the freedmen. Undoubtedly thinking that blacks ought to labor for their former masters, when Johnson began to issue pardons he decided that these included the restoration of landed property.

Consequently, he directed Howard to rescind his former circular and issue a new one (September 12, 1865), which in effect returned abandoned lands to former Confederates. Even plantations which had already been worked by Negroes were given back to their former owners.[35]

In a moving passage, Commissioner Howard recorded the reaction of the blacks to the publication of this edict. While Howard himself still had hopes that the President might be induced to change his mind, the freedmen were losing hope. Gathered in a large hall on Edisto Island, they listened politely to the general. "Nobody knows the trouble I feel—nobody knows but Jesus," sang one old lady.[36] Andrew Johnson's ideas were beginning to have an effect.

Just as Johnson used his executive powers to extend pardons and restore land to Southerners, so too, as early as July 1865, he utilized patronage to undermine the radicals' position. Despite warnings to reappoint Republican incumbents in Baltimore, he nominated a conservative postmaster and collector. The President's plans would have powerful supporters in the individual states.[37]

That Johnson had no vital interest in protecting even the most elementary rights of the freedmen was revealed when he upheld Governor Sharkey's attempt to reactivate the Mississippi militia. The excuse for this action was disorder in the state. However, outrages against freedmen caused the disturbances, and General Henry W. Slocum sought to countermand the governor's order. Despite the warnings of Carl Schurz, Johnson overruled the general.[38]

The results of Johnson's policies soon became evident. Conservatives of all types dominated the first postwar conventions in the South. Categorically refusing to enfranchise even the most qualified blacks, they proceeded to reestablish the old order as much as possible. Mississippi refused to ratify the Thirteenth Amendment. South Carolina failed to repeal the Confederate debt. And the conventions enacted black codes, some of which virtually reduced freedmen to serfdom. Although it was evident that Congress was in no mood to accept the senators and representatives chosen by such assemblies and states—Confederate brigadiers, congressmen, and even the Vice President of the defunct government were elected—Andrew Johnson decided to endorse fully the new governments. Evidently he believed his policy had succeeded.[39]

The President's first annual message was a capable state paper. Written by George Bancroft, the eminent historian, the document had grace and force, but the ideas were Johnson's. "I found the States suffering from the effects of a civil war," he began. "Whether the territory within the limits of these States should be held as a conquered territory, under military authority emanating from the President as the head of the Army, was the first question that presented itself for decision." Congratulating himself on having rejected such a policy, he took pride in having reanimated the states and having reestablished government in the South. Then came the crux of his argument concerning the blacks. "The relations of the General Government toward the 4,000,000 inhabitants whom the war has called into freedom have engaged my most serious consideration," he continued. "On the propriety of attempting to make the freedmen electors by the proclamation of the Executive, I took for my counsel the Constitution itself." The Constitution clearly left up to the individual states the right to decide on suffrage qualifications. He had no power to enfranchise anybody. Eventually, he conceded, the freedmen, "if they show patience and manly virtues, will sooner obtain a participation in the elective franchise through the States than through the General Government, even if it had the power to interfere." The Negroes were likely to "receive the kindest usage from some of those on whom they have heretofore most closely depended."[40]

The President's attitude toward the Freedmen's Bureau showed that his solicitude for the Negroes was very limited. When the organization had first been established, he had led General Howard to believe in his friendship. As time went on, however, he became increasingly hostile to the agency.[41] And when, early in 1866, Senator Lyman Trumbull perfected a new Freedmen's Bureau Bill, Johnson determined to veto it.

It was evident that a veto of the Freedmen's Bureau Bill would alienate the influential senator from Illinois, who was chairman of the Senate's Judiciary Committee. Since the President had already been bitterly attacked by the radicals, an argument could be made for the wisdom of seeking to retain the support of moderates like Trumbull. The senator had been trying sincerely to prevent a rift with the administration.[42] Consequently, members of the cabinet, especially Stanton, Harlan, and Speed, expressed misgivings about the President's decision, and even Welles conceded that Trumbull was not a radical.[43] But Johnson's mind was made up; he was not going to approve the bill. Even when William H. Seward, who drafted the veto message, suggested a mild and inoffensive tone, the President disregarded his advice.[44] If white supremacy was to be preserved, the bill must be vetoed, and a veto might be sustained by appealing to racial prejudice.

Johnson clearly expressed his racial feelings at this time in an interview with a delegation of blacks led by Frederick Douglass, who had come to advocate Negro suffrage. Although Douglass told him very plainly that Johnson had it in his power to "save or destroy" the entire black race by giving it the right of suffrage, the President was unimpressed. Asserting that he was fully aware that slaves had looked down on poor whites, Johnson replied that the abolition of slavery had not been one of the objectives of the war. Racial war must be prevented, and the states had the right to determine their own laws of suffrage. Emigration, he suggested, was one of the ways for the Negro to escape harsh treatment in the South.[45]

The interview ended on an acrimonious note. According to Philip Ripley, a reporter for the New York *World*, the President turned to his secretary after the group left. "Those d—d sons of b—s thought they had me in a trap," he said. "I know that d—d Douglass; he's just like any nigger, & he would sooner cut a white man's throat than not."[46] Whether he really expressed himself in these harsh words cannot be determined. It is not impossible, however, for his sentiments were certainly in keeping with their tenor.

The veto message that followed was a forceful one. Not even bothering to express his appreciation of the workings of the existing Freedmen's Bureau, as he had been advised to do, Johnson roundly condemned the proposed measure as unconstitutional, impolitic, and unwise. The government had no powers to care for indigents of any race, he asserted. If the freedmen would but labor faithfully, they would soon overcome their problems. At any rate, Congress ought not to legislate for ten states which were unrepresented. The Republicans attempted to pass the bill over his veto, but the necessary votes were not forthcoming.[47]

The President had defied his opponents. He made his defiance explicit two days after the veto when he virtually called Senator Sumner and Congressman Stevens traitors. The South was either going to be reconstructed according to his ideas, or it would not be reconstructed at all. At least he would do his best to oppose solutions other than his own. He himself might be hurt in the process, but eventually his philosophy would prevail. "I am going through on this line," he said to Orville Browning, to whom he explained his plan on January 2, 1866.[48] To his private secretary he put it even more concisely. "Sir, I am right," he maintained. "I know I am right and I am damned if I do not adhere to it."[49] His opponents would have to take extraordinary measures to deal with him. Some were even beginning to mention impeachment.[50]

Two.

The Radicals and Reconstruction

Johnson's policies of white supremacy might well have led to immediate success. A majority of his countrymen shared his racial prejudices, he was the leader of the dominant political party, and he had at his disposal all the powers of high office. But the radical Republicans stood in his way. In sheer determination, they were more than a match for him. His own intransigence assured them, at least temporarily, of support from the moderates, and their visions of a perfect America were very different from his. Circumstances had made them the country's vanguard for racial justice, and had their efforts to reconstruct Southern society met with success, they might have brought about a lasting adjustment of relations between the races. All Americans, white and black, would have been the winners.

As a group, the radicals did not possess any firm organization. On one occasion a Republican could be a radical, but under altered circumstances he could become a moderate, only to rejoin the radicals later. As long as he sympathized with the radical program at any given time, he was a radical, no matter what his politics earlier or later. The program was very simple. Based on a vision of a free-enterprise America resting upon the foundations of private property and small landholdings, it envisaged the extirpation of the last remnants of slavery and the plantation system in the South. This goal entailed the elevation of the blacks, even their eventual enfranchisement and integration into society. For its time, it was very advanced.

Much has been written about the motivation of the proponents of radical policies. It is probable that some Republican politicians were chiefly interested in safeguarding the future of their party in the South, but it is equally certain that there were others who honestly sought to do justice to the freedmen. In the minds of many there was no real difference between the goal of elevating the blacks and the protection of the Republican party. Speaking in favor of his Reconstruction Bill in 1867, Thaddeus Stevens admitted as much:

> Do you avow the party purpose? exclaims some horror stricken demagogue. I do. For I believe, on my conscience, that on the continued ascendency of that party depends the safety of this great nation. If impartial suffrage is excluded in the rebel States then every one of them is sure to send a solid rebel representative delegation to Congress, and cast a solid rebel electoral vote. . . . For these, among other reasons, I am for negro suffrage in every rebel State.[1]

In the last analysis, he was not wrong. And the motivation made little difference. As William R. Brock has pointed out, the goal was what counted.[2]

In seeking to impose an open society upon the South, the radicals were not primarily vindictive. "I have no desire whatever to say any harsh things of that portion of the country," said Henry Wilson, speaking of the South while introducing a bill to protect the freedmen, "nor of the men who have been engaged in the rebellion. I do not ask their property or their blood; I do not wish to disgrace or degrade them, but I do not wish that they shall be permitted to disgrace, degrade, or oppress anybody else."[3] Benjamin F. Wade also disclaimed any vengeful motives. "I am not the advocate of proceeding against these rebel criminal States with any greater rigor than is necessary to procure entire security for ourselves—indemnity for the past, if you please, and security for the future," he asserted in December 1866. "I for one, will seek nothing more. I will be content with nothing less."[4] And Carl Schurz put it even more succinctly:

> You want magnanimity to a beaten foe. We offer it to you. We demand no blood, no persecution, no revenge. We only insist that

when the Republic distributes the charitable gift of pardon and grace, the safety and rights of her faithful children are entitled to the first consideration. We are ready to grasp the hand of the South. We only want to ascertain whether the blood of our slaughtered friends is already dried on it.[5]

During the war Charles Sumner had successfully opposed retaliatory measures to stop the mistreatment of prisoners of war and had sought to prevent the display in the Capitol of pictures of victory in battle over fellow citizens. After Appomattox, when Johnson was speaking of hanging leading rebels, the senator, still opposed to unnecessary cruelty, favored exiling the defeated Southern statesmen instead.[6] Horace Greeley was known for his insistence upon amnesty and finally went bail for Jefferson Davis.[7] Gerrit Smith consistently stressed magnanimity, while other radicals interceded for individual Southerners held in various places of confinement.[8] If Thaddeus Stevens was more vengeful than others, even he advocated the abolition of the death penalty.[9]

The radicals did not use their demands for justice for the freedmen only as a cloak for certain economic objectives. In 1930, Howard K. Beale asserted that many ultras emphasized Reconstruction questions merely to make their economic programs palatable. They were allegedly more interested in contraction of the currency, high tariffs, and national banking policies than in black suffrage.[10] But since they did not agree on economic measures, these charges cannot be maintained. Among others, Chandler, Wade, and Stevens favored high tariffs; Sumner, Julian, and Chase sympathized with free trade or low rates. Sumner, Julian, and Chandler believed in the importance of hard money, while Stevens, Wade, and Butler advocated inflation.[11] The only economic principles held in common by the radicals were a belief in an open economy based on free enterprise and individual initiative. The details were subjects of great controversy among them, and on such matters as homesteads and debtor relief, Johnson agreed more with the radicals than with some of his political allies.[12]

In spite of the great differences between the President and the radicals, especially in later years, most of them were loath to break with him. Seeking for months to achieve some modus vivendi, they were slow to realize how determined Johnson really was. In June 1865, when the President's program was just getting under way, several party leaders tried to warn him. Pointing out that the North Carolina proclamation was fraught with danger, Carl Schurz suggested changes be made in dealing with other states.[13] On June 21, Robert Dale Owen, the famous socialist's son, sent the President a nineteen-page letter. If the Negroes were not enfranchised, he pointed out, Southerners would have more political power than the people of the North, something no democratic government could afford. Did not the obligation to guarantee republican government and the power to grant pardons also imply the right to make pardons contingent upon certain conditions? And should not these conditions include impartial suffrage regardless of color or race?[14] Even Thaddeus Stevens, who had never been an admirer of Johnson, ventured to offer advice. None of his friends, he pointed out, approved of the President's policy. If carried out it would certainly destroy the Republican party and ruin the country. Could not the President await the meeting of Congress and, in the meantime, establish military governments in the South?[15]

Warnings continued during the summer and fall. In September 1865, Joseph Medill of the Chicago *Tribune* pointed out that Northerners would no longer tolerate any sort of vassalage to the Southern aristocracy. "Can you afford to quarrel with these two millions of voters?" he asked the President. "Can you afford to *Tylerize* your party?"[16] Others cautioned Johnson not to let the experiment of reconciliation go too far. "Your motives are no doubt excellent," wrote one correspondent. "Perhaps you wish to imitate the kindness of your lamented predecessor. Sir, but Providence has called you to power for a different purpose, & you cannot be like him."[17]

Some radicals attempted to sway the President in personal interviews. Late in June, Wade and Davis came to Washington. In a series of meetings Wade pressed his views upon Johnson. Suggesting the appointment of Ben Butler to the cabinet, he was not entirely discouraged with the outlook. Although the senator no longer trusted the President, Johnson had not specifically rejected the proffered advice.[18] Henry Wilson and other senators visited him in September,[19] and Charles Sumner, on the whole well disposed, came to the White House in December shortly before Congress met. His visit was a disaster. As he put it, much that he heard was "painful, from its prejudice, ignorance, and perversity." That the President inadvertently used the senator's hat as a spittoon did not help matters.[20] Nevertheless, even Sumner's experience did not wholly discourage all radicals. As late as December 29, Boutwell still expressed hope that a compromise might be worked out.[21]

The reluctance of the radicals to bring about an open break with Johnson was due to many factors. They found it hard to give up all hope after the brilliant victories of the spring of 1865. "You have received the North Carolina Proclamation," Sumner wrote to Wade on June 9. "If that is followed we have before us controversy and an agony of strife. How easy it was to be right."[22] Thaddeus Stevens expressed similar sentiments when he queried whether there was any way to arrest the course of events.[23] If Congress were to take hold of Reconstruction, presidential cooperation, at least to some degree, would be highly desirable.

There were also elections to be won. The President's patronage was an important consideration, and the Democrats were making approaches to him. In the fall campaign it was preferable to avoid an open break with Johnson, and in state after state efforts were made to hide the increasing differences between the President and many Republicans.[24]

Even had the radicals been willing to disregard these factors, they knew that in attempting to challenge the President they would encounter severe problems. In the winter of 1865–66 they constituted only a minority of the party. The great majority of Congressional Republicans were even more reluctant to break with the President than the ultras, and while these moderates were seeking a minimum of guarantees for the freedmen in the South, they were not primarily interested in racial questions. In addition, they disliked many of the radical leaders. Sumner, especially, was unpopular with his colleagues; his haughty demeanor, scholarly ostentation, and intellectual pretentiousness irked many.[25] Ben Wade had offended many senators by his immoderate remarks during three terms in Congress, even before his ill-considered co-sponsorship of the Wade-Davis Manifesto.[26] Boutwell was thought a narrow partisan and Butler a dangerous firebrand.[27] Thaddeus Stevens, while respected, was never particularly popular in the House of Representatives.[28]

That the moderates were anxious for peace is not surprising. Four years of war, emancipation, and attempted confiscation had taxed the nation heavily; burgeoning industries needed Congressional attention; and the financial system was in disarray. Under these circumstances an open break with the President seemed unappealing to a majority of the party. "Sumner and Boutwell and . . . some foolish men among us . . . seem to be anxious to make a rupture with Johnson," Congressman James A. Garfield wrote to his friend Burke Hinsdale on December 11, 1865. "I think we should assume that he is with us, treat him kindly . . . leaving him to make the break."[29] John Sherman delivered speeches calling for unity between President and Congress; William M. Stewart conferred with Johnson prior to the Freedmen's Bureau Bill veto, seeking to avoid a break; Trumbull tried to act as peacemaker between the two branches of government; and William P. Fessenden and James W. Grimes made it clear that they detested the radical leadership.[30] But even they went along with Congress' refusal to admit the representatives and senators from the reconstructed states and the establishment of a Joint Committee on Reconstruction to deal with the problem.[31] If the President refused the most elementary safeguards for the Republican party, they might overcome their distrust and support an antiexecutive policy. Reconstruction would be delayed in the meantime, but from the President's point of view this would not necessarily be a calamity. Much as he favored speedy restoration of the seceded states, in the long run he might consider delay preferable to Congressional interference and Negro suffrage.

The most difficult problem for the radicals was the persistent prejudice against blacks, not only in the South, but also in the North. Some of the ultras themselves were not free from anti-Negro sentiments, but, knowing these notions to be prejudices, they sought to counteract them.[32] Less committed Northerners gave free rein to their bias. Either by law or custom, blacks were deprived of civil and political rights. Segregation of the races in schools, public conveyances, inns, and places of entertainment was the rule. Social contacts were frowned upon, and the army maintained black units commanded by whites. In 1865 the voters in Connecticut, Wisconsin, and Minnesota defeated propositions for Negro suffrage; those in Michigan, Ohio, and Kansas followed in subsequent years.[33] Widespread commitment to white supremacy was a fact of life in nineteenth-century America.

The evidence for the persistence of virulent bias during these years was overwhelming, and the radicals knew it. As one of his correspondents wrote to Chase in June 1864: "Let me say that there has been a change in public opinion, but on negro social equality there has been none. Hatred to rebels has made thousands eager to abolish slavery, but no one is less prejudiced against negro social equality."[34] Fully aware of the problem, the chief justice, in February 1865, confided to Francis Lieber that those who held the suffrage already would require a great deal of education before they shared it with those "whom they regard as an inferior class."[35]

The prejudice did not disappear after the war. In April 1865 the Vermont abolitionist, J. W. Phelps, suggested to Sumner that blacks be employed as troops to suppress the slave trade in Africa. "But," he warned, "I am entirely convinced that we shall be plagued as long as we try to keep them among us."[36] In August, Governor Marcus L. Ward received a letter informing him that the Negro suffrage question made it difficult for Republicans to campaign in New Jersey.[37] When Congress met in December, Alphonso Taft of Ohio cautioned Stevens that the most he could hope for was Negro suffrage for the District of Columbia, as well as a constitutional amendment sanctioning a tax on exports and authorizing representation based on actual voters. "Negro prejudice does not stand in the way of these two measures," Taft concluded.[38]

Even in far off Oregon prejudice against blacks was so strong as to induce Senator George H. Williams to write an apologetic letter defending his votes for the Freedmen's Bureau and Civil Rights bills.[39] And in the 1866 campaign as determined a radical as Thaddeus Stevens was afraid that public display of Negro social equality at radical conventions would harm the ticket.[40]

What was clear to the radicals was certainly evident to the moderates. Trumbull's informants did not mince words. "The prejudice against the negro is not wholly overborne," wrote Dr. Charles H. Ray, the Chicago Republican whose skill had contributed in 1860 to the nomination of Abraham Lincoln.

> Say what we may, you and I share it; and what is true of us is doubly true of others. . . . [W]e have a sense of duty, a desire to be faithful to principle and a profound if not always active belief in the much talked-of "brotherhood of man". . . . [T]he masses give way to prejudice uncontrolled; and to dislike, I will not say to hate a negro is just as natural as to distinguish black from white.

Another correspondent made it clear to the senator that if the Republicans advocated Negro suffrage, they would be sunk so deep politically that he doubted "if they would have time enough to hear Gabriel's trumpet sound at the great day of Resurrection."[41] John Sherman heard arguments against Negro equality from his brother, the general, and no one could be in doubt about the strength of anti-Negro feeling.[42]

And yet there was a chance to bring about Negro suffrage and a modicum of racial equality in the South. Immediately after the war, conditions were such that even racially prejudiced Northerners might have gone along with the forcible introduction of reform in the former Confederate States. "Looking at the matter for the white men and not the negro," Horatio Woodman, the Boston journalist wrote to the secretary of war in April 1865:

> I should say that if there is no other clear guarantee against the old oligarchy in each state getting control again, then either keep them out of Congress, or find a way to let the negroes vote,—and this prac-

tically and not theoretically or philanthropically. We have them now under a control which we must not lose, even if we hold them as military dependencies.[43]

The same point occurred to George W. Julian. The Negroes' "fitness for the ballot was a subordinate question," he pointed out. "A great national emergency pleaded for the right to it on other and far more important grounds. The question involved the welfare of both races, and the issues of the war. It involved not merely the fate of the negro, but the safety of society."[44] But the President was unwilling to take the necessary steps.

Economic questions also made the radical program difficult to execute. The financial condition of the United States after the Civil War troubled many businessmen. Believing in sound money and the primacy of financial questions, they deplored the distractions caused by the struggle over Reconstruction. When, in the fall of 1867, many radicals were already advocating impeachment of the President, Johnson learned that the business community stood in the way: ". . . all the great Northern capitalists are afraid of the consequences of impeachment," an informant wrote him. "To use the words of one of them, 'The President might be crushed, but the finances and the country would go to ruin.' "[45] Moreover, since radicals like Stevens, Butler, and Wade advocated inflationary policies, they did not enjoy the confidence of the bankers.[46]

Because of these difficulties, at first the radicals were careful not to precipitate matters. Accordingly, when Congress met in December it did not immediately challenge the President. True, it refused to seat any of the Southern members-elect, even from undoubtedly loyal districts, and referred all questions of Reconstruction to a Joint Committee of Fifteen. But as Professors John H. and LaWanda Cox have pointed out, this action did not necessarily constitute a break with the President.[47] Although such radicals as Stevens and Boutwell played important roles as members of the committee, it was chaired by William P. Fessenden, a leader of the moderates. On January 6, 1866, upon Stevens' motion, a subcommittee to wait upon the President was appointed. It was to ask him to defer action until the committee had acted. Johnson met the emissaries politely. Asserting that he desired to cooperate, he promised not to take any further steps.[48] And in view of the fact that he came from Tennessee, rumors were soon rife that the committee would admit the state in return for his cooperation.[49]

The President, however, determined to defeat Negro suffrage and the integration of the freedmen, could not cooperate. While the Tennessee problem was pending, he vetoed the Freedmen's Bureau Bill.[50] Although the Republicans, by breaking a pair to unseat Senator John Stockton of New Jersey, succeeded in obtaining a two-thirds majority in the Senate, Johnson continued to defy them. He decided to veto Trumbull's Civil Rights Bill as well.

The Civil Rights Bill was not a radical measure. Conferring citizenship upon Negroes, it sought to guarantee their equal treatment under state law by setting up elaborate procedures of enforcement. Considering the effect of the Southern black codes upon Northern lawmakers, it is not surprising that only three Republicans opposed it in the Senate and four in the House. Moreover, while the measure was being drawn up, the President had frequently conferred with Trumbull, who was led to believe that Johnson would approve its main provisions. At least that was the senator's understanding, no matter what the President may really have had in mind. Andrew Johnson was very adept at hiding his true intentions. He had always intended to veto the bill.[51]

The veto message was again defiant. Declaring that federal citizenship did not confer state citizenship, the President took exception to the citizenship clause. The entire bill seemed to him a violation of states rights. Beyond that, it offended his racial sensibilities since it proposed to outlaw all discrimination between the races. Would it not enable Congress to repeal state laws forbidding interracial marriage, he argued. And, quoting Chancellor Kent, was not such a prospect "revolting and . . . an offense against public decorum?"

The President cited further objections to the measure. Maintaining his racial theme, he declared that he did not believe in

making invidious distinctions between "large numbers of intelligent, worthy, and patriotic foreigners," in favor of the Negro who
had just emerged from bondage. How could the government establish for "the security of the colored race safeguards" which went
"infinitely beyond any that . . . [it had] ever provided for the white
race?"[52] The bill did not accord with his view of a white South;
consequently, he disapproved it. As Senator Edgar Cowan, the
Pennsylvania conservative, had pointed out to him, the measure
would enable Congress to confer suffrage on the Negro "or anybody."[53]

That the President had finally declared war on Congress was
evident to all. Moderates like John Sherman had said publicly that
there was no real difference between the President and Congress;
that Johnson had not appointed any Copperheads to office; and
that if he signed the Civil Rights Bill he would prove that the
senator was right. Then the President sent in his veto.[54] Trumbull,
who had been anxious to come to terms with Johnson, declared
that the President had misled him, and the radical press minced no
words denouncing the action.[55] In addition to vetoing the bill, the
President had barely refrained from openly opposing Republican
candidates in the Connecticut state election.[56] Furthermore, he
challenged Congress by a proclamation declaring the rebellion to
be at an end everywhere except in Texas. As justification he cited
his Senate resolution of July 1861, part of which stated that the
war was not being waged for the purpose of interfering with the
established institutions of the states.[57] Because of the difficulties
confronting them, however, many Republicans still sought to
patch up the quarrel.

The best chance to come to an agreement lay in the attempts of
the Reconstruction committee to frame an amendment to the
Constitution. Many Republicans were anxious to neutralize the
effects of the lapse of the three-fifths compromise and the continued withholding of the ballot from Southern blacks. They
sought to write into the Constitution a definition of citizenship,
to keep leading Confederates from voting, and to outlaw the Confederate debt. Although the ultraradicals would have liked to

amend the Constitution so as to make Negro suffrage mandatory, it was obvious that neither Congress nor the states would accept such a proposition. Consequently, the party considered various schemes of adjustment, among them plans of universal amnesty coupled with universal suffrage, as proposed by Senator William M. Stewart of Nevada and Robert Dale Owen. Ben Butler, then unhappy about the increasingly favorable presidential prospects of General Grant, even approached the President with a similar plan for compromise. Finally, the Joint Committee on Reconstruction reported an amendment similar to the later Fourteenth Amendment, except that it contained no definition of citizenship and would have disfranchised leading Confederates until 1870. After the Senate had added the citizenship clause and milder disfranchisement provisions, the present amendment was adopted by the almost unanimous vote of the Republican party.[58]

Because of the moderate nature of the amendment, which made it very unpopular with the extreme radicals, Johnson might easily have accepted it. Had he done so the controversy would have been settled. As late as October the radical General James A. Brisbin still believed the President would take this course. The antiradical New York *Herald* considered the amendment a triumph for Johnson, and many Republicans predicted its success.[59]

But the President was adamant. He could no more accept the Fourteenth Amendment than the Civil Rights Bill; it violated his notions of constitutional procedure and threatened the survival of the Union "as it was." Even when such a moderate senator as Edwin D. Morgan asked Secretary Welles if he did not think the amendment could bridge the gap between Congress and the President, Welles, undoubtedly speaking for his chief, answered in the negative. No amendment could be countenanced as long as eleven states remained unrepresented, he said.[60] And the President, whose duty it was to transmit the proposed constitutional change to the states, put his opposition on the same grounds. Declaring that "a proper appreciation of the Constitution" might "well suggest a doubt whether any amendment ought to be proposed by Congress

... until after the admission of the now unrepresented States," he made his hostility to it a matter of public record.[61]

Johnson's real objections to the amendment were not merely procedural, but substantive. As Secretary of the Interior Orville H. Browning wrote in a letter published with the President's explicit endorsement, the adoption of the amendment would revolutionize the entire structure of the government. The due process clause would confer enormous power upon Congress. And for what purpose? "[N]egro suffrage is the real and only substantial cause of controversy between the Executive and Legislative branches of the Government," he stated. "Had the President consented to join Congress in forcing negro suffrage on the South, all would have been fair and smooth, and instead of being denounced as a fiend he would now be worshipped as an idol by those who so bitterly and unrelentingly assail him."[62] Johnson was ready to defy Congress on the matter of Negro rights. In April 1866, in order to discredit the Freedmen's Bureau, he sent two of his supporters, Generals Joseph S. Fullerton and James Steedman, on a tour of inspection to the South. When Congress nevertheless passed a second Freedmen's Bureau Bill in July, he vetoed it, although it was passed over his objections.[63] While Andrew Johnson was President he would utilize the entire resources of his high office to keep the South a white man's country.

The President's bitter antagonism left the radicals—and most moderates—no choice. In one way or another, they would have to checkmate him. Perhaps the executive could still be made to see that neither they nor the majority of the Republican party would permit the fruits of victory to be taken away from them. Should he refuse to heed their advice, they would seek to govern with their two-thirds majority. But government under such circumstances would be difficult. Further steps might have to be taken.

Three.

The Widening Breach

President Johnson's veto of the Civil Rights Bill and his opposition to the Fourteenth Amendment merely underlined what had been evident all along: his determination to have his own way in reconstructing the South, whether Congress agreed with him or not. Neither the President nor his immediate supporters were unaware of the danger of political isolation; they sought, however, to organize a new political grouping designed to appeal to widespread conservative sentiments. Combining conservative Republicans and loyal war Democrats, they believed they would be able to obtain a majority for their policy of Reconstruction. While recognizing the end of slavery, they would otherwise leave the country's prewar institutions intact. As a matter of course, these institutions included states rights and white supremacy.

The President's efforts to create a new party have been expertly traced by LaWanda and John Cox.[1] Relying on the political skills of Secretary of State William H. Seward and his mentor, Thurlow Weed, as well as on other former Whigs and Democrats, the President, aided by Senators James H. Doolittle of Wisconsin, James Dixon of Connecticut, and Edgar Cowan of Pennsylvania, made careful preparations to convene a National Union Convention in August 1866. Long before the call went out, however, it became apparent that there would be difficulty in winning over enough Republicans to make the movement viable. There were simply too many Democrats actively engaged in the cause to convince Republicans that the President's Union party was not merely the old Democracy under a different name.

This was especially true when Johnson vetoed the Civil Rights Bill. Civil rights for the freedmen seemed so logical an outcome of the war that opposition to the measure was hard to justify. Even congressmen friendly to Johnson deserted him. Assuring the President that he had no desire to break with him, William A. Newall of New Jersey wrote that a vote to sustain the veto would not only have contravened his conscience, but the will of his constituents as well. "They strongly desire protection to the freedmen," he explained, "and fear that the States would be slow to accord it."[2] Relatively conservative senators like Morgan and Waitman T. Willey voted to override, and only a remnant of Republican conservatives stood by the President.

Even the ultraconservatives were finding difficulties in their way. The President was, ultimately, dependent on the Democrats, who sympathized wholly with his views on race and states rights. For tactical reasons he might have liked to keep them somewhat in the background, but this was impossible. They demanded offices and visible signs of his appreciation. S. M. L. Barlow, one of the proprietors of the New York *World*, had long before made this truth perfectly clear. In December 1865, writing to James Hughes, his Washington lawyer, he instructed him to tell the President that New York Democrats completely supported the administration, but they could do nothing if all the offices were held by their political opponents. Consequently, Johnson would have to appoint some officers acceptable to the Democrats.[3] The resulting cooperation between the administration and the opposition party greatly lessened its appeal even to conservative Republicans.

How difficult this situation was for Republicans loyal to Johnson can be gauged from the diary of Benjamin B. French. French had been an enthusiastic follower of Lincoln, but he was biased against blacks and admired Johnson. Nevertheless, in February 1866, he wrote: "The political cauldron is boiling with a vengeance. . . . I have the honor of agreeing with the President. . . . *But*, it vexes me beyond measure to see the copperheads, who have opposed the President and his war policy throughout, endeavoring, now, to seize upon him, and drag him, by main strength, into their ranks."[4] A few weeks later he was even more uneasy. Hoping that the political differences between Congress and the White House might be settled, he worried about Democratic influence. "Although I sustain the President," he commented, "I do hope and pray that he will say to the Copperheads, 'stand thou a little further off.' "[5]

Despite these complications, Johnson might conceivably have convinced the country and some moderate Republicans of the need for a new party and the desirability of his policies if his own plan of Reconstruction had not caused such difficulty for Unionists and Negroes in the South. In the former Confederate States, the President had not merely opposed Congress; he had actually blocked Congressional efforts to protect loyal elements by giving succor and hope to Southern conservatives.

The encouragement Johnson gave to Southern conservatives was very real. Because of his mild Reconstruction policies, in state after state Southern conservatives displaced moderate Unionists; the Negroes were either persecuted or pushed back into occupations little different from those they had pursued as slaves; and the old Southern leaders were making a rapid comeback. In North Carolina a Confederate general, Jonathan Worth, replaced the moderate W. W. Holden; in Georgia the former Vice President of the Confederacy, Alexander H. Stephens, was elected United States senator; in Mississippi another Confederate general, Benjamin G. Humphreys, occupied the governor's chair; and in New Orleans the active former Confederate John T. Monroe was elected mayor. Where there were several factions seeking to control a Southern state, as in Florida, the more conservative groups were certain of presidential support. They reciprocated by expressions of undying gratitude.[6]

The net effect of Johnson's Southern policy was the continued subordination of the blacks to their former masters. It was clear to his Southern admirers that the President was one with them in believing this goal to be just and desirable. In 1871, looking back on the history of Reconstruction, Christopher Memminger, the former Confederate secretary of the treasury, agreed with Carl

Schurz that had the South originally adopted a different attitude toward the Negroes, it would have escaped later difficulties. But, he rejoined: "it was as impossible, as for us to have emancipated them before the war. The then President [Johnson] held up before us the hope of a 'white man's government,' and thus led us to set aside negro suffrage."[7]

His recollection was correct. R. W. Flournoy, a former Mississippi slaveholder who became a radical after the war, in November 1865 pointed out to Thaddeus Stevens that the Republican party ought to protect Mississippi blacks. Instead, they were being persecuted. "Whatever genuine Union sentiment was forming and would in time have grown up [in the state]," he declared, "has been checked by Mr. Johnson's course. He is now the favorite of all the diseffected [*sic*] elements here. . . ."[8] Former Tennessee friends, who had later parted with him because of his Unionism, acknowledged the President's great services. A. O. P. Nicholson, one of the state's leading prewar Democrats whom Johnson had pardoned, thanked him profusely and assured him that at no time had the President so enjoyed the confidence of the people as since his policy had developed.[9] The superintendent of the Virginia & Tennessee Railroad, a convinced secessionist, took pride in the fact that he had saved Johnson from a lynching in 1861. "We hope and pray that you may remain at the head of our Government," he wrote.[10] And in Raleigh, North Carolina, the *Daily Sentinel* rebuked readers who were suggesting General Grant for President. According to the paper, it would be ingratitude for any Southerner not to bring Johnson forward.[11] As Kenneth Rayner, the former North Carolina Whig, put it, "President Johnson is our only hope."[12]

While former secessionists rejoiced, Unionists were discouraged. "It is almost intolerable, Sir, to submit to such rulers as President Johnson has allowed to be placed over us," a South Carolinian protested to Thaddeus Stevens, whom he implored not to leave the Negroes to the tender mercies of their former masters.[13] A Virginia Unionist likewise complained. "I am sorry that Andrew Johnson should turn his back on his friends that elected and trusted him," he wrote to Trumbull: ". . . his policy is doing more to prevent a quiet settlement of the country than all other things together." As he saw it, Johnson's actions had brought back all the former secessionists and put them into power.[14] Similar intelligence came from New Orleans, and Chief Justice Chase felt constrained to write his daughter that he was dismayed at the sufferings of Southern Unionists. "The President must recede from his position," he concluded.[15]

The most active Southern Unionists were among the worst sufferers. Elizabeth Van Lew—Crazy Bet, her neighbors called her—had been a staunch loyalist in Richmond throughout the war. Steadfastly, she had provided intelligence for Federal forces, even hiding the body of Ulric Dahlgren, the admiral's son, killed in an unsuccessful raid upon the Southern capital. Upon the entry of Federal troops, she had been the first to display the Stars and Stripes in the fallen city. But less than one year later she had become despondent. "Now dear friend I want really to come up to the exigencies of the times," she wrote to Senator Doolittle. "To demonstrate that in all ignorance and sincerity I was loyal. . . . I want now to be radical a real out and out secessionist. It certainly is the best thing. . . . You cannot doubt this? Witness everything around us. Who receive all favors? . . . The secessionists. Who are the true Pariahs . . . ? The loyal people of the South. To be a Unionist or a Negro are both unpardonable marks of caste."[16] While the disappointed loyalist was exaggerating, the trends she described were unmistakable.

What Johnson's policy meant for the freedmen was at best second-class citizenship and at worst intimidation, terror, and murder. The conservative governments and black codes were bad enough; in addition, the newspapers and correspondence of leading radicals were full of reports of individual outrages. In Florida the courts were so partial toward whites that blacks regarded them as "only engines of oppression to the race." In Louisiana there were reports of fieldhands whipped and physically assaulted by their employers; in Arkansas one of Thaddeus Stevens' confidants reported a regular massacre of freedmen; in Kentucky, Joseph

Holt was informed that black women were being ruthlessly beaten by the police. Everywhere in the South freedmen's rights were habitually disregarded.[17] While some of these facts may not have been generally known, news of the riot in Memphis in April and May 1866 could not be concealed.

The Memphis riot was one of the worst excesses to occur early in 1866. After an altercation with discharged black soldiers, local police officers ran amok and an infuriated mob indiscriminately killed Negro men, women, and children. Not until General George Stoneman brought in Federal troops was the massacre ended.[18] In view of Johnson's assertion that peace and order were reigning in the South, the bloodshed and terror were difficult to explain.

Nevertheless, the President continued to insist that the South was ready for immediate resumption of federal relations. When Congress passed another Freedman's Bureau Bill, he vetoed it again. The veto was overridden, yet he persevered by protesting against the admission of Tennessee on the ground that the state was already in the Union. He had previously disapproved of a bill for the admission of Colorado, in part because eleven states were still unrepresented.[19]

In addition, Johnson was busy perfecting his plan for a new party. Inviting delegates from all the thirty-six states and the District of Columbia, on June 25 his friends issued a call for a National Union Convention to meet at Philadelphia on August 14. The call asserted that each state had "the undoubted right to prescribe the qualifications of its own electors"; no external power rightfully could "or ought to, dictate, control, or influence the free and voluntary action of the States in the exercise of that right."[20] "A convention is to be held next month for the formation of a new political party . . . ," commented the *National Anti-Slavery Standard*. "All who agree that this is a white man's government . . . may consider themselves entitled to attend."[21]

How isolated the President was becoming from the main body of the Republican party became evident when longtime supporters began to leave him. Already shaken by the suicide of his friend,

Senator James Lane of Kansas, Johnson was faced with the resignation of Postmaster General William Dennison, on July 11. Five days later Attorney General James Speed followed suit, and shortly afterward Secretary of the Interior Harlan also retired. In addition, Hannibal Hamlin, Johnson's predecessor as Vice President, handed in his resignation as Collector of Boston. Only Edwin M. Stanton, the secretary of war, though for some time at odds with Johnson, remained in the cabinet despite his disapproval of the President's policies.[22]

Stanton was a commanding figure. An eminent lawyer in Pittsburgh and Washington and long opposed to slavery, he joined Buchanan's cabinet as attorney general in December 1860. Using his position to strengthen the President's resolve, Stanton was even then secretly negotiating with the incoming Republicans. In spite of his widely publicized criticisms of Abraham Lincoln, in January 1862 he was appointed secretary of war, a post which he filled with ability and vigor. Some called him the American Carnot, and when Lincoln was assassinated Stanton became, for a short time, the most powerful man in Washington.

Andrew Johnson retained Stanton, along with the rest of the cabinet. To the secretary of war he entrusted the task of drawing up a plan of Reconstruction, parts of which became the model for his own plan. As time went on, however, Stanton came more and more to disagree with the President's approach, until he finally regarded himself as the radicals' representative in the cabinet. Although Johnson was fully aware of this attitude, until 1867 he took no steps to rid himself of his uncongenial adviser.[23]

The President's campaign soon ran into new trouble. In New Orleans, where after some misgivings Johnson had sanctioned the election of Mayor John T. Monroe, a notorious secessionist, a riot took place even more serious than the Memphis affair. The radicals of Louisiana, hopelessly outvoted because of the conservatives' resurgence under the President's Reconstruction scheme, were anxious to reverse their fortunes by enfranchising the blacks. For this purpose they sought to reconvene the adjourned constitutional convention of 1864. The dominant conservatives, considering this move illegal, were determined to prevent it at any price, including the forcible suppression of the convention and the arrest of the delegates.[24]

In order to perfect their plans the conservatives sought the support of the military. On July 25, Mayor Monroe wrote to the commanding general, Absalom Baird. Inquiring whether the projected convention had the general's approbation, the mayor called the meeting subversive and informed Baird of his intention to disperse it.[25] Baird answered at once. Neither approving nor disapproving of the assembly, he pointed out that all citizens had the right to gather peacefully. At any rate, he remarked, he failed to understand how Monroe, a mere mayor, could presume to interfere with a state convention. Later Baird personally informed the lieutenant governor and the mayor that he would protect the right of assembly.[26]

The conservatives also tried to enlist the President's help. Naturally believing the administration to be friendly toward them, they telegraphed to Washington. Would the military be likely to interfere with any processes of the courts should a riot result from their planned interference with the convention? Lieutenant Governor Albert Voorhees and Attorney General Andrew J. Herron asked Johnson. "The military will be expected to sustain and not to interfere with the proceedings of the Court," the President wired back. At the same time, he requested the governor of Louisiana to give him information concerning the proposed meeting, only to hear that it had been called by authority of the presiding officer.[27] Because of the uncertainty surrounding the meeting, which was sanctioned by the governor but considered illegal by the lieutenant governor and the city authorities, on July 28 General Baird sought instructions from Secretary of War Stanton. He did not receive a reply.[28]

The result of this confusion was the New Orleans riot. On July 30 the convention met at noon in the Mechanics' Institute. Because General Baird had mistakenly assumed the call to have been for 6 P.M., no military protection was available. A mob began to fire upon a procession of radicals outside the hall and finally upon the delegates within. Over forty people were killed and many more wounded; the victims were almost exclusively blacks and white radicals.[29]

It was apparent from the very beginning that the riot would damage Johnson's political plans. Radical papers pointed out the lesson of the carnage: Johnson maintained that peace had been restored in the South, but in Louisiana over forty persons had been murdered in cold blood. Clearly, sterner measures were required to complete Reconstruction. Although the President charged (and believed) that the riot had its origin with radical congressmen in Washington—a theory he sought to bolster with the fact that Stanton had never shown him Baird's telegram of July 28—the public remained unconvinced.[30] The President himself had been fully aware of the critical situation in New Orleans, and although he directed Herron to arrest members of the assembly on July 30, he issued no clear-cut instructions to the army until it was too late.[31] If an affray such as the New Orleans massacre could happen, obviously Johnson's policy was not working.

Two weeks after the riot, the Union convention met in Philadelphia. Highlighted by a parade of Northern and Southern delegates—headed by General Darius Couch of Massachusetts arm-in-arm with James L. Orr of South Carolina—the convention passed a series of resolutions endorsing the President's policies. Its proceedings were marred by the presence of so many notorious Peace Democrats that Republican orators had no difficulty in finding campaign material for the ensuing canvass. The President enthusiastically endorsed the results of the convention.[32] On August 20, despite ample evidence of widespread disturbances in Texas, he declared the insurrection to be at an end in that state. "Peace, order, tranquility, and civil authority now exist throughout the whole of the United States of America," he declared.[33] His supporters, much to the detriment of the regular Republicans, were rewarded with desirable offices.[34]

The Union Convention in Philadelphia was the first of four political gatherings to be held that summer and fall. Southern loyalists met with their sympathizers at Philadelphia on September 3 to proclaim their support of Congress and the proposed amendment; a convention of soldiers and sailors loyal to the President assembled at Cleveland on September 18; and a similar group favoring Congress came together at Pittsburgh on September 25 and 26 to hear harangues against Johnson by General Butler and others.[35]

But above all, it was the President whose activities rendered the campaign noteworthy. Taking advantage of cornerstone-laying ceremonies at Chicago for a monument to Stephen A. Douglas, Johnson set out upon a "swing around the circle." Addressing crowds wherever he went, he sought support for his policies, but sometimes the heckling was so disturbing as to provoke him to make undignified replies. He incessantly repeated the story of his rise from alderman to President, emphasized the known facts about his loyalty to the Constitution, and reiterated his conviction that the Southern states should be readmitted forthwith. "For myself, I want no better constitutional league as that formed by Washington and his compeers."[36] He expressed nothing but contempt for the radical Congress, which he had earlier referred to as "a body called, or which assumes to be, the Congress of the United States, while in fact it is a Congress of only a part of the States."[37]

In some ways it was appropriate that Johnson undertook a trip to honor Senator Douglas. Like the senator, Johnson had been a Jacksonian Democrat, and while he no longer believed with Douglas that it made no difference whether slavery was voted up or down as long as it was voted upon, he evidently still shared many of the senator's racial attitudes. As he told an assembled crowd in St. Louis, the radicals were anxious to enfranchise the blacks in Louisiana while taking away votes from the whites. Congress, he continued, was "to determine that a Government established on negro votes was to be the Government of Louisiana." A voice cried "Never," and cheers and hurrahs ensued. The President's solution of the race question manifestly held little hope for the blacks.[38]

The radicals, on the other hand, in spite of their awareness of

the dangerous political implications of the almost universal prejudice against nonwhites, did not hestitate to call for justice for the
Southern blacks. "The great issue to be met at the election is the
question of negro rights," Thaddeus Stevens said at Bedford,
Pennsylvania, on September 4. ". . . In this Republic the same laws
must and shall apply to every mortal, American, Irishman, African,
German, or Turk."[39] Ben Wade, Ben Butler, Horace Greeley,
and others likewise asked for protection of the freedmen.[40] And
while these demands did not constitute the main theme of the
campaign, which continued to center upon the need for measures
stronger than the President's Reconstruction plan, they nevertheless underlined the great difference between Johnson and the
Congress.

The election results were most heartening for the Congressional
Republicans. Significantly improving their position in the Northern states, they secured a two-thirds majority in both houses of
Congress. The President's successes in the South merely pointed
up what had already become painfully evident. As James G. Blaine
recalled years later, "The unhappy indication of the whole result
was that President Johnson's policy had inspired the South with
a determination not to submit to the legitimate results of the
war. . . ."[41]

Republican observers were elated. Commenting that the results
exceeded all expectations, Senator Fessenden advised Secretary Mc-
Culloch that the people of the North "would prefer another war to
admitting the confederates to an equal share of the government
before we have made some adequate security for their future good
conduct, and an equal participation of all men in civil and political rights and privileges."[42] Congressman Samuel Shallabarger
declared the elections showed that Johnson's drunkenness at the
inauguration could be forgiven, "yet for him who presumes to
take the sacred life of the government this nation has an axe." If
the President disregarded the warning, he would be ousted.[43] The
radical *Independent* commented that the result had determined
the new Congress would be favorably inclined; consequently, the
old one must move forward to enact universal suffrage.[44] Carl

Schurz considered the Republican victory to have been necessary because Johnson was a very narrow man who had delayed Reconstruction by inflaming the South against Congress.[45] While Senator Grimes warned Gideon Welles that the President must now accept the terms offered by Congress or else face more severe ones, *Harper's Weekly* concluded that the elections had decided once and for all in favor of the Fourteenth Amendment.[46]

Under these circumstances, any number of advisers warned the President to give in. E. G. Cook of Buffalo wrote to Seward in October that the outlook was bleak and that Johnson ought to accept the Fourteenth Amendment.[47] W. B. Phillips of the New York *Herald* likewise urged an accommodation with Congress. "Proscriptive and objectionable as the constitutional amendment is," he counseled the President, "I do not think any more favorable terms can be obtained for the South."[48] Hiram Ketchum, loyal to Johnson, pointed out that the President had done all that could be reasonably expected of him; he need not do any more.[49] James G. Blaine was absolutely right when he wrote: "The defeat was so decisive that if the President had been wise he would have sought a return of friendly relations with the party which had elected him, or at least some form of compromise which would have avoided constant collision, with its certainty of defeat and humiliation."[50]

Nevertheless, in spite of some initial hesitation,[51] the President had no intention of yielding. What he was after was not a temporary election victory, a passing majority in Congress, but the principle of Reconstruction as he understood it. His policy was founded upon the conviction that the people would eventually sustain him. In the meantime, all he had to do was to hold fast and persevere.

How determined the President was not to give in he showed in his annual message to Congress. Refusing to make the slightest concession to the victorious Republican party, he forcefully reiterated all the propositions upon which his policies were based. According to his view, peace, order, tranquillity, and civil authority had been restored throughout the United States, and all that remained was to admit the loyal senators and representatives from the reconstructed states. "The Constitution of the United States makes it the duty of the President to recommend to the consideration of Congress 'such measures as he shall judge necessary or expedient,' " he declared. "I know of no measure more imperatively demanded by every consideration of national interest . . . than the admission of loyal members from the now unrepresented States." To justify this position, he not only recounted his conviction that all the states were still legally within the Union, but cited the Johnson-Crittenden resolutions, part of which he quoted, not omitting the portion denying any intention of interfering with the domestic institutions of the states.[52] Johnson would not cooperate, no matter what measures Congress might devise.

The most provocative example of Johnson's total rejection of all advice to compromise was his continued opposition to the Fourteenth Amendment. Despite advice to the contrary, he still fought it with all the powers at his disposal. In Alabama, for example, the legislature might still have considered ratifying the proposition. But when word came of the President's opposition, it refused to do so.[53] In justification of his action, and to squelch a move to reconsider the vote of the legislature, Johnson wrote on January 17 to ex-Governor Lewis E. Parsons:

> What possible good can be attained by reconsidering the constitutional amendment? I know of none in the present posture of affairs. I do not believe that the people of the whole country will sustain any set of individuals in attempts to change the whole character of our Government. . . . I believe on the contrary that they will eventually uphold all who have patriotism and courage to stand by the Constitution, and who place their confidence in the people. There should be no faltering on the part of those who are honest in their determination to sustain the several coordinate departments of the Government, in accordance with its original design.[54]

The result of Johnson's stubborn opposition to the amendment was that it was finally rejected by every unrepresented Southern state. The President had his way.[55] It is true that by January 1867 he was ready to consider an amendment giving suffrage to all citizens who could read and write or owned two hundred and fifty dollars' worth of taxable property, but exempting previous voters from these conditions. Should this measure be adopted, he was willing to endorse a modified form of the Fourteenth Amendment.[56] But this patent attempt to exclude most Negroes from the suffrage had no chance of success. All it did was to highlight Johnson's opposition to fundamental changes in the Southern way of life.

It was becoming ever more apparent that this was, indeed, the President's aim. Never for a moment hesitating to disapprove of a bill for black suffrage in the District of Columbia, in his veto message he averred that he could not give his sanction to a measure opposed by the people of the District. "Great danger is . . . to be apprehended from an untimely extension of the elective franchise to any new class in our country," he stated, "especially when the large majority of that class, in wielding the power thus placed in their hands, cannot be expected correctly to comprehend the duties and responsibilities which pertain to suffrage."[57]

Of course the Republicans in Congress did not remain inactive. Hampered as they were by the President's obstructions, they sought to implement their policies without him. To the South, some still held out hopes of speedy restoration in case of ratification of the amendment.[58] To the North, their determination seemed to guarantee safeguarding the results of the elections: the Southern states would not be readmitted without adequate protection against a resurgence of Confederate power.

In order to achieve this goal, allowances had to be made for the continued opposition of the White House. As early as July 1866 the Republicans had reduced to eight the number of Supreme Court justices. It is not clear whether this act was designed to prevent the President from filling vacancies, but it was later so interpreted.[59] In January 1867 the dominant party passed a law calling the Fortieth Congress into session immediately after the expiration of the Thirty-ninth, and during the short session (December 1866–March 1867) they began to work on a measure to curb the Executive's patronage.[60]

The outcome of this endeavor was the Tenure of Office Act. It was clear to every radical officeholder that the President's control of patronage was a grave danger to the Republican party. While at first removals had been few, during the campaign of 1866 their pace quickened: 1,644 postmasters were removed between July 28 and December 6—1,283 of these for political reasons.[61] "I do not care about being the only Republican left, surrounded entirely by Copperheads and so called Democrats," Louis Weichman wrote to Joseph Holt. "I am hopeful of the future, and I am convinced that Congress . . . will not be guilty of another adjournment without passing some bills to protect themselves, and their brave constitutents, men who by hundreds are being 'kicked out of office.' . . ."[62]   .

Congress responded to this and similar requests. On December 3, the first day of the session, George Williams of Oregon introduced a Tenure of Office Bill in the Senate. On January 10 the measure came up for debate, the controversy centering upon a section exempting cabinet members. One week later Senator T. O. Howe of Wisconsin offered an amendment to include the secretaries. Did not the New York *Herald* openly predict that Edgar Cowan would be the next secretary of war? His arguments proved unavailing, and the amendment was lost.[63]

The issue of the cabinet was not yet settled, however. After the House had voted down an amendment to include cabinet officers, Congressman John H. Farquhar moved to reconsider. His motion prevailed, and the members of the cabinet were included by a vote of 75 to 66.[64]

In the Senate, too, the issue was kept alive. Some of the more radical senators had become acutely aware of the implications of the measure. Charles Sumner, for one, was insistent on the inclusion of the secretaries. Every constitutional government had ministers objectionable to the executive, he argued in a dinner conversation with John Hay. The secretary of war was especially on his mind, and he expressed the opinion that it should be made impossible for Johnson to remove Stanton.[65] While the committee of conference refused to accept the House version without alterations, Senator John Sherman of Ohio perfected a compromise formula that proved acceptable to both chambers. Cabinet officers were to "hold their offices respectively for and during the term of the President by whom they may have been appointed and for one month thereafter, subject to removal by and with the advice and consent of the Senate."[66] Whether or not Stanton, who had been originally appointed by Lincoln, was covered by this compromise was questionable.

Congress also took into account the danger that Johnson might interfere with the army. When Congressman Boutwell arrived in Washington in December, he received from the secretary of war a letter asking him to call at the department. Arriving at the War Department, Boutwell was told by Stanton that he was more worried about public affairs than at any time during the war. Johnson was issuing orders to the army without informing either Stanton or Grant. There was even a possibility that he might send the general away from Washington. Then, at Secretary Stanton's suggestion, Boutwell wrote out a bill to tie the President's hands as Commander-in-Chief of the Army and Navy. He showed it to Thaddeus Stevens and with the latter's help piloted it through Congress. In its final form, a section of the Military Appropriations Bill for 1867, it provided that the headquarters of the general of the army were to be located in Washington. All orders to the army were to be issued through the general of the army, who could not be removed except with the approval of the Senate. A separate section provided for the dissolution of the militia of the Southern states.[67]

Another measure to curtail the President's power was an act repealing prior legislation giving him the right to issue pardons by proclamation. It was doubtful that the bill would have any effect at all because of the constitutional provisions for presidential pardons. Although Johnson permitted it to become law without his signature, his pardoning policy was not affected.[68] Finally, after it had become clear that none of the Southern states would ratify the amendment because of the President's opposition, Congress passed the first Reconstruction Act.

The Act for the More Efficient Government of the Rebel States was a far-reaching measure. Declaring that no legal governments existed in the South, it provided for the reestablishment of military government in the disaffected region. The President was to appoint five military commanders for the Southern states. Civil government was to be restored after the population had, by universal male suffrage (with the exception of some Confederate officers), ratified a constitution providing for universal male suffrage and accepted the Fourteenth Amendment.[69] Radical Reconstruction was about to begin.

From Johnson's point of view the Reconstruction Act was an abomination. "The BLACKEST RECORD ever made by an assembly of the representatives of a free people," the *National Intelligencer*, his Washington organ, called it while the bill was still pending.[70] When the journalist Charles Nordhoff came to see him weeks before the final version had been perfected, Johnson grew excited. Declaring that the proposed bill was nothing but anarchy and chaos, he expressed the opinion that the people of the South were to be trodden underfoot "to protect niggers."[71] To his secretary he said that rather than sign a measure that deprived American citizens of the right of habeas corpus, subordinated the civil government to the military, and denied the right to trial by jury, he would sever his right arm from his body.[72] Consequently, he disregarded numerous suggestions from friends that he sign the bill to end the impasse with Congress.[73] Undoubtedly agreeing with Francis Blair, Sr., that the bill was a scheme "sacrificing the Constitution and the South together & our white to the black race," he entrusted the writing of the veto message to Jeremiah S. Black and Henry Stanbery. With their help, he prepared a paper of singular strength.[74]

The veto of the Reconstruction Bill summed up all of Johnson's well-known positions on Reconstruction. He attacked the measure as one "without precedent and without authority, in palpable conflict with the plainest provisions of the Constitution." It interfered with civil government, established military dictatorship, and denied all rights for which "our race" had struggled for centuries.

In addition, he once again expressed his philosophy about race relations in the South:

> The purpose and object of the bill, the general intent which pervades it from beginning to end, is to change the entire structure and character of the State governments, and to compel them by force to the adoption of organic laws they are unwilling to accept if left to themselves. The negroes have not asked for the privilege of voting; the vast majority of them have no idea what it means. . . . Without pausing here to consider the policy or impolicy of Africanizing the southern part of our territory, I would simply ask the attention of Congress to that manifest rule of constitutional law which declares that the Federal Government has no jurisdiction, authority, or power to regulate such subjects for any State. To force the right of suffrage out of the hands of the white people and into the hands of the negroes is an arbitrary violation of this principle.

Just prior to the expiration of the session, Congress overrode his objections with little trouble.[75]

Thus the Republican party had sought to protect itself against an Executive whose policies were different from its own. Indeed, it had done almost everything it could to circumvent presidential opposition. But there remained one final possibility. If the President continued to resist the execution of the law, if he maintained his position and made Reconstruction impossible, Congress possessed one ultimate weapon: impeachment.

Four.

First Demands for Impeachment

The President's determined opposition to Congress sooner or later was bound to lead to demands for his removal. At first this ultimate weapon was too drastic to be taken seriously, but there was talk of it as early as October 1865.[1] By the beginning of 1866, anxious correspondents were warning Johnson that the radicals meant to depose him, and when he vetoed the Freedmen's Bureau and Civil Rights bills the Chicago *Tribune* took up the cry. "We believe . . . that the President should be impeached for high treason," it concluded, specifying as his offenses interference with Reconstruction, his alleged abuse of the pardoning power, and his lapse from sobriety.[2] In the fall of 1866, discussion of a possible trial became more general. The New York *Herald* predicted that a radical victory in the elections would result in the President's ouster.[3]

Long before the idea of impeachment enjoyed any great popularity, a number of radical politicians made the subject particularly their own. Perhaps the best known of these was General Benjamin F. Butler. Politician, soldier, and demagogue, Butler was a very controversial figure. A pronounced proslavery Democrat in Republican Massachusetts before the war, in 1861 he was appointed brigadier general of Massachusetts Volunteers. After leading his troops to Washington to lift the virtual isolation of the capital, he defied his superiors by entering Baltimore without orders in order to secure the city for the Union. Promoted to the rank of major general, he was sent to Fort Monroe, where he made a name for himself by declaring Confederate slaves "contrabands" of war. But his reputation rested finally upon his exploits as commander of the Federal troops in New Orleans in 1862. Firmly holding the city despite the restlessness of the hostile population, he maintained discipline, secured his command against yellow fever, and made himself feared as well as hated in the South. When a local gambler tore down the American flag, he hanged him. When rebellious Southerners displeased him, he imprisoned them. And when females annoyed his soldiers, he issued his celebrated General Order No. 28. Citing repeated insults to the army "from the women calling themselves ladies of New Orleans," it directed that "hereafter, when any female shall, by word, gesture, or movement, insult or show contempt for any officer or soldier of the United States, she shall be regarded and held liable to be treated as a woman of the town plying her avocation." The order fulfilled its purpose. The insults ceased, but ever after the general was known as "Beast Butler" in the South. His popularity in the North increased accordingly.

While in New Orleans, Butler was gradually converted to radicalism, and he raised one of the first Negro regiments in the country. Recalled amid charges of graft and high-handed treatment of foreign consuls—he was even accused of having personally stolen silver spoons—he succeeded in obtaining command of the Army of the James, which was supposed to cooperate with Grant in the operations against Richmond in 1864. His military record in Virginia and at Fort Fisher proved so wanting that early in 1865 he was once more relieved. But his popularity was still high; in 1866 his reputation as a radical and his superb political organization enabled him to run for Congress. At that time he was anxious to end the political career of General Grant, who had severely insulted him in his final report.[4]

James M. Ashley of Ohio was another radical eager to impeach the President. Chairman of the House Committee on Territories, in early 1866 Ashley held a more responsible position than Butler, but his vagaries were such that his influence among his colleagues was limited. It is true that Ashley, a former Democrat, was one of the founders of the Republican party; it is also true that he was an early advocate of black suffrage and the sponsor of the Thirteenth Amendment in the House. But he was considered a fanatic. One of his peculiar notions was the idea that every Vice President who had ever completed the term of a deceased President had somehow been involved in the death of his predecessor. Believing in this conspiracy theory, he suspected Johnson as soon as the President proved to be closer to the conservatives than to the radicals.[5] According to the New York *Herald*, in the summer of 1866 Ashley vowed to "give neither sleep to his eyes nor slumber to his eyelids" until he had brought articles of impeachment against the President. It was Ashley who introduced the original resolutions against Johnson.[6]

Other radicals—men like Zachariah Chandler, the forceful senator from Michigan; George S. Boutwell, then a representative from Massachusetts and later secretary of the treasury; Benjamin F. Loan of Missouri, a former Union officer; and Thomas Williams, one of the founders of the Republican party in Pennsylvania—were also identified with early efforts to impeach the President. Old abolitionists like Wendell Phillips and William Lloyd Garrison naturally suported the movement, as did radical newspapers like the *Independent* and *Wilkes' Spirit of the Times*. And Thaddeus Stevens, while not yet prominent in advocating the President's deposition, would soon be the leading champion of his removal.[7]

Of all the important radicals in the House, Thaddeus Stevens has been the subject of more speculation than any other. Born club-footed in 1792 in Vermont and abandoned by his father in childhood, Stevens adored his mother, who saw to it that he received a good education. He never married. In 1815 he moved to Pennsylvania, where he practiced law—first in Gettysburg and then in Lancaster. Soon he played an important role in his adopted state as an eminent member of the bar, industrialist, and politician. An ardent anti-Mason and later Whig and Republican, Stevens became a determined foe of slavery, a stance he steadfastly maintained after entering the House in 1858. By 1863 "the Commoner," as he was often called, had become chairman of the Ways and Means Committee, a position he used to great advantage in securing the radical objectives of uplifting the blacks. His parliamentary skill, his sarcasm, and the relentless pursuit of his aims became proverbial; in 1866 he was generally conceded to be the leader of the radicals in the House. Determined as he was, his original contempt for Johnson eventually turned to hatred. The removal of "the great obstruction" thereafter became one of Stevens' principal goals.[8]

But impeachment was not a step to be undertaken lightly. While there was unmistakable constitutional authority for proceedings against federal officials, the fundamental law was nevertheless very specific on the question of what constituted impeachable offenses. Article Two, Section Four of the Constitution clearly reads: "The President, Vice President and all civil Officers of the United States, shall be removed from Office on Impeachment for, and Conviction of, Treason, Bribery, or other high Crimes and Misdemeanors." In the entire history of the United States, the procedure had been used only five times. In 1797, Senator William Blount of Tennessee was impeached for having participated in planning an invasion of Florida and Louisiana, but two years later, after he had been expelled from the Senate, the charges were dismissed for want of jurisdiction. During Thomas Jefferson's administration, United States District Court Judge John Pickering and Supreme Court Justice Samuel Chase were impeached. Pickering was removed from the court in New Hampshire, after a mental breakdown, for conduct unbecoming a justice, while Chase was acquitted of abusing his office by making bitterly partisan charges to a jury. In 1831, Judge James S. Peck of the Federal District Court in Missouri was also impeached, but he was found not guilty of having improperly imposed citations for contempt of court. Finally, in 1862, Judge West H. Humphreys of the Federal District Court in Tennessee was convicted of having accepted office under the Confederate government. No President had ever been impeached, and, though most modern authorities disagree, in the trial of Justice Chase most of the senators who acquitted him apparently believed that no one could be found guilty except for indictable offenses.[9]

In addition to the constitutional difficulty of impeachment, it was obvious that any proceeding so radical in nature was bound to cause great upheavals in the country. Businessmen feared its unsettling effect upon commerce; politicians were afraid of its impact on elections; and the average citizen was not excited enough to sustain policies so contrary to normal American experience.[10]

For popular speakers like Ben Butler, these considerations did not seem to pose any obstacles. In the wake of reports that he had sought to include an impeachment plank at the radical Soldiers and Sailors Convention at Pittsburgh, his friends announced that if he were elected to Congress he would press for immediate action.[11] Early in October he delivered a speech at Cincinnati. As he saw it, the duty of Congress was evident. Without waiting until the President should commit any other overt "act of mischief," it ought to impeach him at once.[12] Within the next few weeks the general repeated this demand in speeches at Chicago and Brooklyn. At the Brooklyn Academy of Music he accused the President of having violated the Constitution, citing over a dozen specifications to substantiate his charges. Johnson had allegedly brought Congress into disrepute; he had incited people to disobey the law; he had abused the pardoning power; he had illegally restored property to rebels. Butler waxed more enthusiastic as he continued. Had not the President also appointed state governors without sanction of the law? Had he not nominated rebels to office, instituted his own Reconstruction policy, and unilaterally proclaimed the cessation of hostilities? Then the general turned to the affairs of Louisiana. Accusing Johnson of interference in the domestic affairs of the state, he asserted that the President had conspired with insurgents in New Orleans prior to the riot. In addition, he charged that Johnson had corruptly interfered with elections, made temporary appointments of persons already rejected by the Senate, and failed to enforce the laws. He concluded by once again attacking the President's personal habits, his alleged drunkenness, and his improper use of the army during the Fenian invasions of Canada. For all these offenses, Butler not only wanted the President impeached, but suspended from office during the trial.[13]

Other would-be impeachers were less specific, but they too sought to oust the President. George Wilkes, the vitriolic editor of *Wilkes' Spirit of the Times*, demanded that Johnson be impeached for calling Congress a factious body, for blaming the New Orleans massacre on Congress, and for misbehaving during the "swing around the circle." [14] Thaddeus Stevens, nurturing an ever growing hatred for the man whom he held responsible for the country's woes, sought to impeach him for corrupt use of patronage. Robert Schenck, chairman of the House Committee on Military Affairs, believed Johnson's incitement to revolution by referring to Congress as an illegal and usurping body constituted grounds for a trial. [15] Chandler called the President a traitor, and Thomas Williams specified a list of alleged offenses similar to Butler's. [16] With radical newspapers emphasizing the subject, and public figures like Simon Cameron and George S. Boutwell lecturing on it, it was not surprising that even moderates like John A. Bingham of Ohio indicated they might conceivably favor impeachment. If Johnson asserted officially what he had already said unofficially—that Congress was not a legal body—Bingham declared that he would support steps leading to his removal. Speculation was rife whether Congress would really institute proceedings against the President. [17]

At first sight, the Republicans were in a strong position when Congress met in December 1866. Their control of both houses had been confirmed and made more secure by the fall elections; they had the votes to override any veto the President might interpose; and they seemingly enjoyed the confidence of the electorate. But they were by no means in agreement about policies: moderates controlled many an important committee, and questions of finance, foreign affairs, and political strategy seriously divided the party. [18]

As a result, observers agreed that it would not be easy to impeach the President. If definite charges against him could be proven, moderates might go along with efforts to depose him; if the impeachers failed to make good, they would be unable to convince the Republican majority of the necessity of so drastic a step. [19] And Andrew Johnson had been extremely careful never specifically to violate any law. In this respect, his tactics had been exceedingly prudent.

These tactics did not discourage the most determined advocates of impeachment. Boutwell introduced the subject in a caucus on the evening of December 1.[20] Nothing specific was decided, but other radicals, flushed with victory and believing that the Republican majority in both houses could be induced to go along with them, determined to rid themselves of "the great obstruction." On December 17, James M. Ashley introduced a motion for the suspension of the rules to enable him to report from the Committee on Territories a resolution for the appointment of a select committee of seven to investigate the question of impeaching the President. Although he was able to muster a vote of 90 to 49 for this motion, he was unable to obtain the necessary two-thirds, and it failed.[21]

But Ashley would not give up. When a Republican caucus met on January 5, Representative Rufus P. Spalding of Ohio moved that no measure looking toward the impeachment of the President be presented unless agreed upon in caucus. Stevens tried unsuccessfully to table the motion, and after an amendment to refer all resolutions concerning impeachment to the Judiciary Committee was accepted, the amended resolution passed. Ashley now announced that he would offer the resolution. In his determination he found support from Stevens, who argued strongly that Reconstruction could not be carried out until the President was removed. Johnson controlled the army, and without his cooperation no laws could be properly executed.[22] As usual, the Commoner had been very candid. Johnson's obstruction did indeed make Reconstruction impossible.

The difficulties of impeaching the President, however, were too great to convince the majority of the party. Although it was clear to most Republicans that Johnson stood in the way of Reconstruction, the broad center of the party was wary of taking a step as extreme as impeachment. Johnson had not committed an indictable offense; mere speeches were not enough to convict anybody; and the other charges against him were too vague to serve as a basis for his removal. Accordingly, the caucus decided to refer all motions on the subject, not to a special committee, conceivably chaired by Ashley, but to the Committee on the Judiciary, a move which was widely interpreted as a defeat for the impeachers. They might introduce their resolutions, but the resolutions would be safely referred to a moderate committee.[23]

Despite the setback suffered in caucus, the impeachers went ahead with their plans. On January 7 they introduced in the House a series of resolutions looking toward the impeachment of the President. Benjamin F. Loan of Missouri, a former Union general and a determined radical, submitted resolutions for the impeachment of Johnson for the purpose "of securing the fruits of the victories of the Republic." In accordance with the caucus decision, it was referred to the Judiciary Committee, only to be followed by a similar one offered by his colleague, John R. Kelso. Because the morning hour had expired, this resolution was held over. Then Ashley, as a question of privilege, rose to offer new resolutions directly impeaching the President. After briefly remarking that he would have preferred to have more experienced members offer his resolutions, he moved the main point. He charged Johnson with high crimes and misdemeanors, usurpation of power, corrupt usage of the appointing, pardoning, and veto power, corruption in disposing of the public property, and interference with elections. His motion was passed and referred to the Judiciary Committee.[24]

The action of the House caused a sensation. While the New York *Herald* pointed out that there was really no popular clamor for so extreme a measure, and the cabinet generally treated the matter lightly, Gideon Welles believed that "infamous charges, infamous testimony, and infamous proceedings" would be produced "as easily . . . as Butler could get spoons in New Orleans."[25] The Chicago *Tribune* predicted that "startling circumstantial evidence" would be developed; Ashley spoke of the necessity for speed because of the availability of witnesses in Washington; and the London *Times* concluded that the move foreshadowed a revolution. In Paris, newspapers also warned of great dangers ahead.[26]

Knowledgeable insiders, however, were not impressed. As the

Washington *National Intelligencer* pointed out, had the Republicans really been serious about impeachment, they would have pursued it vigorously instead of leaving it in Ashley's hands. The Chicago *Tribune's* Washington reporter called attention to the evident defeat of the impeachers in caucus because of the decision to refer their motions to the Judiciary Committee.[27] Many observers agreed. "I have been greatly inclined to the opinion that Mr. Ashley's scheme would amount to nothing," J. H. Rhodes wrote to James A. Garfield.[28] In Ashley's home town the Toledo *Commercial* concluded that there was no chance of conviction, since there were at least fourteen conservatives and Democrats in the Senate.[29] The cabinet largely discounted the chances of the President's deposition.[30] *The New York Times* expressed the opinion of many when it stated: "The impeachment question, let us hope, is at rest for the session. The proposition which was to accomplish wonders has been presented and disposed of; it produced no great excitement—hardly a flurry, and its referral to the Judiciary Committee strips it of nearly all its danger."[31] Even so loyal a Republican periodical as *Harper's Weekly* concluded that Ashley must give the Judiciary Committee "indisputable and conclusive evidence of criminal act and design." As the editor put it, "If Mr. Ashley knows no more than we all know, then we venture to say the country does not demand an impeachment and it would therefore be a highly inexpedient movement."[32]

The Judiciary Committee, to which Ashley's resolutions were referred, was chaired by James F. Wilson, a Republican from Iowa who was impervious to improper pressure. A highly respected lawyer, Wilson had been in Congress since 1861 and had distinguished himself by his legal acumen. Among other measures for the prosecution of the war, he had sponsored one of the first resolutions favoring an amendment abolishing slavery. Undoubtedly appalled by the President's policies, Wilson was nevertheless too good a lawyer to be swayed by unsubstantiated charges and was by no means identified with the ultra wing of the party. The same degree of moderation was characteristic of Frederick E. Woodbridge of Vermont, Daniel Morris of New York, and Francis

Thomas of Maryland, to say nothing of the Democratic member, Andrew J. Rogers of New Jersey. George S. Boutwell, Burton C. Cook of Illinois, Thomas Williams, and William Lawrence of Ohio were radicals, but they were in the minority.[33]

In keeping with the charge of the House, the committee began its investigations in February. Giving a lot of leeway to Ashley, it looked into a number of rumors and reports of the President's alleged acts. Lafayette C. Baker, the controversial War Department detective, testified that he knew of letters addressed to Jefferson Davis with Johnson's signature. He was never able to produce them, but he continued to regale the committee with stories of spies whom he had sent to the White House to expose the nefarious acts of pardon brokers. Although Ashley himself questioned Baker, nothing of substance developed.[34]

Another charge the committee sought to investigate was one of general corruption. The members vainly examined disappointed office seekers and the former governor of Colorado Territory, John Evans. Johnson had allegedly sought to secure Evans' claim to a Senate seat in return for pledges of support. Since the radical members of Congress, rather than the President, were then the main instigators of the Colorado statehood movement, this imputation also proved to lead nowhere.[35]

But there was always the mystery of the assassination of Lincoln. Ashley was then, and later, convinced that Johnson had had some connection with the crime.[36] Benjamin F. Loan publicly voiced similar suspicions in the House, and the committee proceeded to investigate.[37] Accordingly, it summoned the judge advocate general, Joseph Holt, who had been in charge of the prosecution of the assassins. Holt was unable to shed much light on the matter, but he gave the committee Booth's diary. Testifying that eighteen pages of the document were missing, Holt hinted that they might possibly have contained some incriminating evidence. His insinuations, however, were much too vague to serve as the basis for any serious accusation.[38]

In its search for further clues the committee also looked into Johnson's bank drafts, loans, and dealings with various railroad companies. In addition, it investigated his connection with the New Orleans riot, his appointment policies, and his relations with the provisional governors whom he had commissioned.[39] But before the inquiry had made much headway the term of the Thirty-ninth Congress expired, and the committee decided not to submit a definitive report. "The Committee not having fully investigated all the charges preferred against the President of the United States," it concluded, "it is deemed inexpedient to submit any conclusion, beyond the statement that sufficient testimony has been brought to its notice to justify and demand a further prosecution of the investigation." The Democratic member disagreed. In view of the lack of substantial facts, Rogers could see "no good in the continuation of the investigation."[40] It was apparent that the matter would be kept pending when the new Congress assembled.

Whether or not the impeachment agitation would be successful remained a favorite topic of political speculation. The New York *World* expressed the opinion that impeachment would be carried because it was a party necessity. According to the Democratic paper, the Republicans simply could not permit the existing situation to continue for two more years.[41] It was a common assumption that the resolutions were a club to be held over Johnson in order to induce him to sign the Reconstruction Bill. *The New York Times* quoted a Democratic observer to this effect as early as January 6, although the editor warned that the theory was to be taken *"cum grano salis."*[42] Francis P. Blair, Sr., in an angry letter to the President, expressed his sense of outrage at the passage of the Reconstruction Bill with the threat of impeachment hanging over Johnson.[43] Charles Nordhoff also commented on the connection between the two measures. There was an impression in Congress, he wrote to William Cullen Bryant, that if the President opposed the Reconstruction Bill he would be impeached.[44] Late in the session a friendly observer strongly urged Johnson to sign the bill, an action that would reconcile the moderates. A veto, on the other hand, would result in impeachment. "If a veto should precipitate impeachment & your approval would prevent it," he concluded, "then you ought to sign the Bill—for no man can tell the injury your country would receive if you should be deprived of your high office."[45]

It was generally concluded that the most determined radicals would have to persist in their quest. As Welles put it on January 8: "It is a necessity for the Radicals to get rid of the President. Unless they do, they cannot carry out their plans . . . of Reconstruction." Three days later he again expressed his conviction that the "Radical leaders intend to try to get rid of" the President. Since the Supreme Court was opposed to their schemes, he thought they would have to enlarge the number of justices. In order to obtain justices friendly to their Reconstruction policies, however, they would have to control the executive branch, and this they could do only by "displacing Johnson and getting Wade or one like him to take his place."[46] Gustavus V. Fox, the wartime assistant secretary of the navy, also thought that the radicals were determined to remove the President and that impeachment was most likely.[47] The New York *Herald* agreed. The Judiciary Committee would make its report in favor of impeachment before the close of the session, it predicted; a committee would be appointed to impeach Johnson; and the Senate would try the President during the next session.[48]

Nevertheless, there persisted a general disbelief in the probability of impeachment. Important business interests, among others, were opposed to any rash proceeding. Even before Ashley's resolutions had been presented, Wall Street was reported less than enthusiastic. After the resolutions' referral to the Judiciary Committee, rumors were rife that Wall Street bears in New York City were responsible for the whole excitement.[49] Others believed that Ashley was the tool of certain gold speculators who had allegedly paid him $50,000 to press impeachment.[50] It was not generally known that the Ohio congressman was at that time desperately trying to raise money in New York, and finding very disturbing the havoc he himself had created.[51] At any rate, the financial community could not be expected to be favorably inclined to a movement in which General Butler was believed to be the chief instigator. His inflationary theories were considered too dangerous.[52] And practical congressmen like James A. Garfield looked upon the whole issue as an unnecessary interruption of the important business of the country.[53]

Despite these difficulties, the chief impeachers were not discouraged. Butler delivered speeches in various cities demanding speed in bringing the President to justice.[54] Notwithstanding the fact that Johnson would eventually have to be tried in the Senate, Senator Chandler, much to the annoyance of his colleagues, spoke in favor of impeachment on the Senate floor, and *Wilkes' Spirit of the Times* consistently demanded that the House take action.[55] With Ashley's home organ praising his wisdom and Phillips and Garrison indefatigably working for the cause, it was evident that at least some Republicans thought that they might succeed.[56]

One of the most important questions about the impeachment of the President was who, in case of conviction, would take his place. As the law then stood, the presiding officer of the Senate was third in line for the presidency. Since the term of Lafayette S. Foster, the president *pro tem* of the Senate, was about to expire, a new senator would have to be chosen for the position. With impeachment resolutions already under investigation, the election would have important implications.

The person most frequently mentioned for the position was Senator Benjamin F. Wade of Ohio. With a massive head, glowing black eyes, strong jaws, and clean-shaven face, the sixty-six-year-old archradical had originally been elected to the Senate in 1851 because of his opposition to the Fugitive Slave Law. He soon established for himself a reputation as an outspoken, courageous foe of slavery who knew how to deal with Southerners on their own terms. If anyone wanted to challenge him, Wade was said to have stated, he stood ready to fight with squirrel rifles at thirty paces, with a disk as large as a silver dollar pinned over his heart. During the war Wade was chairman of both the Joint Committee on the Conduct of the War and the Senate Committee on Territories. In this latter capacity he came to blows with Lincoln on the question of Reconstruction. When Lincoln pocketed the Wade-Davis Bill, the senator, together with Henry Winter Davis, signed the Wade-Davis Manifesto, which accused the President of attempting to set up executive satrapies in the South. Known to be honest, outspoken, and committed to radical Reconstruction, Wade was also identified with views favoring high tariffs and government aid to industry.[57]

William Pitt Fessenden, the moderate senator from Maine who had served briefly in Lincoln's cabinet as secretary of the treasury, was also mentioned as a possible choice for presiding officer. Fessenden not only personally disliked Wade, but differed markedly from him in philosophy. His cautious, legalistic approach was the antithesis of Wade's radical bluster, and his advocacy of hard money contrasted sharply with Wade's inflationary views. Slightly built, with a large head resting stiffly on his neck, Fessenden's manner was cold, dry, and severe. As chairman of the Joint Committee on Reconstruction, he had long acted as a brake upon the more radical members. But he was not particularly friendly to Johnson. Like most Republicans, Fessenden felt that the South would have to meet certain conditions before it could resume its place in the Union.[58]

It had been rumored for some time that some Republicans were thinking of Wade as Johnson's successor. As early as July 1866, Montgomery Blair told Welles that the radicals wanted to elect Wade president of the Senate, impeach Johnson, carry out their Reconstruction program, and exclude the Southern states from the 1868 presidential elections.[59] Other observers also cited the coming elections as a reason for Wade's probable elevation. His firmness was deemed sufficient guarantee that he would refuse to open ballots from the South when counting the electoral votes in 1869.[60] In October, John Bigelow, the American minister in France, heard that if the 1866 elections went strongly against the President, Foster would resign, Wade would be put in his place, and Johnson would be impeached and deposed.[61] In November, John W. Forney, the editor of the Washington *Daily Chronicle* and the Philadelphia *Press*, suggested to Senator Chandler that Wade be elected even before Foster's term expired. "Politeness to the incumbent should have nothing to do with this great duty," he emphasized. Wade's election would give peace and security to all business circles and would "consolidate our ranks" more than anything else.[62] Chandler then exerted himself on his friend's behalf, and by late November the New York *Herald* was predicting that Wade would be the radicals' choice.[63]

At the end of the year, the Supreme Court, in its decision in the Milligan case, cast serious doubt on the constitutionality of the establishment of military governments in the South. An added reason was now advanced for impeachment. As Henry Cooke explained it to his brother, the famous Philadelphia banker, the radicals were planning a revolution: they would get rid of Johnson, elect Fessenden or Wade president of the Senate, and make either senator President even while the trial was still going on. Then new justices would be appointed to the Supreme Court and the Reconstruction of the South completed.[64]

By February the speculation about the election of a new presiding officer in the Senate had become general. Either Wade or Fessenden would be elected, Senator Doolittle predicted.[65] *Harper's Weekly* suggested that Fessenden would be the man to inspire the greatest confidence, and John Bigelow, now back from France, observed that Wade's election would be regarded as a triumph for the impeachers, although he himself did not agree with this assessment.[66] When on March 1 the Republican caucus met, Wade won by a vote of 22 to Fessenden's 7, and on the next day the Senate officially ratified the decision.[67]

That Wade's election had not been based on the senator's skills as a presiding officer was conceded by all. He himself admitted that he was no parliamentarian and asked for the forbearance of the chamber.[68] But it was widely understood that the party had been anxious to have a firm radical as acting Vice President as long as impeachment was pending. "It is doubtless in view of this contingency that Wade has received this nomination," commented the New York *Herald*,[69] an assessment with which the Democratic New York *World* fully agreed. As it commented, "The nomination of Senator Wade for the Presidency of the Senate . . . is part of the impeachment programme." [70] The radical Toledo *Blade* was more succinct. "He may make an inferior President of the Senate," it observed, "but he would make a glorious President of the United States." [71]

Whether the movement toward impeachment had really been strengthened by Wade's election is doubtful. The senator was so outspoken and had so many enemies that his selection as Johnson's successor actually made impeachment more difficult, and it is possible that some moderates voted for him for this very reason. As Alexander McClure recalled many years later, "The entering wedge for the division of the Republican forces that led to the acquittal of Johnson was the election of Senator Wade as President *pro tem* of the Senate." [72] On the day before the election John Bigelow had come to the same conclusion, [73] and a few months later, in a newspaper interview, Thaddeus Stevens concurred. Much as he desired impeachment, he said, now that Wade was president *pro tem* of the Senate, Wade's enemies would prevent the President's removal. [74] At most, Wade's elevation may have been a warning to the President. But Johnson was shrewd enough to realize that his position had not really been weakened.

Another development being carefully watched because of its possible bearing on impeachment was the attempt to strengthen the Republican party by the admission of new Western states, especially Nebraska and Colorado. Four additional Republican senators might have an important impact upon any effort to impeach the President.

The question of the admission of Nebraska and Colorado had been pending for some time. Although neither territory had the required population for the federal ratio, the admission in 1864 of Nevada for partisan purposes furnished a good precedent. Accordingly, in the spring of 1866 a bill for the admission of Colorado, which had already failed, was reconsidered and passed by both houses. On May 15, emphasizing the paucity of the population and the fact that eleven old states were still unrepresented, Johnson vetoed it. The measure was not taken up again during the session. [75]

Wade became interested in strengthening the party. As chairman of the Senate Committee on Territories, he thought the admission of new states his special province, and rather than bring forward the vetoed Colorado Bill he turned to Nebraska instead. That territory had more inhabitants; its senators-elect had not been involved in the disgraceful Chivington massacre, which he himself, as chairman of the investigating committee, had severely condemned; and the prospects of success were better. In spite of Charles Sumner's opposition—because of the limitation of the suffrage in Nebraska to whites—the bill passed, only to be pocketed by the President.[76]

When Congress met for the short session in December the problem of the two territories came up again. Wade prepared new bills for the admission of both, and after extensive debate on the question of suffrage they were passed. A proviso requiring the legislatures of both to assent to a declaration of equality for all citizens salved the consciences of radical legislators. Wade's skill in piloting the measures through the Senate—he proved to be infinitely more practical than the doctrinaire Sumner—enhanced his chances for election as presiding officer.[77]

Andrew Johnson was fully cognizant of the problems of the two territories. He had made careful inquiries and at one time even sought to win support from the senators-elect.[78] Since this was not forthcoming, he decided to veto the bills. He could hardly countenance the admission of any more hostile Republican senators.

The President's veto messages again showed his determination to block radical Reconstruction. After pointing out that the proposed states did not have the population requisite for the ratio of representation, and that there was some doubt whether the people of Colorado even wanted statehood, he took issue with the provisions concerning the equality of all citizens: ". . . this condition is in clear violation of the Federal Constitution, under the provisions of which from the very foundation of the Government, each State has been left free to determine for itself the qualifications necessary for the exercise of suffrage within its limits."[79] Andrew

Johnson was not going to permit Negro suffrage to be imposed by Congress if he could help it.

The Nebraska Bill was passed over the President's veto in February,[80] but the Colorado Bill did not fare as well. In the Rocky Mountain territory, one house of the legislature had actually demonstrated against statehood, and the population had declined.[81] Nevertheless, after the President's veto, Wade tried once more to secure statehood for Colorado. Late at night on February 28, when the Senate was not well attended, he believed that the measure had a chance. He encountered serious opposition, however, when he moved to postpone all prior orders and to take up the Colorado Bill. "Sir, we are not without being observed," rejoined Senator Doolittle.

> The world stands looking on. The people of the United States know what is transpiring in this body, and there are peculiar reasons which connect themselves with the Senator from Ohio, which will draw some attention to him, and to the course he is pursuing on this occasion. We all know, that Senator, in pressing this matter of Colorado, has said over and over that his purpose was to reinforce a majority in this body, already more than two thirds. And for what, sir?

The measure failed. According to David Miller DeWitt, "the high water mark of the impeachment had been reached."[82]

In view of Wade's long-standing interest in the admission of the two states in order to strengthen the radicals in Congress, Doolittle's insinuation that Wade wanted to reach the presidency through the votes of two additional senators was probably a piece of political oratory on the part of a determined opponent. Impeachment was so uncertain in February 1867 that Wade, who had not even been elected Foster's successor, could hardly have been thinking only of his own future. Furthermore, he was so oblivious of his own advantage that three months later he greatly embarrassed the party and hurt himself by endorsing women's rights and a new deal for labor.[83] But the charge has stuck, and in view of the fact that the President was later acquitted by one vote, it has always seemed to have had a certain plausibility.[84] It is, however, a plausibility based upon events which occurred a year later.

When the Fortieth Congress met, the relations between the executive and legislative branches were extremely strained. Impeachment had been mentioned as a possibility, but as long as there was any other way of dealing with the President, the Republican party would seek to do so. Within the confines of his policy, Johnson had not conducted his affairs unwisely. Blocking Congress by legal means, he had carefully avoided furnishing his enemies with an excuse to proceed against him. Only continued obstruction on the part of the White House, obstruction so flagrant as to make impeachment feasible and to render Reconstruction totally impossible, could still lead to so radical a step.

Five.

Presidential Defiance

Neither the threat of impeachment nor the passage of legislation designed to curtail his power was able to discourage the President. Firmly convinced that he was right, and determined to defeat radical Reconstruction despite his enemies' two-thirds majority in Congress, he shrewdly proceeded to employ all the powers of his office to hamstring the Republican program. But he refused to be pressured into premature action. He considered carefully both his methods and his timing. He had no doubt that in the long run the electorate would sustain him.[1]

Johnson's stubborn attitude was characteristic. He told his private secretary, Colonel W. G. Moore, that he was right, that he knew he was right, and that he would be damned if he did not adhere to it. On another occasion he told the colonel: "There is nothing like starting out on principle. When you start out right with principles clearly defined, you can hardly go astray." Asserting that he had all his life been guided by certain political ideals, he maintained that he was guided by them still.[2] Thus it was not surprising that Johnson became furious when, in the fall of 1866, Democratic Congressman Samuel S. Cox suggested he might possibly compromise with his opponents. "He got ugly as the devil," Cox reported. "He was regularly mad." He considered the Southern states full members of the Union and no Reconstruction Act could change his opinion. The measure was "nothing but anarchy and chaos," he said.[3] The prospect of an even more hostile Congress held no terror for him.

Inflexible as Johnson was by nature, he was not immune to

favorable popular response, and encouraging support from all over the country must have fortified his resolve. Especially in the South, he was regarded as a hero. Ever since the break with Congress he had received letters assuring him that he was considered the savior and protector of his native section. In April 1866 a former officer of the Confederate army wrote him from Mississippi that twelve months earlier he had been as bitter as possible toward Johnson. He had regarded the President as the "exponent of that faction in the North who made, and still make it their religion to insult and oppress the people of the South." "I do not entertain any better feeling toward that party now," he confessed, "but as for yourself, you have created an admiration and enthusiasm in my breast that really astonishes myself. I look upon you as the savior of the South."[4] Similar assurances came from other states, and Alexander H. Stephens offered his full cooperation.[5] Since this adulation tended to grow with time, it is not surprising that Johnson was flattered.

Not only Southerners congratulated the President. He also received ample evidence of support from Northern Democrats, and it did not seem to upset him that such backers were somewhat incongruous for a President elected by the Union party.[6] He had always been, and still was, a Jacksonian. According to testimony before the Judiciary Committee, in 1865 he told an old party associate, ". . . if the country is ever to be saved, it is to be done through the old democratic party."[7] In view of his attitude, and his close association with Welles and the Blairs, the testimony seems to have been substantially accurate.

When the Fortieth Congress met immediately after the adjournment of its predecessor, Johnson was in a battling mood. Having just vetoed the Reconstruction and Tenure of Office bills, and having signed the Command of the Army measure under protest, he was in no frame of mind to come to an understanding with his opponents. Consequently, when Congress passed within a few weeks another Reconstruction Bill to correct the omissions of the first—in not specifying the exact process of initiating elections for Southern conventions—he again wrote a vigorous veto. He objected to the oath required of registrants; he criticized the sweeping powers of the commanding generals; and he asserted that the Southern states already had valid constitutions. But he did not confine himself to these objections. Negro suffrage was the issue which he again singled out for special mention. "What . . . in the opinion of Congress is necessary to make the constitution of a State 'loyal and republican'?" he queried. "The original act answers the question. It is universal negro suffrage." By these standards, he suggested, the work of Reconstruction might "as well begin in Ohio as in Virginia, in Pennsylvania as in North Carolina." The bill was promptly passed over his veto, but he had again made his point. And he had once more appealed to the racial prejudices of the people, the radicals' perennial problem.[8]

In spite of Johnson's steady adherence to what he considered principle, he was not given to useless obstruction. In keeping with his policy of astute caution, at first he did not seek to circumvent the Reconstruction acts by appointing only conservative generals to carry out the law. John M. Schofield in Virginia, it is true, was a conservative, but neither Edward O. C. Ord in Mississippi and Arkansas, nor John Pope in Alabama, Georgia, and Florida could be so described. Daniel Sickles in the Carolinas and Sheridan in Louisiana and Texas were well-known radicals. Apparently anxious to remain on good terms with the army and Grant, Johnson simply agreed to the suggestions of Stanton and the general. These suggestions were made from the point of view of the army rather than that of the President.[9] Nevertheless, there were frequent rumors that the President intended to interfere with the commanding generals or that he was about to remove the more radical ones.[10]

Johnson's seeming compliance with the Reconstruction acts lessened the demands for his impeachment. As long as he confined himself to vetoes, it was difficult to convince the moderates that drastic steps for his removal ought to be taken. His appointments might be rejected by the Senate and resolutions to meet again in July, if necessary, might pass both houses,[11] but the same conditions which had originally caused the moderate majority to refer impeachment to the Judiciary Committee still existed. Whether the President was deliberately pursuing a policy of delay, or whether his actions automatically had this effect, he was in fact conducting himself with great prudence.

It is true that the advocates of impeachment renewed the investigation in the new Congress. But they did so only after another failure in caucus to appoint a special committee of thirteen. Although Ben Butler, who had now entered the House as a representative from the Essex district in Massachusetts, and John Covode, an archradical from western Pennsylvania, had strongly advocated this tactic, neither the party nor the country was ready for so radical a step.[12] As a result, on March 7, Ashley made a motion to enable the Judiciary Committee to continue its investigation. In a violent harangue accompanying his motion, he asserted that the nation was crying out to Congress to deliver it from the shame and disgrace which "the acting President" had brought upon it and demanded that the "loathing incubus" who had "blotted" the country's history "with its foulest blot" be removed. "Is there an insane asylum here?" interjected the Pennsylvania Democrat, Samuel J. Randall, and the Speaker cautioned Ashley about the violence of his language.[13] Nevertheless, the resolution was passed, and the committee resumed its hearings. As the New York *Herald* had already pointed out, all Johnson had to do to stop the proceeding was to abandon his Southern policy and make peace with Congress.[14] But the investigation was not of such a nature as to put strong pressure upon him.

The committee, which now included John C. Churchill, a New York Republican, and two Democrats, Charles A. Eldridge of Wisconsin and Samuel S. Marshall of Illinois, replacing Cook, Morris, and Rogers, attempted to track down every possible clue. Much to Johnson's annoyance, it again examined his bank account and called witnesses who had taken down his speeches derogatory of Congress. Members of the cabinet were summoned. The secretary of state was questioned about Johnson's pardoning policy, and in view of the fact that, on May 13, Jefferson Davis was released on bail, the committee was especially anxious to learn the reasons for the failure to prosecute the Confederate President effectively.

It even called the chief justice to testify about the case. The secretary of the treasury gave evidence about appointment policies, the postmaster general about patronage, and the attorney general about pardoning practices. Former Secretary of State Jeremiah S. Black, who had written portions of the veto message of the First Reconstruction Bill, reluctantly testified while advising Johnson about the veto of the second, and the secretary of war freely discussed a number of subjects ranging from Booth's diary, the pardoning of deserters, and the New Orleans riot, to the surrender terms Sherman had offered the insurgents in 1865.[15]

Other topics were also investigated. Such varied subjects as the land policies of the Freedmen's Bureau, the capture of John Wilkes Booth, and presidential opposition to the Fourteenth Amendment all came under discussion. Ashley was permitted to pursue his false clues about Mrs. Lucy Cobb, a pardon broker of ill repute who had had access to the White House. But in spite of all efforts and a House resolution requesting a report at the next meeting of Congress, the committee was unable to find anything substantial.[16]

General Butler played a peculiar role in the renewed investigation. One of the original advocates of impeachment, Butler was dissatisfied with the slow progress of his favorite scheme. He was interested not only in seeking to oust Johnson, but also in keeping his enemy, General Grant, from benefiting by the impeachment movement. As Wade's succession to the presidency might be the answer to his problems, Butler consistently attempted to speed up the proceedings. Thus he clashed bitterly with John A. Bingham on the floor of the House, accusing him of having mutilated Booth's diary. The implications were that the missing pages would have shed some light on Johnson's alleged connection with the assassin.[17] General Butler also charged that the President had deliberately pardoned one hundred and fifty deserters in West Virginia in order to enable them to vote against the radicals in 1866.[18] The committee permitted him to examine witnesses, but Butler was unable to produce any more significant facts than the members had been able to elicit.[19] And although the President heard rumors that the committee would seek to manufacture evidence against him, neither the chairman nor the majority of his colleagues believed that there was sufficient cause to impeach Johnson.[20]

Because of the committee's reluctance to proceed without proper cause, on June 3 it voted to adjourn. A minority of four (Boutwell, Lawrence, Thomas, and Williams) favored an impeachment resolution, but they were outvoted by Wilson, Churchill, Woodbridge, Eldridge, and Marshall. It is true that at the same time, by a strict party vote of 7 to 2, the committee, declaring Johnson guilty of acts meriting the condemnation of the people, passed a resolution censuring the President.[21] It was evident that impeachment had failed again. The President's shrewd tactics had not provided the impeachers with anything substantial, and the most they could hope for was a renewal of the investigation in time for action by the summer session of Congress.

Whether or not such a session would be called was one of the issues troubling the lawmakers. Because of the hostility between the President and Congress, the problem of adjournment had become perennial. The first session of the Fortieth Congress had been called to meet in March because of the widespread conviction that Johnson could not be trusted and thus needed watching. When the business of the session was completed, the moderate Republicans desired to adjourn until the customary first Monday in December. But the radicals objected. "Andrew Johnson is a bad man," insisted Butler, who maintained that adjournment would amount to endorsing the President's policies. Moreover, he demanded action on impeachment. Blaine scoffed at this argument on grounds that there was no real demand for so extreme a step, only to be attacked by Stevens. Blaine preferred Johnson to Wade, the Commoner charged. After acrimonious debates, the two houses finally agreed to meet again in July if necessary.[22]

The President's outward compliance with the Reconstruction acts did not conceal the fact that he was determined to weaken them as much as he could. Congress had hardly adjourned when Attorney General Henry Stanbery submitted an opinion interpret-ing the law in such a way as to curtail the power of the registrars. In addition, he held that the number of people disfranchised for rebellion was strictly limited.[23] In June he submitted further portions of his opinion, in which he denied the power of commanding generals to remove civil officials. Secretary Stanton openly challenged this interpretation in cabinet, but Johnson and the other secretaries accepted it as their own.[24]

The attorney general's opinions greatly sharpened the controversy that had long been developing between Johnson and the army. Because the President's encouragement of conservatives made it difficult for military commanders to exercise their powers under the Reconstruction acts, the generals believed that they must have authority to interfere with state officials. In March, firm in this conviction, Sheridan removed a judge, the mayor of New Orleans, the attorney general, and later the governor of Louisiana, among others. In spite of the administration's evident displeasure, he secured Grant's solid support. "The fact is there is a decided hostility to the Congressional plan of reconstruction, at the 'White House,' and a disposition to remove you. . . ," the commanding general informed him. "Both the Secretary of War and myself will oppose any such move, as will the mass of the people."[25] Sheridan nevertheless took the precaution of letting Congressional leaders know that a summer session would be needed to protect him.[26] In other districts, similar problems arose.[27] When Stanbery's opinion appeared, Sickles went so far as to attempt to resign, and Sheridan, in a series of angry protests, took issue with presidential directions ordering him to extend his stipulated period for voting registration in Louisiana.[28]

Johnson's reaction to his generals' contumacy demonstrated his deliberation in dealing with his opponents. In spite of the severe provocation of Grant's and his subordinates' actions, he persisted in his attempts to woo the commanding general and refused to dismiss either Sheridan or Sickles until the time was ripe. Congress was about to meet again in July, and the President was not going to give it additional cause for interference.

That there would be a summer session was certain. It was precisely because of fears of Johnson's actions that the lawmakers had voted to reconvene in July if necessary, and the attorney general's opinion had made a revision of the Reconstruction acts imperative. Consequently, Congress reassembled on July 3.

When the session met, the legislators were in a state of excitement. The two opinions of the attorney general and General Sheridan's reaction to them—his dispatch to General Grant about registration had been published[29]—had sharpened the issues at stake. Amid continuing talk of the removal of various district commanders and renewed demand for impeachment, Congress began its work.[30] The weather was awful; the enervating heat made even a firebrand like General Butler unhappy with the session. "I do not think that we shall do anything to the purpose here," he wrote to his wife. "Probably pass an act that the President shall do no wrong and then he will go on as before."[31] Senator Timothy Q. Howe shared the general's dismay at the prospects, but he believed that it was necessary for him to be present. A quorum was needed to keep watch on the President.[32]

The physical discomfort of the lawmakers and the comparative weakness of the radicals redounded to Johnson's advantage. In spite of radical protests, the session voted to confine itself to the consideration of a supplementary Reconstruction Act.[33] But this preoccupation was closely tied in with the impeachment question, and there were many Republicans in and out of Congress who sought to keep impeachment alive.[34]

The impeachers' strength was limited, however, a fact once again highlighted by the actions of the Judiciary Committee. Reassembling on June 26, it resumed its examination of witnesses. Once more it sought to bring out all the facts shedding light on the assassination of Lincoln, Johnson's practices concerning patronage, pardons, and the restoration of confiscated property, as well as the failure to try Jefferson Davis. It examined former Secretaries Harlan and Speed and questioned Mrs. Surratt's daughter. Horace Greeley, who had gone bail for Davis, was also summoned.[35] But the members could not agree on any definitive action. On July 10, Chairman Wilson reported that the committee was split 5 to 4 and would not be ready with its findings before the next session of Congress.[36]

The failure of the committee to recommend impeachment was a source of great dissatisfaction to the radicals. Still hoping to take advantage of the summer session to achieve their design, they employed all their skill to induce the committee to proceed against the President. It was not only Ashley, Butler, Boutwell, and Lawrence who were now in the forefront of the movement, but Thaddeus Stevens as well. The Commoner had always been politically astute. Just as he had recognized, earlier than most others, that without a redistribution of land, emancipation would be incomplete, so he had now convinced himself, not without reason, that as long as Johnson remained President it would be impossible to carry out the Reconstruction acts. In addition, as Fawn Brodie has pointed out, "punishing the President had become an obsession Stevens could not abandon."[37]

It is true that, during the summer of 1867, Stevens was not very hopeful of success. Although he thought Johnson ought to be impeached for the effort to set up unlawful states in the South, on July 8 the Commoner pointed out to a New York *Herald* reporter that impeachment would fail. Conservative congressmen had "no bone in their backs and no blood in their veins." At any rate, they were jealous of Ben Wade. "This Congress will never vote impeachment. We don't want any of Ben Wade's 'Shellywaggers' around the White House," Blaine had allegedly said on the floor of the House.[38]

Nevertheless, Stevens sought to induce the committee to take action. His opportunity arose when, on July 10, Wilson informed the House that he was not ready to report. The chairman's statement led to debate. The country demanded impeachment, Stevens declared. Boutwell supported him, but for parliamentary reasons the subject was laid over until the following day.

On July 11 the Commoner renewed his assaults. Introducing a resolution calling on the committee to report during the current session, he pleaded for impeachment. But Wilson's opposition was too much for him. The chairman saw to it that the committee was given leave to wait until Congress reassembled, and Stevens gave up in disgust.[39]

Other radicals were also dismayed, but efforts to hasten impeachment continued. The Pennsylvania ultra, John Covode, introduced a resolution charging the committee with the investigation of a presidential pardon granted to Stephen F. Cameron, a former member of Mosby's band of raiders, who had been needed in the trial of John H. Surratt. The resolution passed, and there were further efforts to induce the committee at least to publish its testimony in July.[40] Chairman Wilson, however, had his way. The report would not be made until the fall.[41]

The failure to proceed with impeachment and the ever increasing likelihood of Grant's presidential candidacy greatly irked General Butler. Hoping against hope that he might find some evidence incriminating Johnson in the assassination of Lincoln, he took advantage of the pending trial of John H. Surratt, one of the conspirators who had just been extradited from abroad, to prevail upon Congress to set up a select committee to investigate the assassination.[42] In company with Ashley, he had for several months been in contact with Charles A. Dunham, also known as Sanford Conover, a convicted perjurer who volunteered additional evidence against the President in order to obtain a pardon. Nothing came of this contact; Conover had originally been convicted for falsely testifying in connection with the first investigation of the crime, but neither Butler nor Ashley was willing to give up.[43] The Select Committee on the Assassination might exploit the evidence, even if the Judiciary Committee remained unconvinced. Johnson's Washington organ in turn aired wartime charges against Butler.[44]

The main business of the extra session was the preparation of a supplementary Reconstruction Act to set aside the attorney general's opinions. This task, with the aid of Secretary Stanton and the secret support of General Grant, was quickly accomplished.[45] On July 13 both houses passed the Third Reconstruction Bill. Specifically reversing Stanbery's interpretations, the measure provided that the generals commanding the military districts had full power to remove civil officers and that the registrars had the right to disqualify persons attempting to take the oath. It also spelled out in more detail the disfranchisement provisions of the earlier acts.[46]

Naturally Johnson vetoed the measure soon after it reached him. In unusually pointed language he once more denounced the establishment of military rule in the South. Moreover, he considered Congress' denial of the legitimacy of Southern state governments wholly unjustified. How could these states have ratified the Thirteenth Amendment and refused to accept the Fourteenth if they were not competent states? In addition he pointed out that the granting of power to military officers to supersede state officials was not only unconstitutional, but interfered with the prerogatives of their superior, the President of the United States. Johnson complained:

> Within a period of less than a year, the legislation of Congress has attempted to strip the executive department of the Government of some of its essential power. . . . Whilst I hold the chief executive authority of the United States, whilst the obligation rests upon me to see that the laws are faithfully executed, I can never willingly surrender that trust and the powers which accompany it to any other executive officer, high or low.

Once more emphasizing the conviction that the remedy for the evils of the South must come from the people, he expressed the hope that "in the end the rod of despotism" would be broken.[47] The veto was another expression of his policy of fighting a rearguard action until the people could come to his rescue.

When the message reached the House the principal impeachers, despite setbacks, believed their chance had come. Although Stevens was pressing for a swift vote to override, Boutwell rose to warn his colleagues: "The language of this document convinces me of that which indeed I had little doubted before, that from the oppression . . . of this man . . . upon twelve million people . . . there is no relief except in the assertion of that great power which resides in this House alone." In Boutwell's view, it was useless to attempt

77

to protect the freedmen and to reconstruct the South upon a loyal basis as long as "the executive authority of the country, the command of the Army and the Navy, the power of nominating to office are in the hands of Andrew Johnson." Upon Randall's taunts that the radicals dared not proceed with impeachment, Butler admitted the truth of the accusation. "We dare not do our duty," he said, again demanding action.

Wilson defeated all efforts to force his hand. Outraged that Boutwell and Lawrence had revealed some of the proceedings of the committee, he averred that no amount of political pressure would turn him aside from a conscientious discharge of his duty. "I will be controlled by the law and the facts, and by nothing else," he shouted amid great applause. Congress, after overriding the veto, adjourned until the second Tuesday in November.[48] Although some of the more radical members finally sought to prevent the printing of merely partial evidence, the vote was widely interpreted as a defeat for them.[49] The committee had called further witnesses, among them Secretary McCulloch and even General Grant, but it adjourned on July 20.[50] Johnson had again succeeded in holding Congress at bay. Unless he interfered further with Reconstruction, even the most radical publications admitted that impeachment was dead.[51]

But the President had merely been waiting for Congress to adjourn in order to continue his policy of obstruction. That he was consciously attempting to shore up whatever power he retained in order to continue delaying the Reconstruction process became clear when he made his next move: the removal of the secretary of war.

Johnson's relations with Stanton had become increasingly strained. Many of the administration's supporters had never been able to understand why he had retained the secretary of war after the resignation of the other dissatisfied cabinet members. As one of his Michigan friends wrote in the summer of 1866, Stanton was staying in the cabinet merely to act as a watchdog for the radicals.[52] Such influential advisers as Senator Doolittle and Francis P. Blair strongly urged Secretary Stanton's dismissal.[53] The well-known Pennsylvania Democrat, Samuel Randall, agreed. Stanton must go, he warned. The people would approve.[54]

But the President retained Stanton even when it became increasingly apparent that the secretary, opposing the vetoes of the District of Columbia suffrage, the admission of Nebraska and Colorado as new states, and Reconstruction bills, was wholly out of sympathy with the administration's policies.[55] Although Stanton disapproved so vocally of the Tenure of Office law that Johnson, in order to embarrass him, asked him to prepare the veto message, the President was under no illusions about his adviser. As he said to his private secretary in April, the entire Reconstruction struggle would have ended long since had it not been for Stanton. Convinced of Stanton's duplicity, he called him obsequious.[56] For the time being, however, for substantial reasons of his own, he hesitated and did not dismiss the secretary of war.

Johnson's reluctance to rid himself of his hostile counselor was a good example of his cunning in seeking to thwart Congress. The replacement of Harlan, Dennison, and Speed had caused no problem because all three had resigned voluntarily. Stanton, however, remained in the cabinet. To dismiss him meant challenging the administration's foes on Capitol Hill. It might also mean challenging the army, and Johnson was anxious to retain Grant's good will. That the commanding general and the secretary of war were cooperating to foil the administration could not have been entirely unknown to the White House, but the President must also have been aware of the personal differences between Stanton and Grant.[57] The general's presidential ambitions were popular in conservative circles,[58] and his hostility to Butler made him a potential ally against the impeachers.[59] Consequently, Johnson awaited an appropriate moment to dismiss Stanton, and at the same time tie Grant more closely to the administration.

By the spring and summer of 1867 it became evident that Stanton and the President were bitter enemies. In company with Grant, who was anxious to protect the army from interference by the courts and to simplify the task of military Reconstruction, the war secretary was quietly sabotaging Johnson's Reconstruction policies.[60] Johnson was outraged, and after the veto of the Third Reconstruction Bill rumors of Stanton's dismissal began to appear in the press.[61]

But the President was too shrewd to take action at once. Biding his time, he waited until Congress had adjourned. Then, when Sheridan again defied him by removing the governor of Texas,[62] he became more than ever convinced of the necessity of removing not only the general commanding in New Orleans, but his protector as well.

A series of developments soon gave him the opening for which he had long been waiting. The first of these was the application of a pardon for the perjurer Sanford Conover. After his intrigues with Ashley and Butler had failed to secure his release from prison, Conover turned to the President. Hoping to gain Johnson's favor, he now approached him and accused his former associates of attempting to manufacture evidence. Johnson was incensed at this revelation of his opponents' tactics, and the story made for good newspaper publicity at a time when he was preparing to move against Stanton. Consequently, the administration saw to it that this information was released to the press.[63]

When, on July 29, Johnson learned about Conover's maneuvers, he finally decided to remove the secretary of war. Anxious to retain Grant's support, he conferred with the general and told him both Stanton and Sheridan must go. Grant warned that Stanton was very popular and that he could not be removed without the consent of the Senate. On the subject of Sheridan he was even more emphatic. He pointed out that Sheridan, who had administered his district well, was one of the best loved Union officers. Although it was obvious that Johnson could get little help from Grant, the general nevertheless stated that he would not shrink from duty. Grant would accept Johnson's offer of the War Department, and the President told his private secretary to prepare a letter asking Stanton to resign.[64]

A second development facilitated Johnson's designs. On August 5, as a result of the trial of John H. Surratt, he learned that a recommendation for mercy for Mrs. Surratt had never been shown to him. Since the secretary of war had been in charge of the prosecution, the President could and did blame Stanton for the omission.[65] The story would again make good reading in the press, and therefore on the very same day Johnson sent Stanton a demand for his resignation. He did not really expect the fiery secretary to leave voluntarily, but he also said that he could not understand how Stanton could fail to comply.[66]

The secretary of war decided to refuse Johnson's request. Convinced that he must protect the interests of the Republican party and the army, he sent the President a curt reply:

> SIR: Your note of this day has been received, stating that public considerations of a high character constrain you to say that my resignation as Secretary of War will be accepted.
>
> In reply, I have the honor to say that public considerations of a high character, which alone have induced me to continue at the head of this Department, constrain me not to resign the office of Secretary of War before the next meeting of Congress.[67]

But Johnson was now sure of his course. Strengthened by support both within and outside of the cabinet,[68] he decided to remove Stanton without his consent. On Sunday, August 11, he called in General Grant. Would the general accept the position of secretary of war *ad interim*, he asked. When Grant hesitated, Johnson wanted to know if there were any real differences between them. There was nothing personal, replied Grant, merely a difference of opinion on the Reconstruction acts and the Fourteenth Amendment. The interview ended with Grant's acceptance, and Johnson ordered his private secretary to bring him the letter suspending Stanton. "SIR," it read,

> By virtue of the power and authority vested in me as President by the Constitution and laws of the United States, you are hereby suspended from office as Secretary of War, and will cease to exercise any

and all functions pertaining to the same. You will at once transfer to General Ulysses S. Grant, who has this day been authorized and empowered to act as Secretary of War *ad interim,* all records, books, papers, and other public property now your custody and charge.

He dated it August 12 and calmly went to church.[69]

When Stanton received the order, he protested. However, in view of "superior force," as he put it, he had no alternative but to comply. Johnson had won the first round. "The turning point has come; the Rubicon is crossed," he said.[70]

The removal of the secretary of war paved the way for other changes. Contrary to the advice of Grant and of the cabinet, and sustained only by Welles, on August 17 the President finally recalled Sheridan.[71] Two weeks later Sickles, too, was asked to surrender his command. And to clinch matters, after first appointing George H. Thomas as Sheridan's successor, Johnson later determined to replace Thomas with Winfield S. Hancock, one of the most conservative generals in the army. To complete his attack on Congressional Reconstruction, Johnson also issued a proclamation of amnesty to all but a mere handful of Confederates, a document in which he once more invoked the authority of the Johnson-Crittenden resolutions.[72]

The President's seeming assault on the Reconstruction policy of Congress greatly agitated the country. Not only the radicals were incensed; moderate Republicans also believed that the Chief Executive had gone too far. "Stanton has been suspended by the President," the moderate John Bigelow noted in his diary. "This is an outrage which makes forbearance toward Johnson no longer a virtue. Impeachment is now probable." He was so stirred that he even sent a letter of sympathy to the ousted secretary of war.[73] Garfield's friend, Hinsdale, was also perturbed. "Johnson is rampant again," he wrote to the future President, then vacationing in Europe. "Hitherto I have been opposed to impeachment, but I am beginning to think Johnson must be put out of the way."[74] Thomas A. Jenckes, a moderate representative from Rhode Island, heard that Stanton's removal met with the unmitigated condemnation of Union men.[75] Even conservatives who tended to favor the President were uneasy. "What in God's name has gotten into Johnson?" one of Thurlow Weed's confidants queried him. "The people are with Stanton, who has done his whole duty in saving the government from ruin during old Buck's administration and from disgrace under Johnson's. The removal of Sheridan will be an additional argument with Ashley and others for impeaching him, and they will put him on trial as sure as he is a living man."[76] As Senator Henry B. Anthony wrote to Seward, he had been trying to mollify the feeling against Johnson. But there was now "no defending" of what he was doing. He was risking impeachment, which would be bad for the country and himself.[77]

Johnson had not struck blindly, however. Although his friends were uneasy—Dixon thought the removals had come too late and that Johnson should never have appointed Sickles and Sheridan in the first place, and the cabinet, with the exception of Welles, had advised against Sheridan's recall[78]—for the time being he held the upper hand. He had acted strictly within the law.

It is true that demands for impeachment became more insistent as a result of the President's assertion of power. The Chicago *Tribune*, which in spite of its early broaching of the issue had been opposing impeachment for some time, now again demanded that the President be brought to trial.[79] Radical journals redoubled their efforts,[80] and private observers became convinced that the removal of the President was merely a matter of time. "Should the President proceed in his recently manifest line of action, in my opinion, no power this side of God's throne will prevent his impeachment and removal from office," A. N. Cole wrote to the secretary of the treasury. He himself had long been opposed to impeachment, he averred, but the President's policy of delay and obstruction would not work.[81] Carl Schurz decided that Johnson was a madman, virtually certain of impeachment, and even Fessenden wrote to McCulloch that the outlook was grim. Formerly, the sentiment of New England had generally condemned the impeachers and opposed "Wade, Butler & Co." But now, he continued, "I meet not a man who is not in favor of impeachment if any decent pretense for it can be found. It does seem as if Johnson was resolved upon destruction." Schuyler Colfax agreed. He thought impeachment was certain to come.[82]

But the man in the White House continued on his course. Convinced that in the long run the people would support him, Johnson was carefully marshaling his strength. Neither the fears of the cabinet nor the threats of his enemies disturbed him. Congress was not in session. He had succeeded in including Grant in his cabinet. Elections were approaching, and there were indications that popular dissatisfaction with Negro suffrage might yet redound to his advantage. He was willing to take his chances.

Six.

The Election of 1867

President Johnson's persistent opposition to Congress probably could not have been sustained had it not been for his
unwavering faith in ultimate vindication by the people. As he saw
it, radical Congressmen might for a time triumph over him, but
in the long run he was certain that the American people would
come to his rescue. The voters would see to it that his views of
"the Constitution as it is" and "the Union as it was" prevailed in
the end.

Johnson had always believed in the ultimate wisdom of the people. Popular support had sustained him in his rise from alderman
to senator. Faith in democracy, as he understood it, had enabled
him to risk life and property in defying secession in a slave state,
and the broad mass of voters had elected him Vice President. His
struggle with Congress, he thought, was still a contest for popular
supremacy. As he said on February 10, 1866, to a committee of the
Virginia legislature:

> I know that some are distrustful, but I am one of those who have con-
> fidence in the judgment, in the integrity, in the intelligence, in the
> virtue of the great mass of the American people; and having such
> confidence, I am willing to trust them. . . . I feel that the day is not
> far distant—I speak confidingly of the great mass of the American
> people—when they will determine that this Union shall be made
> whole, and the great right of representation in the councils of the
> nation be acknowledged.

Twelve days later, in his reply to the Washington's Birthday
serenade, he returned to the same theme. "Yes," he said, "there is a

groundswell coming, of popular judgment and indignation. The American people will speak, and by their instinct, if in no other way, know who are their friends. . . . All that is wanting is time, until the American people can understand what is going on, and be ready to accept the view just as it appears to me."[1]

Johnson's belief in final popular vindication played a significant role in his attempt to form a new party. As he explained in August 1866, when receiving the delegation from the Philadelphia National Union Convention, "I said on a previous occasion, and repeat now, that all that was necessary in this great contest against tyranny and despotism was that the struggle be sufficiently audible for the American people to hear and properly understand the issues involved." And during the "Swing around the Circle," he again emphasized his trust in the electorate. "All that is wanting in the great struggle in which we are engaged is simply to develop the popular heart of the nation," he assured a New York audience. "It is like a latent fire." Repeating the same argument when concluding a speech at St. Louis, he unmistakably predicted, "with the confidence I have always had, that the people will ultimately redress all wrongs and set the Government right."[2]

The defeat which the President suffered in 1866 did not discourage him. The results could be explained away on the grounds that the elections had turned on a false issue—an effect of radical charges of administration favor to rebels—and Johnson maintained his hard line in spite of the seeming reversal. He was looking with perfect confidence for his vindication "to the justice of that future" which he was certain could not long be delayed, he told the New York satirist, Charles G. Halpine, in March 1867.[3]

Because of this outlook, Johnson was eagerly watching for every possible sign of popular approval. A minor victory in Iowa was encouraging, and he had great expectations of the 1867 spring elections in Connecticut. "If Connecticut repudiates radicalism . . . , it will change the whole aspect of things in Washington," James F. Babcock, the New Haven newspaperman and politician, predicted.[4] When James E. English was elected governor in April, the President was much gratified about the victory. It was the turn of the current, he remarked.[5]

The election of 1867 did not generally turn upon competition for national office, but although most of the fall contests would be local in nature, Johnson attached great importance to them. If he could demonstrate that popular opinion was turning in his direction, it would be very difficult for Congress to impeach him. His cause—the cause of the immediate restoration of the *white* South— would be greatly strengthened. And, based as it was on white supremacy, it provided a weapon to weaken his enemies: the race question.

Because the Reconstruction acts had imposed Negro suffrage upon the South, the continued exclusion of nonwhites from the electorate in a number of Northern states was becoming increasingly embarrassing for the Republicans. Accordingly, the party sought to remove racial voting barriers whenever feasible. In 1867 the question of enfranchising the blacks appeared on the ballot in Kansas, Ohio, and Minnesota. In other states it also became an issue because of the Republicans' commitment to equal rights. But in spite of Democratic charges that all their opponents wanted was to secure black votes, popular prejudice against blacks was so great that the experiment was very dangerous for the party sponsoring it.

The Democrats and Johnson's supporters enthusiastically espoused the issue of white superiority. "[The radicals] have at last split on the rock of Negro supremacy—a very different thing, they will find, as a party cry, from 'War for the Union,' " Senator Dixon wrote exultingly to Welles in September 1867.[6] Consequently, the administration's friends exploited the controversial issue to the fullest. "Any Democrat who did not manage to hint in his speech that the negro is a degenerate gorilla, would be considered lacking in enthusiasm," commented Georges Clemenceau, then a young reporter on a tour of the United States.[7] The New York *Herald*, which had reversed itself to come to the support of the administration, warned that the radicals were trying to give the South over to Negroes. Let Northern Republicans free themselves![8] In Ohio, wagons filled with girls dressed in white bearing banners inscribed "FATHERS, SAVE US FROM NEGRO EQUALITY" rolled through the streets.[9]

The election in the Buckeye State was one of the most crucial that fall. In spite of many misgivings, the Republicans included a suffrage plank in their platform and saw to it that a referendum on a constitutional amendment for extending the right to vote to Negroes appeared on the ballot. In addition, a new governor and legislature were to be elected. Since Senator Wade's term would expire in 1869, the new senate and assembly would have to choose his successor.[10] This fact, as much as the suffrage amendment, focused national attention on the contest. Its outcome was sure to be regarded as a referendum on Reconstruction.

When Ohio Republicans first adopted the suffrage plank, delegates from the southern part of the state strongly opposed it. But although it was certain that general distaste for racial equality would alienate many voters, the radical leadership insisted on the inclusion of the reform. It was a difficult burden to carry.[11]

Wade's candidacy for reelection also posed problems for his party. The old senator had long been known for his radicalism. In the forefront of the struggle for a Homestead Act, he had also been the champion of high tariffs and wage earners.[12] In the summer of 1867, however, he went further. In company with other members of Congress he set out on a railroad excursion to the West. When he stopped at the Eldridge House in Lawrence, Kansas, he was serenaded by a crowd and delivered an impromptu speech from the balcony. Just as he had been in the forefront of the fight against slavery, he said, so he would now take the same position in the beginning contest for the rights of women. If he had not thought that his wife had enough sense to vote, he would never have married her. Radicalism in this and all other questions was righteousness; conservatism, hypocrisy and cowardice. Then he turned to Reconstruction. The South now had the mildest terms it would ever obtain, and if it accepted them everything would work out well. If not, "another turn would be given to the screw." But it was his final point that really brought him notoriety. The next great question facing the nation, he predicted, would be that of the relationship between capital and labor. Was it just that the laborer should receive so small a reward for his toil? A more equitable distribution of property must be worked out. Congress, which had done so much for the slave, could not quietly regard the terrible distinction between the man who labored and him who did not. "If you dullheads can't see this, the women will," he added, "and will act accordingly."[13]

The speech caused a sensation. "Agrarianism—Equal Division of Property—Woman's Suffrage—Moonshine and Green Cheese—Reconstruction and Misconstruction," the New York *Herald* headlined its report of the event. The *Times* called Wade worse than Stevens, Butler, or Phillips, and the *National Intelligencer* predicted that the Acting Vice President's behavior had effectively killed impeachment.[14] The senator sought to defend himself by maintaining he had been quoted incorrectly, but in an interview with the Cincinnati *Commercial,* he repeated his criticism of the existing order. "That system of labor which degrades the poor man and elevates the rich; which makes the rich richer and the poor poorer . . . is wrong," he said.[15] The general tenor of his remarks could not be denied. He was evidently as radical on matters affecting the economy and society as on those pertaining to race relations.

Another difficulty facing Ohio Republicans was the financial question. The state Democratic leader, George H. Pendleton, was the author of the Pendleton Plan, the payment of federal bonds in greenbacks instead of gold. Despite the fact that Wade was also an advocate of soft money, Chase's hard-money views tended to identify his party with deflation. As a result, many a greenbacker was attracted to the Democratic ticket.[16]

That these factors were rendering the result doubtful became evident early in the campaign. Party leaders privately expressed their misgivings, and the New York *World* charged that they were secretly abandoning the suffrage plank because of their fear of the issue.[17] The President was greatly encouraged.

The Democrats made the most of their opponents' dilemma.

Undaunted by his wartime record of persistent criticism of the national effort and his reputation as the country's most prominent Copperhead, Clement L. Vallandigham continually stressed the suffrage issue. "I am not in the habit of pandering to the hates or prejudices of the Democratic Party on the question of the negro," he said on August 14 at Middletown. "I leave all allusions to his curly head, his thick lips, his flat nose and eboo shins to the slang wangers of the Democratic Party. . . ." Asserting that he was not going to discuss the question of Negro equality, he assured his audience that he was certain the blacks had so far failed to show any capacity for self-government. The government was made for white men, and God had placed an unbridgeable barrier between the two races. "The wolf is now at your doors," he warned, calling upon the electorate to protect itself against the threatened black danger.[18]

The Republicans desperately attempted to counter this argument. Stressing the need for equal justice, prominent figures from Ohio and other areas canvassed the state.[19] Wade was especially active in attempting to meet the racial questions head on. Given to private prejudices himself, he had no hesitation in urging his listeners to overcome theirs. "The right of the colored man to Suffrage is but the legitimate logical deduction from what you had done before," he said. "There are no doubt men here who have strong prejudice against the colored men, the result of education. Men are not to blame for that, but they are to blame if they suffer what they know to be prejudice to do injustice to anybody."[20] The chief justice himself also campaigned for the party and its platform, but the Republicans' efforts to overcome the bigoted notions of their constituents proved fruitless. Encouraged by a victory in California early in September and a reduction of Republican strength in Maine a few days later, the Democrats swept on to victory. They captured the state legislature, defeated the suffrage amendment, and rendered Wade's reelection impossible. Although Rutherford B. Hayes, the Republican candidate for governor, managed to squeeze through, the result was a severe setback for Johnson's opponents.[21]

The defeat in Ohio coincided with a local Democratic success in Pennsylvania. Although no suffrage amendment was on the ballot, the race problem figured prominently in the Pennsylvania campaign. In its address to the voters the Democratic State Committee warned that Congress was assuming the right to regulate local rules of suffrage: ". . . the negro is, by law, made the equal of the white man in all public places, and authorized to hold offices and sit on juries in the capital." To prevent the perpetuation and spread of such conditions, it asked Pennsylvanians to support the Democratic ticket. This they did in overwhelming numbers, and the Democratic candidates, especially the party's choice for a vacancy on the state supreme court, were successful.[22]

With the October setbacks setting an example, the November elections also proved disappointing for the Republicans. The Democrats won clear-cut victories in New York, New Jersey, and Maryland, defeated Negro suffrage in Kansas and Minnesota, and reduced Republican majorities elsewhere. Since the Republicans had endorsed black enfranchisement in New Jersey and were known to favor it in the pending New York constitution, the issue played a significant role in both states despite its failure to be voted upon directly.[23] Thus Johnson could pride himself on having been sustained on his Reconstruction policy and opposition to racial equality. While the result did not materially affect relative party strength in Congress, it nevertheless appeared to give some substance to the President's assertions of popular support.

Johnson's reaction to the Democratic victories was enthusiastic. Here at last was the popular vindication for which he had been waiting. Elated at the election results, he sent a congratulatory telegram to the victors in Ohio, while the *National Intelligencer* exulted: "The Impeachers Impeached. While Ben Wade and Ashley are howling for the impeachment of the President, they have themselves been impeached . . . by the people of their own State."[24]

The President's conservative supporters were equally cheered by the Democratic successes. The elections had exceeded his expectations, Senator Dixon wrote to Welles. They vindicated fully the position conservatives had taken. "One year ago," he continued, we had to encounter what to superficial observers, seemed to be popular sentiment. Of course we knew then that the results of the el[ection]s at that time, were no real test of public opinion. . . . Now the most blind & bigotted [*sic*] partisans cannot fail to see that the people & the President are together against the mad policy of Congress.[25]

Babcock rejoiced at "these signs of the triumph of our principles," and Lewis Campbell believed the administration majority would have been even greater had not the Democrats insisted on pushing forward "men of the Vallandigham type."[26]

If conservatives were delighted, Democrats expressed their satisfaction even more strongly. "The long and cheerless night of violence is drawing to a close," John A. McClernand wrote enthusiastically to Johnson. "The elections in Pa. and O. have struck the death knell of radicalism. Thank God, the people, and the President for it." Other Democrats asked Johnson to remove Republican officeholders. As Horatio Seymour, the wartime Democratic governor of New York, summed up the feelings of his associates in a letter to Johnson: "We have gone through a great contest, the results of which . . . have cheered your heart. In this contest you had a deeper personal influence than any other living mortal."[27] And while Johnson was reputed to have commented that the Ohio results constituted a rebuke to both extremes—the Thurman Democracy and Wade radicalism[28]—there was little difference between his position and that of the Democrats.

The reasons for the Republican defeats were easy to see. While the Democrats everywhere campaigned against radical Reconstruction, the Negro suffrage question had loomed as their strongest point. Not in vain had Johnson chosen this issue as one of his main weapons in the struggle with Congress. Campbell gloated that he had always been right. He had predicted to the President that if the question of Negro enfranchisement ever came up, it would be voted down in Ohio. Events had borne him out. The elder Ewing agreed. The vote on black suffrage, he thought, had shown the radicals the handwriting on the wall.[29]

What Johnson's supporters welcomed, his opponents deplored. Readily conceding that the "Amendment" caused the defeat, the Ohio Republican, R. C. Parsons, complained to Sumner that "it was to a great extent impossible to get the mass of the people to vote for it—& those who did vote for it . . . did so with great reluctance."[30] Senator Sherman's analysis was similar. The Negro voting question was the first cause of the reverse, he concluded.[31] As Ben Wade put it in language the President could understand, "The nigger whipped us."[32]

The suffrage question also greatly influenced the outcome in states where it was not even on the ballot. In California, where the number of blacks was negligible, it played a major role. "Negro suffrage hurt us here very considerable [*sic*]," a local politician confided to Washburne. "A great many of our party here are mean enough to want it in the South, & not in the North. . . ."[33] Elsewhere the issue was considered to be of significant, if not decisive importance,[34] and in view of the fact that the Democrats everywhere never failed to stress the problem, its importance was self-evident.

In addition to the suffrage issue, local problems played a part in the Republican defeat. In New York, rival contenders, especially partisans of Senator Morgan, were trying to break down Governor Fenton's hold on the party; California Republicans were plagued by factionalism and a history of corruption; and in Maine, Massachusetts, and Wisconsin, the prohibition question reduced Republican majorities.[35] In Ohio, the greenback issue also affected the outcome. Although some distrusted Wade because of his soft-money views, others were strongly influenced by the even more inflationist slogans of George H. Pendleton.[36] Moreover, Wade's economic and social radicalism, buttressed as it was by Stevens' and Butler's demands for confiscation of rebel property, disquieted many well-placed Republicans.[37]

Finally, there was the question of impeachment. Many radicals felt that the defeats were due to Congress' failure to remove the President, while moderates were equally convinced that the agitation about a possible trial had harmed the party.[38] Whatever the explanation, the elections greatly encouraged Southern conservatives.

The renewed strengthening of the President's sympathizers in the South was one of the most important results of the Democratic successes. How difficult it would be to carry the Reconstruction process forward became evident almost immediately. "Rebels are very jubilant over the result of the election in Ohio and Pennsylvania," a Georgia Republican complained to Congressman Samuel Shellabarger. "They talk very confidently of the 'near approach of the day when all Yankees and white niggers will have to leave the south.' "[39] The Richmond *Whig* regarded the reaction in the North "as in the nature of a popular revolt against the rule of ultraism" and hailed with satisfaction the promise it gave "that the bedlamites of the SUMNER and STEVENS school are to be set aside. . . ."[40] Southern Democrats were inspired with hope for the future,[41] and as long as Johnson's policy seemed to find some popular favor in the North, they would never acquiesce in radical Reconstruction.

What the other results of the Republican reverses would be was more difficult to predict. According to many observers, impeachment would have to be given up. Not only conservatives, but even the radical *Independent*'s Washington correspondent considered the impeachment movement "dead, unless the President, by fresh outrages," gave it "a new impetus."[42] Several radicals, on the other hand, believed that it was more than ever necessary to bring the President to trial. Johnson would undoubtedly be " 'ten times more' the child of hell than he was before," thought Parsons.[43] Carl Schurz was convinced that the President, encouraged by the election results, would attempt by executive means to hinder the carrying out of Congressional policy.[44] To prevent further presidential encroachments, renewed demands for impeachment were common.[45]

The most generally accepted conclusion about the elections was that they assured General Grant's nomination. The Republicans would now have no choice except to select the general as their presidential candidate. Conservative enough to appeal to the moderates, Grant would be able to offset recent losses. The radicals, who had long opposed him, would have to accept him or risk defeat. "Since these elections," former Speaker Galusha Grow asserted, "there can be no doubt of [Grant's] nomination. . . . Everybody feels that with him as our candidate our success in the elections would be beyond doubt." Wade had been defeated, the Chase candidacy had received a mortal blow, and the Victor of Appomattox seemed the only way out.[46]

In some quarters it was believed that the effect of the elections would be comparatively small. The Democratic success was not so brilliant after all, as Clemenceau pointed out. By claiming victory for the future, the minority party was frightening Republican moderates. In the long run the elections would have the same effect on Negro suffrage that the battle of Bull Run had had on emancipation. People would get used to it.[47] Many radicals agreed with the young Frenchman. Speaker Colfax vowed that the "standard must not be lowered an inch," and Thaddeus Stevens, though ill, was planning new measures to restrict the President.[48]

Perhaps the most profound interpretation of the elections was offered by James D. Cox, the former governor of Ohio. "In the bare hope that the evidence of our willingness to accept the same rule we apply to the South, would make it possible that the two races there would . . . seek a peaceful solution of their great problem," he had worked earnestly for the adoption of the suffrage amendment, although he was a moderate. But the failure of the suffrage plank had changed everything. Northerners could not expect Southern acquiescence in Negro suffrage when they themselves denied it to the small number of blacks in their midst. "We ourselves have made a new revolution there [in the South] inevitable. . . ," he predicted. "It may take two or three years to complete the dissolution, but as for cure, there would be more hope for a confirmed epileptic." Reconstruction was in serious trouble.[49]

The President could truly congratulate himself. His refusal to compromise with his opponents had at last paid off. "I am gratified, but not surprised at the result of the recent elections," he responded to a group of serenaders at the White House. "I have always had undoubting confidence in the people. They may be misled . . . but never perverted, in the end they are always right. In the gloomiest hours through which I have passed . . . I had still an abiding confidence in the people and felt assured that they in their might would come to the rescue. They have come, and thank God, they have come."[50] Congress, to be sure, was still in the hands of his enemies, but its policies would be more difficult to implement. Buoyed by the victory, he prepared his address on the state of the Union.

Johnson's third annual message showed his newly won confidence and determination. So harsh that it even offended some of his own sympathizers,[51] it restated many of his previous arguments. His objection to the lack of representation of the Southern states, his horror of military rule, his denunciation of the Tenure of Office Act—all were included. But the core of the message dealt with the Negro question, "the subjugation of the States to negro domination," which he considered "worse than the military despotisms under which they are now suffering." Conceding that the freedmen were entitled to good and humane government, he nevertheless pointed out that the qualities which enabled any people to undertake the experiment of self-government were rare. "In the progress of nations," he continued, "negroes have shown less capacity for government than any other race of people. No independent government of any form has ever been successful in their hands. On the contrary, whenever they have been left to their own devices they have shown a constant tendency to relapse into barbarism." Emphasizing that the extension of the suffrage was an exceedingly delicate matter, he insisted that it was particularly inappropriate to confer the vote upon blacks. "The great difference between the two races in physical, mental, and moral characteristics," he concluded,

> will prevent an amalgamation or fusion of them together in one homogeneous mass. If the inferior obtains the ascendency over the

other, it will govern with reference only to its own interests—for it will recognize no common interest—and create such a tyranny as this continent has never yet witnessed. Already the negroes are influenced by promises of confiscation and plunder. They are taught to regard as an enemy every white man who has any respect for the rights of his race. . . . Of all the dangers which our nation has yet encountered, none are equal to those which must result from the success of the effort now making to Africanize the half of our country.[52]

Johnson's outlook had remained unchanged. He was still determined to keep the United States in general and the South in particular a white man's country. As he saw it, his tactics had proven successful, and he was perfectly willing to step up his attacks upon the policies of Congress. The people, he was certain, were with him. Congress would have to meet the challenge.

Seven.

Failure of the First Impeachment

The state and local elections were not the only subjects of political interest during the late summer and fall of 1867. From the moment Johnson suspended Stanton, speculation about the likelihood of impeachment was revived. True, the House Judiciary Committee had decided against the removal of the President, but his renewed defiance of Congress and his evident determination to interfere with the execution of the Reconstruction acts might easily lead one committee member or another to reverse himself. So widespread was the discussion of an impending showdown that Senator Dixon warned the administration not to push matters too far. The President had done enough, he cautioned. Let him not upset things any more.[1] Judge William Lawrence, one of the radical members of the committee, published an article on impeachment in the *American Law Register*, and the newspapers continually kept the subject alive.[2] The administration had to take the threat seriously.

But Johnson was perfectly willing to defy the impeachers. When at the time of the impending dismissal of Stanton the possibility of a trial was mentioned in cabinet, he expressed the utmost contempt for all threats against himself.[3] Whatever might be said about him, no one could accuse him of cowardice.

Contempt for the impeachers did not mean that the President simply disregarded them. On the contrary, he carefully planned to weaken them with all the weapons at his command.

In his efforts to frustrate his enemies' plans for a new South, and in his defense against impeachment threats, Johnson considered his every move with great deliberation.[4] Just as he did not actually suspend the secretary of war until he judged the time opportune, and just as he relentlessly kept up the propaganda against Butler and Ashley, so he also devoted much attention to the choice of a suitable replacement for Stanton. The selection of Grant was a perfect example of his tactics.

The popularity of the Victor of Appomattox was a fact of American political life. Although Francis P. Blair, Jr., was convinced that the general, with Stanton's aid, was grasping for dictatorship, and Johnson himself knew that Grant differed with him, he nevertheless was also aware of Grant's firm hold on public opinion. Undoubtedly he would become a presidential candidate. The moderates liked him and the radicals were afraid of him. If Congress could be induced to confirm any new secretary of war, no one stood a better chance than Grant. Why not attempt to win him over?[5]

It was with this aim in mind that the President asked Grant to take over the War Department, and to the administration's delight a near rupture occurred between the incumbent and his *ad interim* successor. When informing Stanton that he had accepted Johnson's offer, Grant expressed his appreciation of his former superior's "zeal, patriotism, firmness, and ability" in office. Stanton, who was miffed, did not meekly acquiesce in his ouster. "Under a sense of public duty," he replied,

> I am compelled to deny the President's right . . . to suspend me from office as Secretary of War, or to authorize any other person to enter upon the discharge of the duties of that office, or to require me to transfer to you or any other person the records, books, papers, and other property in my official custody. . . . But inasmuch as the President has assumed to suspend me . . . and you have notified me of your acceptance of the appointment of Secretary of War *ad interim*, I have no alternative but to submit, under protest, to the superior force of the President.

Although he acknowledged the general's "kind terms" of notification and assured him of the "cordial reciprocation of the sentiments expressed," Grant considered the letter irksome. He resented the implication that he was Johnson's tool.[6]

So far Johnson's stratagem seemed to be working well, especially since Ben Butler chose early August to launch a renewed attack on Grant. Afraid of the general's ever increasing popularity, Butler had him shadowed with detectives and was even compiling an exposé of his alleged shortcomings. Finally, Butler decided to issue a report blaming the breakdown of wartime prisoner exchanges on Grant. When the document was published, the general's cooperation with the administration appeared to have been made easier.[7]

The President exploited his advantage to the fullest. Having succeeded in inducing Grant to become a member of the cabinet, Johnson carefully sought to keep the general reasonably satisfied. He treated the new secretary with respect, appeared to take him into his confidence, and refused to make an issue of their obvious differences. Thus, while attending his first cabinet meeting, Grant impressed Welles as "not at all displeased with his new position." The Maryland Blairs, unlike Francis P. Blair, Jr., believed Grant would ultimately come over to the administration.[8] It was already being said in radical circles that he had made a fool of himself, and Horace White, editor of the Chicago *Tribune,* feared that the general's presidential prospects had received a setback. He thought the latest developments would confirm the impression that Grant was tainted with Johnsonism.[9]

In view of the general's determination to carry out the Reconstruction acts, Johnson's patience was sorely tested. After deciding to remove Sheridan, the President invited Grant to submit his opinion about the proposed change. Instead of replying verbally, as Johnson had expected, the general prepared a strong protest in writing. "In the name of the patriotic people," he urged that the order not be insisted upon. Maintaining that it was "unmistakably the expressed wish of the country that Gen. Sheridan should not be removed from his present command," he stressed that the United States was a republic in which the will of the people was the law of the land. Sheridan's removal would only be regarded as "an effort to defeat the laws of Congress." The "unreconstructed element in the South, those who did all they could to break up this government by arms," would consider the order a triumph. They would be encouraged to renewed opposition because of the belief that the President was with them.[10] He alerted Sheridan at the same time, assuring him of his firm support. He had already encouraged the general in New Orleans to arrange matters in such a way as to make it difficult for any successor to effect material changes.[11]

In keeping with his determination to separate the general from the mainstream of the Republican party, Johnson met this challenge with firmness and tact. Because Grant had unexpectedly chosen to put his suggestions in writing, the President answered in the same way. Insisting that his orders be carried out, he rejected all intimations of popular disapproval. He was not aware that the question had ever been submitted to the people for determination. Moreover, it would be unjust to the army to assume that Sheridan alone was capable of commanding in Louisiana and Texas. Not only was Thomas a great man, but his administration of the Department of the Cumberland compared most favorably with that of the Fifth Military District, where Sheridan's rule had been "one of absolute tyranny." While conceding that the United States was a republic, Johnson emphasized that it was one based on a written constitution, which made the President commander-in-chief of the army and navy. Concluding with a reminder that he had never been in favor of Sheridan's appointment in the first place, he declared that now "patriotic considerations" demanded that the general be superseded.[12]

The written reply was only one way of meeting Grant's objections. Still anxious to come to some understanding with him, the President invited the general to come to the White House to discuss the matter. At first Grant demurred. It was rumored the transfer in New Orleans was merely the beginning of many more changes, he said. After Sheridan's ouster others would follow. All the generals commanding Southern districts would be relieved, and finally the commanding general himself. Johnson laughed disarmingly. Had he not long ago wanted Grant to act as secretary of war? Flattered, the general answered in the affirmative. Remarking that he did not see the use of a civilian as secretary of war, he intimated that perhaps Stanton's suspension had not been such a bad thing after all. On this note of agreement the conference ended. The President, who had acted contrary to the advice of almost the entire cabinet—Stanbery had told him he would face impeachment if he removed Sheridan—had succeeded beyond expectations.[13]

Johnson persisted in maintaining his course. A showdown with the commanding general had been avoided temporarily, but the controversy was not yet over. Once again, the President, who had a low opinion of Grant's understanding of political problems,[14] succeeded in emerging as the victor without losing the advantages of the general's membership in the cabinet.

The choice of George H. Thomas as Sheridan's successor had been dictated not by preference, but by necessity. Thomas was considered a radical, and Johnson wanted conservative generals in command of the South, officers like Winfield S. Hancock whom he had originally intended to send to Louisiana. However, Thomas fell sick, and his doctor warned that it would be dangerous for him to go to New Orleans.[15]

Johnson welcomed this development. It was a favorable sign that the Lord was helping his work, he remarked. He was now free to appoint Hancock after all, and orders to this effect were accordingly made out. Sheridan would have to leave New Orleans at once.[16]

The renewed change in commanders brought about another clash between Johnson and Grant, and the President once more deftly put the general in his place. During a cabinet meeting on August 27, Grant protested against the new dispositions. No word had yet been received from General Thomas, he protested. It would also be injudicious to recall General Hancock from the Great Plains, where he had varied duties. Would it not be better to carry out the original order and let Sheridan remain until

Thomas could relieve him? At any rate, insisting that the law placed the execution of the Reconstruction acts in his hands, Grant complained that he had not been consulted. Without betraying his anger, Johnson reminded the general that his orders must be carried out. It was the President's duty to see that the laws were executed.[17]

Grant gave in. He even agreed that General Canby would be a very suitable substitute for General Sickles, whom Johnson, after considerable altercation about Sickles' defiance of the federal courts, had also determined to remove. In view of Grant's long support of the commander of the Carolinas, this change also constituted a victory for the President. Moreover, the general asked to be excused from future cabinet discussions concerning purely political matters.[18]

But Grant had not yet given up his opposition to Sheridan's transfer. In another letter admonishing Johnson that Sheridan's recall would be considered an effort to defeat the Reconstruction acts, Grant again protested against the orders. Reiterating his verbal objections, he repeated the argument that nothing had been heard from Thomas. If Sheridan were immediately recalled, no general officer would be left in the Fifth Military District. He also reemphasized his conviction that, since the law made him responsible for the proper execution of the President's orders, he should have been consulted.[19]

The letter infuriated Johnson. Pronouncing it insubordinate in tone, at first he was not even sure whether he would answer it at all. In a terse note acknowledging its receipt, he directed Grant to carry into effect without further delay the order "to which your communication refers."[20] But on the following day he managed to overcome his anger. Reverting to his subtle way of handling the general, he again summoned Grant to a conference. If the letter were published, he said, it would do the general much more harm than himself. Besides, if every order he issued brought forth a political lecture there could not be any cooperation between the two men. Thereupon Grant, chastened by the President's remarks, asked permission to withdraw his letter. Johnson had won. Hancock went to New Orleans, Canby to Charleston, and both Sheridan and Sickles were recalled.[21]

Of course Grant did not abandon his secret and open opposition to the President's Reconstruction policies. In a private note he confided to Sheridan that he considered the change in New Orleans a heavy blow to Reconstruction and an encouragement to its opponents. Assuring the displaced commander of his continued support, he expressed hopes for a speedy personal interview and praised Sheridan's conduct.[22] When the two recalled generals finally came to Washington, Grant received them cordially. In addition, he issued orders forbidding the appointment of Southern officials who had previously been removed by military authority, thus keeping in force as many of Sickles' and Sheridan's policies as possible. Grant also endorsed Sickles' vain request for a court of inquiry.[23]

In spite of these open indications of Grant's lack of sympathy with his policy, the President, though under no illusions, refused to change his course. In order to put some pressure on his secretary of war, early in October he called General Sherman to Washington. Perhaps the general, a conservative who greatly disliked Stanton, could influence Grant.[24] Shortly afterward, on October 12, Johnson visited the War Department to call on its chief. Grant must be aware of the schemes against the President, he said. Should an attempt be made to impeach him and to depose him before a trial and conviction, would he be able to rely on the loyalty of the army? He would expect to obey orders, the general replied. If he changed his mind, he would let the President know. Johnson thought he could now rely on the secretary.[25]

The recurrent electoral victories in the fall greatly strengthened the President's confidence. It was obvious that Republican reverses would complicate the impeachers' task,[26] but Johnson did not rest. Whenever possible, he sought to weaken his opponents still further.

The financial question was the obvious issue at hand to counteract the growing impeachment movement. Although the Democrats were tainted with George Pendleton's inflationary schemes, conservative financiers and many moderate Republicans were more fearful of the unorthodox monetary views of such prominent impeachers as Butler, Stevens, and Wade.[27] Consequently, the President squarely endorsed conservative measures. Not only did he refuse to dismiss his hard-money secretary of the treasury, Hugh McCulloch, against whom opponents had launched a veritable smear campaign,[28] but he also skillfully linked his plan of Reconstruction with deflation. "I submit to the judgment of Congress whether the public credit may not be injuriously affected by a system like this . . . ," he stated in his annual message in reference to radical Reconstruction. "If we repudiate the Constitution, we will not be expected to care much for mere pecuniary obligations."[29]

While the President had thus been laying the groundwork in his defense, the proceedings of the Judiciary Committee became a focus of national interest. Before going home to Iowa, Chairman Wilson had assured McCulloch that there was no cause for worry. If Johnson did nothing rash, and especially if he did not remove Sheridan, there would be no impeachment.[30] But now that the President had refused to follow Wilson's advice, there was speculation that the committee might reverse its 5 to 4 vote of the previous spring. And since many Republicans believed their election reverses were due to the failure to oust the President, not even the Democratic gains during the fall stilled the rumors of impending drastic action.[31]

The committee, which had adjourned on July 20, resumed hearings on November 15. The few witnesses it examined during the following week testified again about such subjects as the pardoning of deserters in West Virginia and the bestowal of patronage on administration newspapers. A few interesting witnesses were recalled, but they failed to add anything substantial to the already voluminously unimpressive record. Colonel Moore was neither willing nor able to shed any new light on his employer's policies in West Virginia, and Baker again testified about his vain efforts to discover a connection between Johnson and Confederate authorities.[32]

The committee's last witness clearly demonstrated that the case against the President was extremely weak. On November 23, Congressman Ashley appeared before the committee. His questioners wanted to know whether he had produced all the testimony in support of his charges. "All that I can present to the committee at this time," he answered. All the evidence? he was asked. "Substantially all," he had to admit. As for Conover, he said he knew nothing about the perjurer's part in the trial of Lincoln's assassins because he had not been there. He had recommended the convict for a pardon when Conover had led him to believe that he could produce a letter linking Johnson with the assassination. Eldridge was not satisfied. Had the witness not asserted that he had evidence about the crime? Ashley could not deny it, but he had an explanation. "It was not that kind of evidence which would satisfy the great mass of men, especially men who do not concur with me in my theory about this matter." Then he told the committee about his hypothesis of foul play by all Vice Presidents who had ever succeeded to office. Such eccentric speculations did not amount to legal evidence, however, as even Ashley had to concede. As a final witness, he made a very poor impression.[33]

The committee's failure to uncover any substantial infractions of the Constitution constituted a tribute to Johnson's caution. Despite his undoubted interference with Reconstruction in the South, his course of action had been so carefully thought out that he had not given his opponents any legal cause upon which conclusive charges could be based. Certainly he had neither committed any "high crimes or misdemeanors" which were indictable, nor offenses serious enough to justify charges on more general grounds, and the investigators' efforts to find some did them more harm than good. The only way in which he could be impeached was for political reasons. But such an indictment would scarcely be sufficient to convince the moderates in the House, to say nothing of its chances of success in the Senate.

The President's meticulous avoidance of illegal or otherwise clearly impeachable actions was not due to lack of encouragement to take the law into his own hands. Ever since the beginning of his differences with Congress, he had been receiving numerous proposals to arrest the radical leaders, seat the Southern representatives by force, or raise an army to resist impeachment.[34] From time to time various papers had printed rumors of armed clashes, while various radicals had speculated about their veracity.[35] The President, however, had resisted all such temptations. Determined not to break with constitutional precedent, neither by word nor deed did he provide his enemies with any real excuse for impeachment.

In spite of its difficulties the Judiciary Committee decided to render a report recommending the impeachment of the President. Congressman Churchill of New York had reversed himself, and on November 25 the majority, consisting of Boutwell, Churchill, Lawrence, Thomas, and Williams, presented its findings.[36] Written by Williams and submitted by Boutwell, it contained seventeen charges against the Chief Executive. Johnson's Reconstruction, pardoning, and appointing policies, his surrender of property to former Confederates, his vetoes, his denial of the legality of the Thirty-ninth Congress, his alleged connection with the New Orleans riot—they were all there. The gravamen of the charges was his attempt to resist efforts to remold Southern society. "Every great abuse, every flagrant departure from the well settled principles of the government, which has been brought home to its present administration . . . ," Boutwell said,

> is referrable to the one great overshadowing purpose of reconstructing the shattered governments of the rebel States in accordance with his own will, in the interests of the great criminals who carried them into the rebellion, and in such a way as to deprive the people of the loyal States of all chances of indemnity for the past and security for the future. . . .

Chairman Wilson refused to endorse the report. Together with Woodbridge, his remaining Republican colleague on the committee, he submitted a minority opinion. While critical of the President's policies, it pointed out that none of the majority's accusations constituted indictable offenses; consequently, according to the minority, there were no grounds for impeachment. The two Democratic members naturally agreed with the minority, but they strongly rejected Wilson's condemnation of the President's course. With a stinging reminder that the impeachers had just been "themselves impeached" in the fall elections, the Democrats castigated the majority for "trifling with the peace, safety, and prosperity of the country by precipitating on it this dangerous question." [37]

The reports created tremendous excitement. The majority of the Judiciary Committee of the House of Representatives believed that the President of the United States ought to be arraigned on charges of high crimes and misdemeanors. While it was generally conceded that the chances for passage of the impeachment resolutions were slim, the drama about to be enacted in Congress attracted universal attention. Newspapers were filled with stories about the case, and vast crowds converged upon Capitol Hill. Was the struggle between Johnson and Congress about to reach a climax? [38]

The President himself, however, remained calm. When four days earlier he had first heard of the impending majority report, his friend Edmund Cooper told him that Churchill had been bought. Johnson doubted the accuracy of the information about the majority report. If it were correct, however, and impeachment was to be recommended, "so let it be," he said. [39]

Nevertheless, the President did not remain idle. Late in the summer and early fall, there had been some talk of suspending the Chief Executive during any contemplated impeachment trial. When the majority introduced its report and suspension bills were offered in Congress, Johnson took up the problem with his cabinet. Could the President be deposed in any other manner than on impeachment for and conviction of high crimes and misdemeanors? Could he be suspended in any way prior to conviction? If a law were to be passed suspending the President, should he obey it or resist? And would the deposition of the President at the instigation of Congress be any less unconstitutional than a similar attempt by private persons? He solicited his advisers' opinions on these questions, and the cabinet unanimously agreed that resistance to suspension was justified. [40] But Congress never passed a suspension law.

Johnson was fully aware of the strength of his position. With a feeling of exultation about the unanimous support of his advisors, he reminded Colonel Moore of his earlier statement that the Rubicon had been crossed. The time for defense had passed, and now he could stand on the offensive in view of the Constitution and the country.[41]

The President's confidence was not misplaced. Despite all the agitation and the constant rumors, the impeachment movement was not popular with large segments of the Republican party. In the first place, its success was highly problematical. Many moderates disliked so extreme a step, and there were more than enough of them, together with the conservatives and Democrats, to provide the one-third of the Senate votes the President needed for acquittal. This was so well known that chances of impeachment in the House were greatly diminished, and two days before the committee submitted its reports, *The New York Times* forecast the probable vote with astonishing accuracy.[42] Nor were the elections calculated to convince moderates of the feasibility of impeachment. "I have never been more than at this moment impressed with the peril of the Republican party," the New Hampshire editor and diplomat George G. Fogg wrote to Washburne on November 20. "I see it stated in Washington telegrams . . . that we are to have the new 'radical' issue of 'impeachment' upon us. I had hoped the late elections had taught us something. I had hoped we could be allowed to breathe before being rushed forward into new disasters under the lead of men who are now little better than paroled prisoners of war."[43] His views were shared by others. Their reverses had made many Republicans cautious.[44]

Even more difficult for the radicals was the problem of the currency. By the fall of 1867 such prominent advocates of impeachment as Stevens, Butler, and Wade had become closely identified with propositions to pay the principal of federal bonds in greenbacks. This stance badly frightened opponents of inflation. "The great question in America's politics today is the financial question, and must, ought to override the reconstruction and impeachment questions," Senator Grimes wrote to the famous Boston economist Edward Atkinson. The senator, who for some time had been worrying about the effect of impeachment upon the financial structure, believed that if Butler and Stevens had their way the government "would not last twelve months." Atkinson himself, though friendly with Sumner, had already confided to Secretary McCulloch that the demand for impeachment was on the wane because of fear of the consequences.[45] Henry L. Dawes, the moderate congressman from Massachusetts, was also warned that impeachment was most unpopular. The party already had enough trouble with repudiation schemes. At a time when many moderates feared that the movement to depose the President would depress the rate of the national bonds, Johnson's hard-money stand was extremely helpful to him.[46]

Another problem was the widespread conviction that the President had already been sufficiently hedged in by Congressional legislation to make him comparatively powerless. Would it pay to make a martyr of him? His political career would soon be over anyway, and it would not do to convict him on insufficient evidence.[47]

Above all, the charges were simply not convincing. "Since the report of the impeachment committee you have gained many friends here," a New York supporter assured the President. "Republicans who *really believed* that you had committed great crimes now say the whole scheme is nothing more nor less than political persecution."[48] Garfield, who had long believed impeachment impractical, after examining the charges came to the conclusion that the majority had failed to make out its case.[49] And Carl Schurz, on a trip to Washington where he was able to speak to members on the floor, urged them to vote against the proposal "because the majority report fell so completely into the muck."[50]

In view of the dim outlook for their scheme, why did the majority propose it at all? The principal advocates of impeachment, men like Ashley, Boutwell, Butler, Lawrence, Stevens, Wade, and Williams, had long persuaded themselves that as long as Johnson was in the executive chair radical Reconstruction would be severely hamstrung. Thus they had been disappointed at the failure of Congress to take steps to oust him in July. Their forebodings seemed to be particularly borne out when Johnson removed Stanton, Sheridan, and Sickles.[51] And while a realist like Stevens was fully aware that the road ahead would be difficult—"impeachment is dead," he said in November[52]—he was neither willing nor able to stem the tide after Churchill reversed his vote. The New York congressman made no secret of the reasons for his change of mind. In a letter to *The New York Times* he explained that up until June he had opposed impeachment. But then Johnson vetoed the Supplementary Reconstruction Bill and fired the secretary of war, and Churchill switched his vote.[53] Convinced of the necessity of removing the President, the radicals tended to disregard the obstacles in their way.

Actually the ultras' assessment of the situation was substantially correct. By reasserting his powers Johnson had effectually encouraged Southern conservatives even before the elections. "The Amnesty Proclamation of the President has greatly elated the unreconstructed here & throughout the South," complained the radical mayor of Woodville, Mississippi, who added that Grant's doubtful position had "served to embolden them to hope that he would uphold the President against Congress." His letter was not the only one of its type to reach Republican members of Congress. It was evident that because of Johnson's policies Reconstruction had once more suffered a reverse.[54]

Former insurgents also expressed themselves forcibly. A policy of delay would yet win white supremacy for the South, J. Barrett Cohen wrote to Stephens from Charleston.[55] Was not the New York *Herald* coming to the support of the President in sustaining the ouster of Stanton? When news of Sheridan's transfer reached New Orleans, a local conservative exulted in a letter to the White House, "There will be tonight many manly, many beautiful lips that invoke the blessing of God on the head of Andrew Johnson."[56] The election results further strengthened Southern confidence. Radical newspapers might well point out that hunted Unionists and persecuted Southern Negroes looked "on impeachment delayed as so many months added to their torture."[57]

Convinced of the necessity of action, however foolhardy, the majority of the committee went ahead. Ten days after presenting the majority report, Boutwell spoke for fifty-five minutes on December 5 in support of his accusation. Then the House adjourned, only to take up the matter on the next day, when the Massachusetts radical finished his speech. The galleries were crowded, especially after the upper house adjourned so that senators could come in large numbers.[58]

Boutwell stuck closely to his theme. While conceding that the President could not be suspended by a mere majority pending a trial, the speaker nevertheless demanded that the House vote to impeach Andrew Johnson. Recounting the various charges already made, he warned that the President was giving aid to Southern white supremacists. Fully aware of many of his colleagues' doubts about the subject, he tried to prove that an indictable offense was not necessary in cases of impeachment. Misconduct in office was enough to convict an incumbent of a misdemeanor.[59]

It was exactly this argument that Wilson, speaking for the minority, sought to demolish. Readily conceding that Johnson was the "worst of Presidents," Wilson pointed out that opposing the Republican party was no crime. Consequently, he moved to table the impeachment resolution. For the time being, however, the motion could not be carried.[60] The climax came on the next day, December 7. After John A. Logan attempted to filibuster against renewed attempts to dispose of the subject by laying it on the table, the impeachers and Wilson reached an agreement. The chairman would withdraw his tabling motion, thus allowing the question to be voted upon directly without debate. The vote was called, and the motion to impeach the President for high crimes and misdemeanors lost by 57 to 108. Sixty-eight of the negative ballots were cast by Republicans.[61]

The result revealed the depth of the split within the Republican party. While radical journals deplored the lack of determination in the House—Wilkes declared that the President was now the master of the situation[62]—many respected newspapers expressed their relief. "Congress deserves well of the country," editorialized the Chicago *Tribune*. "Yesterday . . . the Impeachment resolution was defeated . . . ; thus this source of mischief falls to the ground to be troublesome and distracting no more." Congress could now turn to the important financial questions facing the country, while Johnson had received a warning. The world could realize that the United States, because of its devotion to legal procedure, was great enough to retain even an obnoxious troublemaker.[63] *The New York Times* expressed satisfaction with the "End of the Impeachment Folly," and *Harper's Weekly*, which had already found the majority report unconvincing, did not even bother to comment on the result it had clearly foreseen.[64]

The radicals were naturally disappointed. "You will see how Congress backed down on impeachment & can guess the effect of it on the whole of the South followed by such a message as the last," Julian complained to his wife. "It is pitiful."[65] Thaddeus Stevens, barely recovered from his illness, received a deputation of members of Southern Loyal Leagues. When the conversation turned to the President's ouster, he repeated his long-held conviction that impeachment was not a criminal but a political undertaking. But now the time for it had passed, he feared. Johnson should have been removed a year earlier.[66] At the Brooklyn Academy of Music, Wendell Phillips delivered a lecture entitled "The Surrender of Congress," and other ultras feared that the events of the winter would hurt the cause badly. "The impeachment fizzle, Butler's miserable plea for repudiation, the impudence of the [annual Presidential] message, the vagaries of the [Southern] conventions . . . are, I fear, injuring us with . . . our 'weaker brethren,' but whose aid we must have," wrote one of House Clerk McPherson's correspondents.[67] And although Clemenceau was mistaken in believing that the failure of the impeachment was the first instance in which the radical minority had been helpless to make the majority vote with it,[68] nevertheless the radicals, outfoxed by the President, had suffered a serious reverse.

The reactions of the President's supporters were predictable. Enthusiastic about their opponents' rebuff, they tended to overlook Johnson's continued political isolation. "The Death of Impeachment," read a headline in the *National Intelligencer*, which rejoiced that the "disgrace" was over.[69] Benjamin B. French, Johnson's faithful adherent, was so pleased with developments that he speculated about the possibility of the President's emergence as a martyr. Perhaps Johnson, like Van Buren before him, would be elected President as a result of the Congressional attack upon him.[70]

If the President's Northern friends were encouraged, his Southern allies were greatly relieved. The Richmond *Whig* professed to observe a tremendous change in Northern attitudes, while in the same city the *Enquirer* agreed that the radicals' days were numbered.[71] Under these circumstances it was not surprising that Southern Unionists blamed the retention of Johnson for their increasing difficulties.[72]

Reactions of the Northern Democrats, on the other hand, were cautious. Although they had been opposed to impeachment, they had still refused to identify with the President.[73] They asserted in Congress that had Johnson been impeached on such flimsy evidence he would simply have been reelected by the people.[74] It was no secret that they would not have been too happy about such an outcome.[75]

And Andrew Johnson himself? As far as is known he said little about his success; Welles did not even mention the vote in his diary.[76] Johnson's confidence had been borne out by events, and he resolutely turned to new controversies with Congress.

The President might well have congratulated himself. In spite of his defiance of the party, in spite of his dismissal of Stanton and popular military commanders, he had succeeded in escaping impeachment. His policy of refusing to collaborate with the moderates was paying off. And although he would not be able to prevent the drafting of constitutions conferring suffrage on Negroes in the South, he had nevertheless already helped to lay the groundwork for their ultimate failure. His encouragement of the forces of Southern conservatism at this crucial time would greatly contribute to their survival and ultimate success.

Eight.

Renewed Presidential Defiance

As 1867 drew to a close, Andrew Johnson was more confident than he had been for a long time. The fall elections, the failure of the attempt to impeach him, and the comparative ease with which he had outsmarted Grant gave him hope for the future and put him in a fighting mood. Firm in his conviction that the Rubicon had been crossed, he was determined to resume his offensive against radical Reconstruction.

The President's truculent mood had already been evident when he delivered his uncompromising annual message. A few days later the impeachment failed—an apparent success which was not calculated to make him more cooperative. Believing sincerely that civil government in the South must be supported, he was certain that once military interference ceased the Southern people would know how to deal with their radicals, both black and white.

It was precisely because of this conviction that Johnson had been so anxious to replace radical military commanders with conservatives. As Hancock pointed out in his first order to his district: "The General commanding is gratified to learn that peace and quiet reign in this department. It will be his purpose to maintain this condition of things. As a means to this great end, he regards the maintenance of the civil authorities in the faithful execution of the laws as the most efficient, under existing circumstances."[1]

The President was delighted. Remarking that Grant had looked somewhat downcast when the order had been discussed in cabinet, he attributed it to the contrast between Grant's own behavior and "the manly, statesmanlike course of Hancock." After the defeat of the impeachment effort, he conceived of the idea of sending the lawmakers a request for a vote of thanks to Hancock for his timely assertion of "the principles of American liberty." The more he thought about it, the more he liked the idea, and on December 18 he actually transmitted the message to Congress. Although it was met with laughter, he had not only shown his contempt for the radicals, but had also made a bid for the Democratic nomination. Hancock was a Democrat.[2]

Hancock's order clearly showed the intent of Johnson's Southern policy. In spite of the difficulties he had encountered in implementing it, his effort to ameliorate the effects of the Reconstruction acts seemed to be working well. As he told Colonel Moore, Sheridan's ouster a few months earlier had not been easy. Grant had feared revolution. The cabinet, with one exception, had been bitterly opposed. Browning's face had actually grown thin, and Randall, suggesting delay, had become very nervous. Nevertheless, he had persisted.[3] Two commanding generals had already been replaced; it was time to transfer two more.

The most urgent case, as Johnson saw it, was that of General Pope in the Third Military District. Pope and his collaborator, Wager Swayne, the Freedmen's Bureau assistant commissioner in charge of Alabama, had undoubtedly long stood in the President's way. The commanding general had interfered on behalf of the radical convention in Atlanta when the conservative state treasurer had refused to pay the expenses. Moreover, if Pope (and Swayne) were only suspended, the conservatives in Alabama believed they could defeat the radical constitution then being framed. Acting as their spokesman, John Forsyth, editor of the Mobile *Daily Advertiser and Register*, pleaded with Johnson. Remove Pope and Swayne, and Negro supremacy may yet be avoided, he wrote.[4] The President was only too willing to comply.

In the Fourth Military District (Mississippi and Arkansas) there had been fewer clashes between the commander and the President. But Ord, who had radical leanings, was anxious to be relieved and himself asked for a transfer. The President had no objections.[5]

It was certain that this renewed interference with Reconstruction by means of military transfers would cause an uproar. Again the cabinet was dubious. When Johnson read Forsyth's letter to the secretaries, the attorney general was unimpressed. Nothing should be done because the troubles in the South would induce a popular reaction which would soon "overwhelm" radicalism, he said. The interior secretary agreed with him, and the secretary of the treasury was equally cautious. But McCulloch admitted that at the time of Sheridan's removal he had been mistaken, and he might be wrong again. Johnson thought he was, and on December 28 orders were issued transferring Pope, Ord, and Swayne. The President was determined to have his own way.[6]

In view of Johnson's aggressive attitude, it was natural that rumors about his intention to test the constitutionality of the Tenure of Office Act should appear in the press. It was said that he would induce one of his supporters to make up a court case by contesting removal by a writ of mandamus, and all this would be done before the Stanton case was decided.[7]

The President had different plans, however. Because the twenty days' grace allowed him under the Tenure of Office Act was coming to a close, on December 12 he sent to the Senate a long document explaining his suspension of the secretary of war. Reminding the lawmakers that in Stanton's case "the mutual confidence and general accord" which ought to exist between a President and his advisors had ceased, Johnson explained that he had given the secretary to understand his resignation would be accepted. Stanton had been suspended only when he refused to withdraw. Moreover, his own letters showed that he did not trust the President to fill the office of secretary of war. Especially noteworthy was that all this had been done by a counselor who had emphatically advised Johnson to veto the Tenure of Office Bill, which had never been held to apply to Lincoln's appointees in the cabinet. After references to Stanton's failure to inform his chief of the impending trouble in New Orleans and a reminder of the relationship between the President and his cabinet as one between principal and agents, the paper closed with high praise of Grant. The general, Johnson informed the Senate, had effected substantial savings in the administration of his department.[8] Apparently, the President had not yet abandoned his efforts to drive a wedge between Grant and the majority of the Republican party.

The message, a skillfully worded, dignified document, was well received and was referred to the Committee on Military Affairs. It was evident that Johnson had presented his opponents with a difficult problem.[9]

That winter, as before, the President's aggressiveness again sustained the hopes of Southern conservatives, who were doing their utmost to undermine the Reconstruction acts. Preferring military rule to what they called Negro domination, at first they had sought to defeat the call for constitutional conventions by various means, including a scheme of registering but refusing to vote, thereby denying absolute majorities to the victorious party. When this policy did not work, they changed their tactics. Johnson's removal of radical generals, his escape from impeachment, and the elections of 1867 had given them renewed encouragement, and they began to organize. Conservative conventions, attempting with the President's aid to prevent racial equality, met in several Southern states. Their support grew with the amnesties proclaimed by the White House.[10]

In their quest to frustrate or delay the constitution-making process and to prevent Negro equality, Southern Democrats used every available means. In some states they hoped to defeat the constitutions by again refusing to vote. Because the law required an absolute majority of registered voters to validate the new basic statutes, large-scale abstention might result in rejection. Sometimes the reactionary whites threatened the blacks, and sometimes the former masters even sought to influence their ex-slaves to vote for them.[11] Ultimately, however, they relied on support from Washington.

How closely Southern conservatives worked with the President may be shown in the case of Foster Blodgett, the Republican postmaster of Savannah and a Unionist. Attempting to accuse Blodgett of perjury, the conservative federal district attorney of Savannah, Henry S. Fitch, conferred frequently with Johnson. Fitch was planning to indict other Republicans as well and continued to look to the White House for aid. As he put it, "I sincerely trust, Mr. President, that you will support me. . . . Let it once be made manifest by a few removals that such men shall not be permitted to use positions of trust and profit under the provisional government to oppress and degrade helpless people . . . more moderate counsels will speedily control." The perjury charges were based on a technicality involving an iron-clad oath, but the administration suspended Blodgett.[12] Southern Unionists, both black and white, were the chief victims of Johnson's policies.

Not even the most highly placed Southern Republicans were immune to the all-pervasive hostility against them. "We try to keep our temper under & in spite of a vast amount of slander, persecution & even threats of violence of which no one at a distance can form an adequate concept," Judge John C. Underwood, the presiding officer of the Virginia convention, explained to Horace Greeley. "Indeed God only knows the hardships of a live Union man in this den of rebel lions." He also pleaded with Washburne for "the help of Congress to relieve us from the oppression of our rebel rulers." Unless the convention were given real power, the "rebels with all the offices in their possession" would be able to vote down the constitution.[13]

Conditions worsened after the new year. "The removal of Genls. Pope and Swayne has taken from the work of reconstruction two able and experienced leaders," an Alabama radical complained. "Their loss to the union men of this State is irreparable. . . . No man to-day can enter the canvass and publicly work for reconstruction without taking his life in his hand. . . ."[14] In Georgia, conservatives were rejoicing about the ouster of Pope and bragging that Reconstruction was a failure; in Mississippi, loyal men were ostracized, maligned, and persecuted "in every conceivable manner."[15] At least this was the opinion of radical letter-writers, and they were not far from wrong. As one of the members of the Georgia convention warned Thaddeus Stevens, "Unless Congress affords the delegates . . . immediate relief, we shall all be compelled to leave the State."[16]

This situation created severe problems for the Republican party. Eighteen sixty-eight was an election year. The country was tired of Reconstruction, and party leaders wanted an end of the process—on Republicans terms—as quickly as possible. "Pardon me a line to express the interest we all feel in the labors of your convention," Washburne wrote to Judge Underwood in December. "It is of the most transcendent importance that you should make a constitution that will commend itself to the the enlightened judgment of the country." Exhorting him to proscribe as few persons as feasible, the Congressman pleaded with the judge to make the sessions "as brief as possible."[17] Underwood, in reply, outlined his problems, but the overriding importance of the speedy and successful conclusion of the convention remained very much on his Northern friends' minds. "Our success politically depends so largely on the wise & judicious action of the Southern Constl. Conventions," Colfax cautioned him, "that I watch their proceedings every day with great interest."[18] The Southern question must be solved prior to November, and Johnson must not be allowed to stand in the way. This was especially true since there had long been rumors of Johnson's reliance on the Supreme Court to declare the Reconstruction acts unconstitutional.[19]

In the North, too, the Republicans were confronted with trouble. The failure of the impeachment, as well as the monetary dispute, had accentuated the differences between radicals and moderates. "The trouble is the extreme radical measures are becoming more and more unpopular," William Schouler, the wartime adjutant general of Massachusetts, wrote to Henry Dawes. "The response of the nation to the impeachment folly foreshadows, though it does not really represent this feeling." The nomination of Grant on a moderate platform, he concluded, was the party's only hope.[20] The German-American newspaper editor Frederick Hassaurek, reporting on the state of the party in Ohio, came to the same conclusion. Gloomily describing the falling off of Republican enthusiasm, he expressed his fear that "the desire for change . . . , the negro prejudice, the greenback scheme . . . and other inevitable disadvantages" could only contribute to swelling "the reactionary tide." People were not willing to change the American form of government merely because Johnson occupied the chief place in it; Stanton was not popular, and ordinary folk did not think that cabinet ministers ought to be encouraged not to be gentlemen.[21]

As the Ohio politician had pointed out, the nomination of Grant seemed to be the solution. The more the party encountered difficulties, the more it turned to the popular war hero to rescue it. But because many radicals thoroughly distrusted him, his increased availability for the campaign further emphasized the party's lack of unity. Some doubted even Grant's ability to heal the party's wounds.[22]

In order to meet these challenges the Republicans renewed their offensive. Driven on by the radicals, many moderates believed that the President must be checked further. If the conservatives in the South sought to defeat Reconstruction by abstaining from the ballot, the Reconstruction laws must be changed in order to enable a mere majority of the actual voters to carry the new constitutions. If Southern governments frustrated the intent of Congress, they must be totally superseded. If the President appointed conservative generals, Grant must be put in command of the entire Reconstruction process. If Johnson relied on the Supreme Court, then the high tribunal must be curbed. Above all, the President must not be allowed to suspend the secretary of war.

In view of the comparative weakness of the radicals, it was not easy for them to induce Congress to pass all these measures. Worried about a possible alliance between Johnson and the moderates,[23] the ultras had to be careful. That they were able to achieve even moderate successes was to a large extent due to the indomitable will and parliamentary skill of Thaddeus Stevens.

The Commoner was in very bad health that winter. Over seventy years of age, crippled since birth, and so weak that he had to be carried around by attendants, he had nevertheless not lost his iron determination to make Reconstruction work. When unable to obtain his entire program, he would settle for parts of it, in the meantime making use of every parliamentary device to secure passage of his favorite measures. The Constitution was not for him the shibboleth it represented for others, and since both the President and the Supreme Court were standing in his way, he sought to depose the one and curb the other.[24]

The radicals' distrust of the court dated back to 1866. At that time the tribunal, in *ex parte Milligan*, had declared military trials of civilians unconstitutional when the civil courts were open. Although this decision and opinion referred only to wartime executive action in the Northern states, it encouraged conservatives. *Ex parte Garland* and *Cummings* v. *Missouri*, which held invalid retrospective test oaths for lawyers and various public officials, did not lessen the ultras' fears of the court. To be sure, during the following year, in the Habeas Corpus Act of 1867, Congress actually expanded federal jurisdiction, and the justices seemed to exercise caution in rejecting an injunction against the President and the secretary of war to prevent them from carrying out the Reconstruction acts. As long as the Milligan decision stood, however, the radicals did not feel safe, and the President's reputed reliance on the court increased their distrust.[25] Consequently, when at the beginning of the second session of the Fortieth Congress, the Senate sent to the House a bill establishing five as a quorum for the justices, the House Judiciary Committee added an amendment prohibiting the court from deciding the constitutionality of laws by less than a two-thirds majority. After an unsuccessful radical attempt to require unanimity, the bill was passed by a strict party vote, only one Republican voting in the negative. Possibly because of the outcry against so radical an alternative to American jurisprudence, the more moderate Senate failed to act on the amended bill and it died.[26] But since the Mississippi newspaperman William H. McCardle was at that very time appealing to the Supreme Court for a writ of habeas corpus to protect himself against arrest by the commander of his state, both moderates and radicals were becoming more fearful than ever about the judicial fate of the Reconstruction acts. A new bill to prevent such appeals was speedily prepared.[27]

In addition to its attempt to limit the power of the Supreme Court, the Republican party also sought to strengthen the Reconstruction acts. Bills for this purpose were introduced in both houses, and the House of Representative finally passed two of these. One repealed the majority requirements for the ratification of Southern constitutions so that a mere majority of the voters rather than of those registered would suffice to put the new basic laws into effect. The other denied recognition to existing Southern state governments and conferred most of the military powers heretofore exercised by the President directly upon the commanding general in Washington. Efforts to increase the influence of the conventions failed, and although the Senate finally accepted the voting bill, it never assented to its companion measure. The party was badly divided on the issue.[28]

Finally the party sought to protect itself against the President by rejecting the suspension of the secretary of war. On January 6 the House voted to censure Johnson for transferring Sheridan.[29] On January 7, Jacob Howard of Michigan laid his report on the Stanton case before the Senate Military Affairs Committee, and on January 13, in executive session, the Senate voted to accept it. "[H]aving considered the evidence and reasons given by the President in his report of the 12 December, 1867, for the suspension from the office of Secretary of War of Edwin M. Stanton, the Senate do not concur in such suspension," read the resolution adopted by a vote of 35 to 6. In accordance with the Tenure of Office Act, Johnson would have to reinstate his obstreperous subordinate.[30]

But the President was determined not to countenance Stanton's return to office under any circumstances. Greatly encouraged by the signs of radical disarray—his newspapers printed pointed articles about the problems of his enemies—he decided to rid himself once and for all of his unwelcome adviser. If Grant would cooperate with him, well and good; if not, he had already made up his mind that the general was also expendable.[31]

Johnson's willingness to break with Grant requires some explanation. He was aware that the general's popularity had hardly diminished, and ever since August he had handled Grant successfully and tactfully, sometimes under difficult circumstances. Objection might be made that Johnson needed the general as much in 1868 as before. From the point of view of seeking maximum popular support, it might be said that Johnson blundered in breaking with the popular hero. But the President was not interested in immediate gains. Long-range successes were still his goal, and he now felt that Grant had served his purpose.

It had been clear to the President for some time that the secretary of war *ad interim* was veering toward radicalism. In order to make use of Grant's popular appeal, however, Johnson had always been able to overlook this tendency, and it had seemed from time to time as if he might yet win him over.[32] After the November elections, when it became even more certain that the general would obtain the Republican nomination for the presidency, Johnson found it more difficult to offer him anything. Among the President's friends, the Blairs totally despaired of Grant's usefulness. Doolittle also decided that the conservatives had lost the general. When after the new year even the ultraradical *Independent* found words of praise for Grant, Johnson came to the conclusion that he had already lost the general. Shortly before Congress recessed for Christmas he told Welles that Grant was becoming more and more identified with the tyrannical acts of the district commanders.[33] Since even his most daring actions in the past had been successful, the President must have concluded that he could now afford to dismiss the general if necessary.

Naturally Johnson was anxious to find a possible substitute for Grant. The obvious choice was William T. Sherman, the army's second-ranking officer who was conservative and well disposed toward the President. Whether he could be induced to take part in active politics was a difficult question. Despite his close connections with various conservatives—Thomas Ewing was his father-in-law—he had already expressed his unwillingness to oppose Grant, whom he liked very much and with whom he had collaborated so successfully during the war.[34]

Johnson carefully cultivated Sherman, then in Washington as president of a board to revise army regulations. On January 3 he tendered the general a complimentary dinner at the White House. Thomas Ewing, the attorney general, the secretary of the navy, and their wives were also present. The President and his daughters tried their best to make their guest comfortable.[35] Johnson was laying the groundwork for the future. He would soon call upon Sherman for help.

While the Howard Resolution was still pending, on Saturday, January 11, the President conferred with Grant. Would the general stay in the cabinet in case Stanton's suspension was not upheld? According to Adam Badeau, Johnson offered to pay any fine that might be levied because he wanted to test the constitutionality of the Tenure of Office Act. But he emphasized that he had not really suspended the secretary of war in accordance with that statute. His powers as President under the Constitution were at stake, and he had acted accordingly. Grant refused. As Johnson understood it, however, the general would let him know precisely what he was going to do. If he could not properly resist the action of the Senate, prior to the vote Grant would at least leave the office of secretary of war in the condition in which he had received it.[36]

Grant was not pleased with the position in which he found himself. Naturally slow to make up his mind and not well versed in politics, he was not particularly anxious to see Stanton revert to his position as secretary of war. On the other hand, he was equally unwilling to become the President's pawn. After conferring with Sherman, Grant came to the conclusion that Governor Cox of Ohio would be an excellent compromise candidate; he was opposed to Negro suffrage, but might yet be confirmed by the Senate. Sherman actually made the suggestion to Johnson, who had already heard the same thing from Thomas Ewing.[37] But Johnson was anxious for a test of the Tenure of Office Act, and Cox's appointment did not fit in with his plans.

After the Senate acted, on Monday, January 13, Johnson saw Grant only briefly at a reception. The next morning General Cyrus B. Comstock, a Grant aide, brought Johnson the general's resignation. "I have the honor to enclose herewith," it read,

> copy of official notice received by me, last evening, of the action of the Senate of the United States in the case of the suspension of the Hon. E. M. Stanton, Secretary of War. According to the provisions

of Section 2 of "An Act regulating the Tenure of certain Civil Offices," my functions as Secretary of War, ad interim, ceased from the moment of the receipt of the within notice.

The President was furious. Grant had simply turned over the office to Stanton, contrary to Johnson's understanding that he was to return it into the President's hands. When, in response to a summons, the general appeared at the Tuesday meeting of the cabinet, Johnson asked him whether he had not, on Saturday, promised that he would return the office to him. Exactly what happened afterward soon became a subject of bitter dispute between the two men. The President maintained Grant looked abashed; one cabinet member believed him to have been drunk— but Grant denied it all.[38] In view of the general's unmistakable stand ever since August, the President could not have been greatly surprised at his actions. But since he was about to break with his subordinate, he had to show him in the worst light possible.

The break with Grant was not yet complete. Because of Stanton's imperious actions—he unceremoniously summoned the general to appear at his office the moment he was restored—Grant was still anxious to effect a change in the War Department. Consequently, that afternoon he met Stanton and advised him to resign.[39] Early on the morning of January 15, accompanied by Sherman, Grant appeared at the White House. "For the good of the service," he offered to induce Stanton to withdraw. But he complained grievously about the press. The National Intelligencer had carried an untrue story about his dealings with the President. Johnson replied that he had not yet read the paper. After the general left, however, Johnson asked his private secretary to show it to him. The account was strictly accurate, he told Colonel Moore.[40] A bitter quarrel was in the making.

In spite of his chagrin, Grant was still not totally committed to open war on the President. On January 18 he again told Sherman that he ought to attempt to induce Stanton to resign. On the next day he made an offer to the President that he would go to the War Department for this purpose, but found Johnson cool to the idea. Johnson simply instructed him not to obey any orders issued by the secretary of war unless specifically authorized by himself. And when Grant saw Stanton he discovered that the secretary would not hear of withdrawing.[41]

Grant now moved closer to a complete rift with Johnson. Demanding that the verbal orders concerning the secretary be put in writing, he was preparing for a showdown.[42] And although the general still hesitated—as late as January 26, he told Johnson that Stanton, whose behavior annoyed him, had been reduced to a mere clerk—he soon thought better of it and again demanded written orders. In a letter written on January 28, Grant complained bitterly about "the many and grave misrepresentations affecting my personal honor" which had appeared in the press and proceeded to detail his version of the events of the last two weeks.[43]

Johnson did not permit this challenge to go unanswered. "I have tried to be decent," he said, taking up Grant's letter. "I know my nature and will be damned if some things have not gone about as far as they are to go." Inspired by reading the addresses of Cato, the President promptly endorsed Grant's earlier request with written directions not to obey the secretary of war.[44]

Two days later he sent a full reply to the general. Anxious to discredit Grant, Johnson had already taken special pains to obtain corroboration of his account from his advisers.[45] He pointed out that he had indeed given written orders not to obey the secretary and then turned to the facts as he saw them. The general had deceived him, he charged. The suggested appointment of Cox he considered merely a sort of reparation for Grant's failure to live up to his alleged promise to return the office of secretary of war to him before the Senate acted. Moreover, the cabinet fully sustained him in his recollection of the events of January 14.[46]

Several more letters followed, each becoming more violent than its predecessor. The general charged the President with efforts to involve him in unlawful acts; Johnson retorted that Grant had been insubordinate and devious. In support of his position, the President secured written accounts of the disputed cabinet meeting from the various secretaries. The radical press praised the general, and even moderate Republican papers sided with him.[47] The

House of Representatives called for copies of the correspondence, and the break was so complete that the two men remained bitter enemies for life. Thaddeus Stevens admitted that it was time to take Grant into the radical "church," but the President had shown the general to be less than astute in his political relations.[48]

Johnson had not acted out of mere peevishness. As was his custom, he was engaged in a well-thought-out plan to further his policies. Since the Senate had refused to concur in his suspension of Stanton, and since his tactic of substituting Grant for the secretary had finally not been successful, he was now looking for a new candidate. William T. Sherman was the obvious choice, and, hoping to separate him from Grant, the President attempted to induce Sherman to join the cabinet. For this purpose, he was contemplating the establishment of a new military district with headquarters in Washington and Sherman in command. The general would then be on hand to become secretary *ad interim*. The whole matter might even end up in the courts.[49]

Sherman was not pleased with the proposition. Still distrusting the machinations in the capital, he told the President that he would prefer to return to St. Louis. For the time being, the project had to be shelved,[50] but Johnson did not abandon it.

By the beginning of February the President was in so aggressive a mood that his private secretary recorded the fact in his diary. More than ever determined to secure Sherman's help, on February 6 he issued orders creating the disputed Military Division of the Atlantic. On the next day he countermanded them, only to renew them on February 12. In addition, he nominated Sherman for a full generalship by brevet. Only the general's steadfast refusal— he asked his brother, the senator, to vote against confirmation— frustrated this project.[51] But Johnson, sure of his course, was looking for another secretary *ad interim*. He was ready to employ any legal means to oust Stanton.

It may be argued that by breaking with Grant, the most popular man in the country, the President made a serious mistake. In reality, however, he had little choice. The general was about to be the nominee of the Republican party. True, he was preferred by moderates and opposed by radicals, but it had always been Johnson's policy not to cooperate with the moderates. They simply did not see things the same way he did, especially in reference to the South and Negro suffrage. If Johnson broke with Grant, the general would be pushed farther into the radicals' camp. At the same time, however, Grant would be separated from all those conservatives who still sympathized with him. And Johnson was right. There would be no impeachment as a result of the controversy. His Southern supporters could only be encouraged by it.

It was not that the radicals would not try once more to persuade their colleagues to impeach the President. Thaddeus Stevens, more convinced than ever that the President had to be ousted, thought that his opportunity had come. The obvious tactic was to remove the whole problem from Wilson's Judiciary Committee and take it up in the Reconstruction Committee, in which, as chairman, Stevens wielded considerable power. On February 10 he induced the House to follow his plan; the Reconstruction Committee was promptly summoned to take up the matter. Subpoenaing a correspondent of the New York *World* to testify about Johnson's alleged attempt to influence Grant to violate the law, the committee conducted an investigation. Rumors abounded, and although the President and most of his advisers remained confident, the secretary of the interior feared that Stevens' efforts might succeed.[52]

Browning, as earlier, proved to be a bad prophet. On February 13, Stevens submitted to the committee a resolution for immediate commencement of impeachment proceedings. He supported it by a report charging the President with attempting to induce Grant to violate the Tenure of Office law, and accompanied it with one of his sarcastic speeches. But the moderates were too strong for him. Upon Bingham's motion to table, Fernando C. Beaman, Frederick A. Pike, Calvin T. Hulburd, James B. Beck, and James Brooks voted to sustain him. Only Boutwell and Farnsworth supported Stevens, and a second effort to impeach the President failed.[53]

The old Commoner was furious. Refusing to carry the matter to the floor of the House, he said the Republican party was a group of cowards. He was even angry at Grant, whom he accused of not being forceful enough.[54] It was clear that Johnson had won again. Flushed with success, he was bound to present new challenges to the party.

Nine.

Impeachment of the President

Stevens' attempt to impeach the President after the break with Grant did not deter Johnson from seeking to oust Stanton once and for all. As long as there was no communication between the secretary and his chief, the routine affairs of the War Department naturally suffered. Should the Treasury honor Stanton's drafts? Should the postmaster general forward the department's mail? These were practical, every-day issues, but they merely reinforced Johnson's conviction that he must act. When, on February 14, Welles asked him who was secretary of war, Johnson confidently replied, "That matter will be disposed of in one or two days."[1]

The President was in a fighting mood that winter. For inspiration, he was still turning to Addison's *Cato* and memorizing the speeches. "Have you ever read the Addresses of Cato?" he asked Colonel Moore. "Well, I am more like Lamponius, who, when Cato in the Roman Senate said, 'Others pronounce your thoughts!!' declared 'My voice is still for war,' than Lucius, who responded, 'My thoughts, I must confess are turned on peace.' " Not long afterward, upon returning from church on Sunday, Moore had to read Addison's sentimental tragedy to his chief. The President listened attentively. Cato was a man, he mused, who would not compromise with wrong, but, being right, died before he would yield. The secretary was struck by the evident parallel Johnson was drawing between the ill-fated Roman and himself.[2]

Johnson, however, did not think his position was desperate. If he had any doubts, he was constantly reassured from all parts of the country. But it was especially from the South that he received the most persistent encouragement. "I wish to assure you of how deeply I have sympathized with you in the great and trying public duties which have devolved on you during the past ten months, and to congratulate you on the firmness with which you have met and discharged them," wrote Alexander H. Stephens early in January. Others praised his statesmanship and applauded his "manly course in defense of freedom and white man's government."[3]

But how was he to proceed? If he really wanted to bring about a showdown testing the applicability of the Tenure of Office Act to the cabinet, he had to find some candidate to consent to appointment as secretary of war *ad interim*. Since both Grant and Sherman had definitely refused, lesser-known candidates must be approached.

Among the persons he considered for the position was John Potts, the chief clerk of the War Department. As the legal custodian of the department's papers in case of a vacancy, Potts was an obvious choice. Consequently, on February 15, Johnson asked Colonel Moore to sound him out. Would he accept the appointment until somebody else, possibly General McClellan, could be found, Moore asked him. But Potts was not willing to cooperate. His relations with Stanton were friendly, he retorted. If he did the President's bidding, Stanton would merely fire him. Not even the colonel's reply that Stanton would no longer have any authority to do so once he were removed could budge the clerk. The whole thing would only cause trouble, he objected. Besides, he was grateful to Stanton, who had appointed his son to a position in the army. The President had to look elsewhere.[4]

Four days before the interview with Potts, Gideon Welles suggested to Johnson that he restore General Lorenzo B. Thomas, the adjutant general of the Army, to his old position. Thomas had never been on good terms with Stanton, who in 1863 had sent him to the Mississippi Valley to supervise the recruiting of black troops, the first of many subsequent assignments designed to keep him away from the War Department. The assistant adjutant general, E. D. Townsend, who was too friendly with Stanton to suit the administration, had performed Thomas' duties in the meantime. The President agreed, and on February 12 orders were issued recalling Thomas as adjutant general.[5]

Thomas had no influence with the army; he was old, garrulous, and vainglorious. Nevertheless, it now occurred to the President that the adjutant general could serve as secretary of war *ad interim*, at least until a permanent appointment could be made. Moore cautioned him. Would the appointment carry any weight, he asked. The President conceded that it would not, but he said he had made up his mind to remove Stanton. Self-respect demanded it, and if the people did not support their Chief Executive in such a measure, he ought to resign.[6]

Johnson's aggressive attitude worried some of his advisers. Thomas Ewing thought Stanton ought to be left alone. Public opinion was against him and no risk should be taken "by an imprudent act" to turn it in his favor.[7] Governor H. H. Haight of California, who had benefited from the Republican defeat in 1867, also cautioned the President to let matters run their course. If only he persisted in his policy of "forbearance," he was bound to win at the next election.[8] Stanbery strongly advised against Stanton's expulsion, and even Colonel Moore warned his chief that he must be careful. But Johnson, without even consulting his cabinet, decided to go ahead. He was at last going to solve the Stanton problem.[9]

The President struck on February 21. Briskly entering his office, he dictated four papers to his secretary. The first was a letter to Stanton informing him of his removal. "SIR," it read,

> By virtue of the power and authority vested in me as President by the Constitution and laws of the United States you are hereby removed from the office as Secretary for the Department of War, and your functions as such will terminate upon the receipt of this communication.

It also instructed him to turn over the office to Brevet Major General Lorenzo Thomas.

The second document was a notification to the Senate of Johnson's move. Again he emphasized that he was acting now, as in August, "by virtue of the power and authority vested in the President by the Constitution and laws of the United States," an important point in view of his contention that the Tenure of Office Act did not apply to Stanton.

The third and fourth papers concerned two supporting actions. One was a request to the secretary of state to bring with him to the next cabinet session the nomination of General George B. McClellan as minister to Great Britain, and the other a nomination of General George H. Thomas as lieutenant general and full general by brevet. Johnson was evidently trying to tie Thomas to the administration. Then he sent for the adjutant general, informed him of his decision, and dispatched him to the War Department. Carefully showing him the laws about appointments, he remarked that he wished to proceed according to the Constitution and the laws, and advised Lorenzo Thomas to procure witnesses before delivering the letter to Stanton.[10]

The excited scenes which followed have often been described. When Stanton received the letter from Thomas, he sat down on a sofa and read it. He asked for time to remove his personal property, but after a while gave Thomas to understand that he was not at all certain whether he would obey the order. Then he notified his allies on Capitol Hill.[11]

The reaction in Congress was frantic. In the Senate the President's message arrived while Trumbull was delivering a speech. Colonel Moore delivered the document at the door, a rush took place to the Vice President's desk, and Sumner tore open the package. Then the senators read the contents—the removal of the secretary of war, the appointment of Lorenzo Thomas, the nomination of George H. Thomas for a higher rank, and the now-completed nomination of McClellan. Sumner promptly sent a one-word telegram to Stanton. "Stick," it admonished. Other senators took a carriage to the War Department to urge the secretary to hold fast. They also visited Grant to tell him that he had to support Congress. Upon the receipt of a note from Stanton that Thomas intended to oust him in the morning, Senator Edmunds introduced a resolution disapproving of the President's action. After the substitution of Henry Wilson's version specifically denying the President's power to remove the secretary of war, it was accepted by twenty-eight Republicans and opposed by six—four Democrats, Doolittle, and Edmunds. Twenty senators did not vote. Surprisingly, while moderates like Fessenden, Frelinghuysen, Fowler, Grimes, Henderson, Morgan, Nye, and Sherman were not recorded, a number of others, including Anthony, Ross, Trumbull, Van Winkle, and Willey, voted in the affirmative.[12]

In the House the uproar was even greater. When Colfax announced the receipt of Stanton's communication, excited little clusters of congressmen formed. Thaddeus Stevens, leaning on Bingham's arm, moved about from group to group. "Didn't I tell you so?" he said again and again. "What good did your moderation do you? If you don't kill the beast, it will kill you." After some parliamentary maneuvering, John Covode offered a resolution that the President be impeached "of high crimes and misdemeanors." The resolution was referred to the Reconstruction Committee, and since it was late in the afternoon the House adjourned to take up the question on the following day. It was evident that the impeachment resolution would pass as soon as members had been given an opportunity to be heard.[13]

Stanton was greatly encouraged by these developments. Surrounded by Congressional supporters, he prepared to hold the War Department against all comers. Not only did he physically remain in his office, but he was soon heavily guarded by soldiers outside. General Logan had a cot set up in the department in order to be able to direct the Washington members of the Grand Army of the Republic, which he commanded, should civil war ensue. These preparations might have looked ridiculous, but Stanton was determined not to yield.[14]

Lorenzo Thomas, in the meanwhile, did not seem to be in any particular hurry. Finding time to attend a masked ball during the night of February 21–22, before he left he boasted that he would oust Stanton by force, if necessary, and drank so much that Johnson became alarmed. There were rumors that Thomas would be arrested, and the President asked Colonel Moore to see him first thing in the morning. The rumors proved well founded; early in the morning, upon Stanton's complaint about the adjutant general's violation of the Tenure of Office Act, he was apprehended and brought before Federal Judge David K. Cartter. Upon the attorney general's advice, Thomas went bail, called on the President, and then proceeded to the War Department. Stanton tried to forbid him to act as secretary of war; Thomas relied on the President's authority, and after some contretemps between the two men Thomas remarked that he had had nothing to eat or drink all morning. Stanton produced a bottle of whiskey, put his arms around Thomas' neck, and finally the two contestants took a drink together. "The next time you have me arrested, please do not do it before I get something to eat," said Thomas. Stanton remained in possession of the office.[15]

Johnson was not displeased with these events. If Thomas' case was in the courts, he would be able to test the legality of his action and the constitutionality of the Tenure of Office Act. Some of his advisers thought it would have been better had the general remained in custody and sued for a writ of habeas corpus, and his actions have lent some plausibility to the theory that Johnson's alleged long-standing attempts to seek a court test were a mere afterthought poorly carried out. However, since he had mentioned the matter on January 31 in conversation with Sherman and in a letter to Grant, and since Seward and Browning stated that the issue had played a role at the time of Grant's resignation, it would appear that the thought, at least, had long before occurred to the President. At any rate, he now asserted that the courts were the forum where he wanted the case.[16] Even if the suit against Thomas were dismissed—an event that took place a few days later—Johnson's strategy was one of careful observance of the law, except for the Tenure of Office Act.

The President's determination did not mean he was not worried about the outcome. "The President shows some anxiety," Colonel Moore noted on February 22.

He says, however, that he has made an issue demanded by his self respect and if he cannot be President in fact, he will not be President in name alone. "What advantage," he asked, "would it be . . . to do wrong. I have nothing to gain by a wrong step of this kind. But I am right and I intend to stand by. I do not want to see this Government relapse into a despotism. I have ever battled for the right of the people and their liberties and I am now endeavoring to defend them from arbitrary power." [17]

To a correspondent of the New York *Herald* Johnson said that he had determined his action long ago and acted "carefully, prudently, and moderately." He was still hoping Stanton would see the propriety of resigning, but did not care even if he were impeached. Some thought he was deliberately courting martyrdom for political reasons.[18]

In line with his policy of trying to act within the law (always excepting the Tenure of Office Act) and placing his opponents in the wrong, Johnson naturally disregarded the constant inducements he received to employ violence. People from all over the country were offering him troops to arrest Congress, oust Stanton, or to protect himself. But he simply put the letters into his files. Maintenance of calm and adherence to due process were the policies he was determined to employ. He even sought to bring about a settlement by nominating Thomas Ewing, Sr., an old Whig, as secretary of war.[19]

The Ewing nomination was never considered by the Senate. After adjourning in honor of Washington's Birthday the senators walked across the hall to the House, where an enormous crowd was watching the debates on the impeachment resolution. When Stevens reported it back from committee, he was ready to proceed at once to a vote. The desire for debate was too strong, however, and members discoursed all day on the alleged crimes of Andrew Johnson. Because of the intervening Sunday, it was not until Monday, February 24, that the Covode Resolution finally passed. The President was impeached by a strict party vote of 128 to 47, with fifteen not voting. Stevens and Bingham were appointed to notify the Senate.[20]

Whether Thaddeus Stevens would have hurried along the impeachment in the way he did had he not been ill is problematical. At any rate, it was peculiar for the House to pass an impeachment resolution without first drawing up articles and specifications against the defendant. As it was, a committee for this purpose was only appointed after the vote. Its activities were carefully watched by both sides.[21]

The committee to draw up charges consisted of Bingham, Boutwell, Julian, Logan, Stevens, Wilson, and Hamilton Ward of New York. After interviewing witnesses, it agreed on ten (badly written) articles dealing in various ways with the removal of Stanton, the appointment of Thomas, and the violation of the Tenure of Office Act. The final article accused Johnson of telling General William H. Emory, the commander of the Washington garrison, that the Command of the Army Act was unconstitutional and of seeking to circumvent it. All in all, the articles were strictly legalistic, confined themselves to Johnson's overt acts on February 21 and 22, and contained nothing that was either startling or new.[22]

It was exactly this aspect of the accusation that worried Stevens. Had he been in better health he would doubtless have taken firm charge. But he was now being carried around most of the time by two black servants, and only sheer will power still kept him going.[23] Seeking assistance, he turned to General Butler, who had been kept off the committee because of his enmity for Grant. "Dear General," Stevens wrote on February 28,

> As the Committee are likely to present no articles having any real vigor in them, I submit to you if it is not worth our while to attempt to add at least two others, (and as many as you choose) in the House as amendments, and see whether they will adopt anything worth convicting on. Had I my usual strength I would not ask you to undertake this movement, but I deem it so important that I send you copies which may serve as hints for you to act upon.[24]

Butler did not have to be asked twice. Quickly preparing another article, he sought to indict Johnson for various speeches tending to bring Congress into disrepute. On March 2, when the House voted to adopt the original charges (now reframed to contain eight articles about Stanton and Thomas and a ninth about the Emory interview), Butler's addition was voted down. The House was reluctant to include items which had already been rejected in December. On the next day, however, it changed its mind, and Butler's article became number ten. At the same time a catch-all article framed by Wilson and reworded by Stevens was also adopted as number eleven. It summed up the others by accusing Johnson of attempting to violate acts of Congress in pursuance of his assertion that Congress was not a lawful body. Then a committee of managers was chosen. To emphasize the rallying of the moderates, it consisted of Bingham and Wilson, as well as of the radicals Butler, Boutwell, Logan, Stevens, and Williams. On March 4, in an imposing ceremony, the managers appeared before the Senate, which organized itself into a high court. The great trial was under way.[25]

In view of the moderates' long-time opposition to impeachment, at first glance it seems astonishing how quickly they changed their minds. Respected party leaders like James F. Wilson and John A. Bingham were not easily swayed by intemperate arguments, nor did they have any particular liking for their radical colleagues. Yet they not only voted for the Covode Resolution, but took a prominent part in the ensuing trial.

What were the reasons for this conversion? Among those who had opposed impeachment in December, but who favored it in February (though not always later on), were Bingham, Wilson, Trumbull, and Sherman, all legalistically minded and jealous of the preservation of the balance of power among the three branches of government. It was easy for them to reject Boutwell's report in December. The President had neither violated any specific law nor encroached on the prerogatives of the two houses of Congress. And, in spite of his bluster, he had not threatened anyone directly.

In February the situation was entirely different. By ousting Stanton in apparent contravention of the Tenure of Office Act and by appointing a secretary *ad interim* without the consent of the Senate, Johnson had defied Congress. He had assumed the right to judge the constitutionality of a duly passed law and seemingly denied the power of the Senate to advise and consent to cabinet appointments. In addition, Thomas had made some statements which could be interpreted as threats to use force in ousting Stanton.[26] Under these circumstances, legalistic Republicans might well have felt that the President had finally behaved exactly as the radicals always said he would. He had proven their vote in December to have been premature. He must be impeached.

Johnson's actions between December and February also contributed to the moderates' readiness to join in removing him. In December they had voted against the majority report in the belief that he had been effectively shackled and that the threat of impeachment would be sufficient to keep him in line.[27] Thus they had broken with the radicals. But when the President removed Pope, Swayne, and Ord, and began his quarrel with Grant, the mood of Congress visibly stiffened. Georges Clemenceau attributed the shift to the members' exposure to their anti-Democratic constituents during the holiday recess, but whatever the reason, by January congressmen were infinitely more hostile to Johnson than they had been before Christmas.[28]

All these considerations were closely linked with the Southern question. In the last analysis, it was this problem that was the real cause for the impeachment of Johnson. Many historians have called the attempt to depose the President a radical plot.[29] With the exception of Michael L. Benedict and Harold M. Hyman, who feel Johnson deserved conviction, they have described the proceeding as a senseless effort to humiliate a man stripped of all power, a defense of capitalism against populist anger, or a ploy to change the constitutional system of the United States.[30] But in reality, it was something else. A majority of the Republican party had become convinced that Reconstruction could not be completed successfully as long as Johnson occupied the White House. The Southern problem had become closely identified with the success of the party. It must be solved if the Democrats were to be defeated in 1868.[31] Not merely the radicals, but the moderates had come to this conclusion. And so they voted for impeachment.

How closely impeachment was linked with Reconstruction had been evident ever since 1866. Johnson was "the Great Obstruction," as the radicals called him, in more ways than one. His power, his influence, his patronage made it almost impossible for Congress to prevail in the South. Thus it is not surprising that a desperate party finally took the ill-considered and dangerous step of attempting to get rid of him.

That Southern Unionists believed the impeachment of the President to be indispensable was no secret. A Virginia Republican in July 1867 wrote to the moderate West Virginian, Senator Waitman T. Willey, "As things now stand, they [the Southern conservatives] have all the power in their hands and do not care about reconstruction . . . in the hope that the President is the 'Moses' to lead them out of bondage *without repentance* on their part. . . . As soon as the people of the South perceive that the Congress is in earnest, and will even set the President aside . . . they will move in *solid columns* to reconstruction." Radicals like John Covode heard the same thing. Conditions were very bad in his state, a carpetbagger wrote him from Mississippi. Planters were threatening Negroes with loss of home if they attended political meetings. If Johnson were impeached, Reconstruction would be safe. If he were permitted to escape, it would be a farce.[32]

The correspondent's opinions were borne out by another Mississippian, W. H. Gibbs, the Republican mayor of Woodville. As early as September 1867, he wrote to Washburne: "I have taken grounds that the President should be & will be impeached and I am of the opinion that if it is not done the Republican party will be in great danger of being defeated in the next Presidential Election and such a result would be fatal to Unionists South without regard to color." As time went on Washburne's correspondence was filled with many more letters of a similar nature.[33] And although he had voted against impeachment in December, as one of Grant's principal managers he was very anxious for a Republican South prior to the election of 1868.

Southern demands for the impeachment of Johnson multiplied during the winter of 1867–68. On New Year's Day an Alabama Republican warned a Boston friend:

> I wrote you nearly a year since, that Prest. Johnson ought to be impeached. I wrote thus, from the intimate knowledge I had of the influence he was exerting in opposition to the reconstruction of these States, on the Congressional plan. But for his opposition to Congress, this and the other rebel States, would now be regularly represented in the councils of the Nation. And yet Congress has allowed him to go on, thwarting their efforts at every step, and there is now reason to fear, that the whole scheme of Reconstruction will fail, through his cooperation with men who have brought all the troubles upon the country.[34]

A member of the Georgia convention, pleading with Stevens for help, expressed his conviction that either the legislative or the executive branch must go down. "It is a fierce struggle between Parliament & the King," he wrote. "Our only hope is Congress. For God's sake protect us!"[35] One of his colleagues complained to Sumner that the government was not worthy of the name of republic because it tolerated a despot at its head and "had neither vitality or courage to remove an open Enemy to the Nation itself." His exaggeration was understandable because of his bitter experiences. Andrew Johnson's encouragement of the conservatives had frustrated schemes of radical Reconstruction in his state.[36]

It was not only the radicals in the South who demanded the President's removal. Governor Francis Pierpoint of Virginia, who had long quarreled with the ultras, agreed with them about impeachment. "The late action of the President has very much unsettled the political situation in Virginia," he complained to Willey after Sheridan's removal. "I fear there will be no peace to the country as long as Johnson is in the Presidential Chair. I confess my sympathies heretofore have been against his impeachment. I think the ground is now enlarged and . . . he ought to be removed as soon as Congress assembles."[37]

Early in February the results of Johnson's encouragement of Southern conservatives were once more vividly brought home. In

Alabama, they succeeded in defeating the radical constitution by abstaining from the ballot and thus denying the radicals the necessary majority of registered votes.[38] In Louisiana, General Hancock removed several Negro aldermen who had been elected during Sheridan's tenure.[39] And in Florida, pro-Johnson conservatives seceded from the radical convention to set up one of their own and keep power in the hands of the whites.[40] It was evident that there was some substance to the warnings of Southern Unionists.

In addition to complicating Republican efforts in the South, Johnson's policies also endangered the party in the North. No Republican, moderate or radical, could be expected to welcome the President's courting of the Democrats. Elections were about to be held in Connecticut and in New Hampshire, and in both states the administration's influence was used to further the Republicans' opponents. In a presidential year this situation was calculated to stir up even the most moderate Republicans against the White House.[41]

The Republican party, it is true, was in control of both houses of Congress, but the reverses of 1867 and the evident disunity on the impeachment question in December had caused factional rifts which had weakened it.[42] Should the President succeed in frustrating radical Reconstruction so that reanimated Southern Democrats could cooperate with their Northern counterparts, the political outlook for the Republicans was very bleak. Removal of the President might prevent such developments; moreover, party unity might be restored if it showed firmness in attacking the man in the White House.[43]

Under these circumstances, when Johnson finally ordered the dismissal of Stanton the demand for impeachment grew until it became almost irresistible. The governor of Illinois demanded it because of "the usurpations of Andrew Johnson," the last of which he called the "act of a traitor." In city after city mass meetings petitioned for it, and the rank and file exerted pressure on representatives and senators. It was a current even moderates found too strong to withstand.[44]

If the advocates of caution had not already changed their minds, the events of February 21–24 convinced them. Senator Willey learned that the people in his home state, "by one of those sudden impulses that seem to seize the public mind," saw that it was the President who refused to permit the return to quiet and demanded that "he be put aside."[45] Representative Woodbridge of Vermont, the moderate who had joined with Wilson in dissenting from the majority report in December, confessed that he had no choice but to vote for impeachment; his constituents demanded it.[46] Garfield, who had also long opposed final action against the President, had been told that Johnson's policies in the South might well defeat Reconstruction. Now he must vote for impeachment.[47] John Sherman, who had publicly stated that no gentleman would remain in office if he were not wanted, came to the conclusion that "the alleged *forcible* expulsion of Stanton" constituted a "trespass, an assault, a riot, or a crime."[48] Even Lyman Trumbull, who would later change his mind again, had become convinced of the necessity of impeachment. As he told Shelby Cullom of Illinois, he must vote for the Covode Resolution. Johnson was an obstruction and must be removed.[49]

The impeachment of Andrew Johnson followed. The ultras naturally welcomed it, but they were not alone. Goaded on by the incessant demands of the radicals, mortified by the continual rebuffs they suffered from the President, and worried about the political future of their party and program, most moderates rallied to its support. Thaddeus Stevens and his co-workers finally had their way. The odds against success, however, were tremendous.

In venturing to depose the President, the Republicans were taking a fearful chance. If the process could be speeded up, if the President could be deposed in short order, all might be well. But if the trial dragged on, if the first enthusiasm of the hour were to vanish, they might well fail to convict.[50] In that case Johnson might be more influential than ever. His escape would be interpreted as a stunning defeat for radicalism. Reaction would be revived in the South, and the foes of Reconstruction would be reassured and strengthened. The failure to foresee this contingency was probably one of the greatest mistakes the radicals made.

In view of the emotional atmosphere surrounding the impeach-ment proceedings, however, their actions can easily be understood.

And the President? To the great surprise of his friends, he re-mained very calm. Many of his supporters believed that by goad-ing the House into impeachment he had made a mistake and was likely to be convicted.[51] But they were wrong. Whether or not it was true that he was planning to influence the Democratic Na-tional Committee then meeting in Washington,[52] he had not taken any step without careful deliberation. Ever since the contretemps with Grant, he had tried to find a way to supersede the contuma-cious secretary of war. In challenging his opponents by interpret-ing the Tenure of Office Act in a way with which many of them agreed, he had confronted them with a dilemma. Had not Senator Sherman made his attitude about refractory cabinet members clear? Had not the compromise version of the bill enabled senators who did not want it to apply to the cabinet to vote for it? At the very least, there was considerable doubt about the law's applica-bility to Stanton. Johnson's challenge placed his enemies at a dis-advantage. Since he had carefully refrained from really breaking universally recognized law or principle, they had to prosecute him on dubious grounds. As he remarked after the passage of Covode's resolution, many of those who voted to impeach must have felt more uneasy about the position in which they had put themselves than about the one in which they had put him.[53] Determined to oust Stanton, he knowingly risked impeachment; if he succeeded, his cause, and especially the cause of white supremacy in the South, would be greatly enhanced.

Ten.

The President's Trial

The trial of President Andrew Johnson has often been described as an unequal contest between a sorely harassed, courageous statesman and a vindictive Congress. Allegedly, only the fortitude of seven upright senators saved the President and the Constitution. Whether this picture corresponds to the truth is questionable.

When Johnson presented his final challenge to Congress, he was not really acting from weakness. As he assessed the situation, not for a long time had his opponents faced such problems as early in 1868. Believing that "a decided change of public sentiment in the North" had taken place, he was confident he would be vindicated—if not in the Senate, then at the polls. "One who held fast to principle when a majority was arrayed against him," he said, "is not likely to loosen his hold upon it when so much of the pressure has been removed."[1] Although he exaggerated the Republican reverses, he nevertheless chose wisely the time to test the question of his remaining prerogatives. And the issue with which he confronted his opponents was equally well drawn. He took a gamble; probably he could not foresee the outcome, but the gamble paid off.

The pretext for impeachment that Johnson provided for his opponents was very dubious. In dismissing Stanton and appointing a successor *ad interim*, he maintained, correctly or not, that he was merely seeking a legal decision on the constitutionality of the Tenure of Office Act. Since there was more than a little doubt about the statute—it has not been resolved to this day—it was difficult to quarrel with his purpose.[2] Whether his methods alone were sufficient grounds for the deposition of a President was a question the Senate might well ponder.

In addition, it was not at all certain whether the act applied to Stanton. As the secretary had originally been appointed by Lincoln, it was quite reasonable to interpret the statute in such a way as to exclude him from its operation. Several senators had said so at the time of the bill's passage, and Johnson naturally returned to this argument in his defense.[3] Was it really possible to convict a President for differences of opinion on the interpretation of a vaguely worded law? And if Johnson had indeed possessed the right to dismiss Stanton, could he be found guilty merely for appointing a successor *ad interim* while the Senate was in session?

In spite of these shortcomings the first eight articles hinged upon the challenge to the Tenure of Office Act, and the three remaining accusations did not materially weaken Johnson's case. The Emory interview amounted to a mere conversation; not even some of the radicals put much stock in it.[4] Butler's addition was a rehash of charges rejected a few months before. As *Harper's Weekly* pointed out:

> The House of Representatives did not strengthen in public opinion the indictment against the President by the article offered by General Butler. . . . It is unspeakably shameful and humiliating that a President of the United States should be so far lost to all sense of common propriety as to denounce Senators and Representatives by name. . . . These remarks are charged as a high misdemeanor, but are they of a kind for which a President should be impeached? We think not.[5]

Others agreed with this assessment. It was widely held that the article would merely prolong the proceedings.[6] And Stevens' article, though less impractical, in effect added little that was new. That Johnson had provoked the Republicans to try him on very tenuous grounds was clear from the beginning. "I think Congress did right in the matter of impeachment, although I very much regret the necessity for the act," a Providence supporter wrote to Representative Jenckes. "It strikes me that, if the action had been delayed for a few days, Johnson w[oul]d have been mad enough to commit some further misdemeanor, upon which you could have prosecuted him with the certainty of convicting him."[7] As it was, that certainty was lacking.

There were other factors which rendered the President's position much stronger than it might have been at some other time. In a presidential year no political event could be considered without weighing its effect upon the various candidates for office. To be sure, the Republicans were almost certain to nominate Grant, but it was no secret that the general had not been the radicals' first choice. Stevens blamed him for the failure to impeach Johnson earlier in February; Greeley had long opposed him; Sumner had warned against his candidacy; and Wade had expressed doubts about his political opinions. As for Butler, his hatred for his former superior was notorious; he was still collecting material to substantiate charges of Grant's drunkenness and incompetence.[8]

How the trial would affect the general's candidacy was not entirely clear. As long as he still maintained tolerable relations with Johnson, the impeachment movement had sometimes been interpreted as an effort to favor Chase and defeat him.[9] But the chief justice was now known to be opposed to the deposition of the President, and Grant had broken with the White House.[10] Should Johnson be convicted, Senator Wade, as president *pro tem* of the Senate, would succeed him. In the short time remaining of the President's term, Wade might nevertheless use his patronage powers in such a way as to interfere with Grant's ambitions.[11] Consequently, it was to the advantage of the general's supporters to work for delay of the verdict until the meeting of the Republican convention in May, or at least to protract the trial sufficiently to secure Grant's nomination at that time. Delay was bound to redound to Johnson's advantage.

The likelihood of Wade's succession in itself also weakened the prosecution. The senator had many enemies, especially among the moderates, and some of these were likely to consider even Johnson preferable to "Bluff Ben." In addition, it was generally conceded that, in case of conviction, Wade would have an excellent chance for the vice presidential nomination. Since there were several other candidates for this honor, they too had every incentive at least to delay the trial.[12]

Although Johnson overestimated the Republicans' difficulties in early 1868, they still contributed to the strength of his position. The Negro problem was as much a cause for disquiet as it had been in the fall. It sharpened the differences between moderates and radicals and provided the President with an issue he never failed to exploit.[13] "The whole object of impeachment is partisan . . . ," charged the *National Intelligencer.* "Looking to the same end, nearly three years have been spent in attempts to Africanize ten Southern States."[14] Johnson's propaganda was well attuned to the country's prejudices.

The financial issue, too, would evidently affect the impeachment. The problem of the currency was becoming ever more important. Firm believers in hard money felt threatened by advocates of greenbacks and distrusted all who suggested that the country's money supply ought to be expanded. Conservative Republican financial experts, deploring the inflationist views of Butler, Stevens, and Wade, were deeply perturbed. Edward Atkinson dreaded "Ben Wade on the financial question." Conceding that he appreciated the senator's vigor and pluck as a member of a minority, he reminded Sumner of his distrust for Wade as a leader of the majority. "The one irreparable injury which I think the Executive can do is to tamper with the currency and commit the country to disguised repudiation," he argued. "Upon this question Johnson has been right and Mr. Wade is suspected of being wrong. Should such be the truth I should regard the removal of Johnson a great misfortune in its ultimate effect, while admitting that it appears to be a necessity." And since Wade was also known to be a protectionist, the free-trade element was equally disturbed.[15]

A final factor strengthening the President's position was the attitude of the chief justice. As the presiding officer of the High Court of Impeachment, Chase evidently was in a position of influence. Since it was known that he detested Wade and considered impeachment unwise, that influence would do the President no harm. Moreover, Chase had ambitions for higher office and eventually attempted to court the Democrats.[16]

Johnson took full advantage of this situation. Whether or not he had deliberately precipitated impeachment as some thought,[17] he met the challenge with great prudence. Just as the *National Intelligencer* played up the Negro problem, so it also emphasized Wade's protectionist tendencies.[18] And although the President had grave misgivings about Secretary McCulloch's loyalty—Johnson was constantly warned to dismiss him—he curbed his emotions. The secretary of the treasury was not only permitted to remain, but he continued to keep in contact with deflationists in the opposite camp. Conservative financiers and their supporters had no reason to distrust the White House on monetary matters.[19]

In choosing his defense counsel, Johnson also showed considerable flexibility. Upon the advice of his closest collaborators he selected some of the most eminent legal talent in the country. And because it was necessary to appeal to the moderate senators, he not only sought to include conservative Republicans, but even consented to the choice of William M. Evarts, who only recently had denounced his policies.

As finally constituted, the defense consisted of Evarts, a leading member of the New York bar who later became secretary of state, Benjamin Robbins Curtis, former associate justice of the Supreme Court who had dissented in the Dred Scott case and had since built up a lucrative practice in Boston, and Attorney General Henry Stanbery—all Republicans. In addition, Johnson called on the Tennessee Unionist Thomas A. R. Nelson and his trusted confidant, former Democratic Secretary of State Jeremiah S. Black.[20] Black, however, had to withdraw. (He had championed the case of certain Baltimore investors with claims upon the West Indian guano island of Alta Vela, and his clients' pretensions, which were opposed by Seward, had been endorsed by some of the principal impeachers.) As a replacement, Johnson chose an Ohio War Democrat, William S. Groesbeck, who had participated in the Union Convention of 1866. It was a distinguished group of attorneys.[21]

Perhaps the most important indication of the President's deliberation in dealing with the impeachment crisis was his evident change of tactics. At first he seemed as uncompromising as in the past and freely permitted newspapers to interview him. But then his lawyers protested. Stanbery, who had resigned as attorney general, asked him to place himself entirely in the hands of counsel. He must no longer speak unguardedly to newspapers. Although Johnson was as convinced of the rectitude of his position as ever, he consented. No further fiery presidential interviews appeared in the press.[22]

Because he was convinced of the justice of his case, the President did not find it easy to take his lawyers' advice. When he was summoned before the High Court, he naturally wanted to take the opportunity to justify himself; he had even written a speech for the purpose. But when his attorneys told him not to go, he obeyed. Much as he might chafe at their restraint—they ought to refute the outrageous calumnies made against him by the managers, he complained—he knew better than to break with counsel.[23] He was simply not as undiplomatic as his enemies believed. As time went on, he was even ready to make deals with the moderates. And to all the world he presented a calm, dignified front.[24]

Before long the impeachment trial had become the social event of the season. The public eagerly sought to obtain tickets, and day after day tremendous crowds converged upon Capitol Hill. The diplomatic galleries were filled; the ladies in their crinolines vied for conspicuous seats. Not since the war had there been such excitement in the capital. Whatever the merits of the case, whatever its consequences, it provided Washington with an unparalleled spectacle.[25]

Proceedings began in the Senate on February 25 when Stevens and Bingham appeared at the bar. Pale and emaciated, but speaking in a stern voice, Stevens made his announcements: "Mr. President," he said, "In obedience to the order of the House of Representatives and of all the people of the United States we do impeach Andrew Johnson, President of the United States, of high crimes and misdemeanors in office." He promised to make good the charges by presenting articles in due time.[26]

The managers presented the articles on March 4. The Senate, which had already adopted twenty-five rules of procedure, met again on March 5 in order to permit the chief justice to administer the oath. After Chase himself had been sworn in by Associate Justice Nelson, the senators were called one by one to swear to try the defendant impartially.

The swearing-in caused no great difficulty until Senator Wade's name was called. Upon objections that Wade had a personal interest in the outcome of the trial and therefore should not be sworn, a general discussion ensued. After arguments concerning the equal impropriety of swearing in the President's son-in-law, Senator David T. Patterson of Tennessee, and the right of the state of Ohio to be represented by two senators, on the next day Wade was finally permitted to take the oath. The chief justice had ruled that the articles adopted by the Senate were not in force pending its organization for the purpose of the trial. His ruling was sustained, and the defense gained a point: there was a difference between the High Court and the Senate in its legislative capacity. Ordinary rules of evidence could not simply be disregarded. The President's supporters also made the most of Wade's alleged impropriety.[27]

In the meantime the managers had been busy organizing their case. When they first met, Boutwell was elected chairman. But it was known that Bingham was dissatisfied. As a leading moderate, his cooperation was essential to success. Accordingly, on the next day Boutwell yielded the chairmanship to him. However, the radical Ben Butler, who had been craving for the honor, was given the right to deliver the opening speech. Unfortunately for the prosecution, he determined to try the President in the same way in which he would try a "horse case."[28]

On the day that Wade was sworn in the managers reappeared in the Senate. Upon their request that the defendant be summoned, the Senate set the date for his appearance on Friday, March 13. The sergeant-at-arms then served the summons on the President.[29]

On March 13, the day the summons fell due, an enormous number of spectators again assembled in the galleries. The House of

Representatives adjourned to witness the scene, and the police efficiently kept the throng in order. Two tables were placed in front of the presiding officer's desk: one for the managers and one for the defense. The chief justice directed the sergeant-at-arms to call the accused. "Andrew Johnson, President of the United States," he intoned repeatedly, "Appear and answer to the articles of impeachment exhibited against you by the House of Representatives of the United States." All eyes turned toward the door, but to the onlookers' great merriment only Butler entered, looking like a huge bumble bee with his famous squint and bald pate. Then the President's council walked in. Stanbery, tall and slim, slightly bent forward, and then Curtis, much shorter and thickset, followed by Nelson, of medium height and visibly graying. The defense asked for a delay of forty days to prepare a replication. After considerable debate—"forty days . . . as long as it took God to destroy the world by a flood," exclaimed Butler—ten days were granted.[30]

On March 23, in its replication, the defense emphasized that it was in accordance with his powers as President under the Constitution that Johnson had removed the secretary of war. The Tenure of Office Act, it argued, did not apply to Stanton. This contention also justified Thomas' appointment. Nor had Johnson ever entered into a conspiracy against the law as charged in Articles IV through VII. Turning to the last three articles, counsel pointed out that in his conversation with Emory, the President had committed no overt act but merely expressed an opinion. Because of his right to free speech, he could not be held responsible for his addresses, and what applied to the preceding ten articles also applied to the eleventh. Johnson's line of defense was clear. When his lawyers asked for another thirty days' delay, they were given ten. The trial would begin on March 30.[31]

The day of Butler's opening address again brought a huge crowd to the Capitol. The general was known for his verve, and his impudent sallies had become notorious. But when he began to read his long speech many of his listeners were disappointed. His technicalities, his citing of precedents, his efforts to prove that impeachments could lie for mere misdemeanors rather than statutory crimes, and his insistence that the Senate was not a court of law did not make for drama. As was expected, he sought to prove that Stanton was covered by the Tenure of Office Act so that Thomas' appointment was illegal because no vacancy existed. Warning that Johnson might emulate usurpers like Cromwell and Bonaparte, he shouted, "By murder most foul he succeeded to the Presidency, and is the elect of an assassin to that high office." This final "Butlerism" may have been sensational, but it was not a good tactic to strengthen a weak case.[32]

During the following days, the managers called witnesses and tried to substantiate the accusations. Since most of the facts were not disputed, much of the interest in the trial waned during this time. All the managers were able to accomplish was to submit proof that Thomas had indeed boasted that he would take the War Department by force if necessary. The seriousness of his threats, however, remained in doubt, and the case was not strengthened by the revelation that a fellow citizen from his home state had encouraged Thomas with the remark, "The eyes of Delaware are upon you." The audience burst out in uproarious laughter.[33]

The defense opened on April 9. In a convincing speech which lasted for two days, Justice Curtis ably presented Johnson's case. Stressing the inapplicability of the Tenure of Office Act to the cabinet, he emphasized the President's right of free speech. In addition, he insisted upon the propriety of executive recourse to the courts and the evident truth that mere differences of opinion did not constitute a crime. "It is due to the truth of history to say . . . ," Ben Butler confessed, "That after he [Curtis] had presented the case of his client, in my judgment nothing *more* was said in his behalf, although in the five or six closing speeches presented by his other counsel much *else* was said."[34]

What the defense sought to prove—and in the last analysis proved successfully—was the lawful intent of Johnson's actions. In order to do so it summoned General Sherman and members of Johnson's administration. The managers desperately tried to exclude testimony of this nature, but their efforts only hurt them.

THE HIGH COURT OF IMPEACHMENT. From J. T. Trowbridge, *A Pictorial History of the Desolated States and the Work of Restoration.*

When Senator Reverdy Johnson finally put a direct question to Sherman, the latter, after the prosecutors' objections had been overruled, answered. The President had told him, as he recalled, "If we can bring the case to the courts, it would not stand half an hour." Subsequent testimony of Gideon Welles confirmed Johnson's legitimate purposes of seeking a constitutional test of the Tenure of Office Act.[35] Not in vain had he been careful to abide by the letter of the law.

On April 14 the defense was slowed down because Stanbery had fallen ill. When a few days later Evarts asked for a delay, Butler answered with a furious harangue. "While we are waiting for the Attorney General to get well," he shouted, "and you are asked to delay this trial for that reason, numbers of our fellow citizens are being murdered day by day. There is not a man here who does not know that the moment justice is done on this great criminal these murders will cease." The trial continued, but the defense was virtually finished. The final arguments were scheduled for the week of April 20.[36]

While the trial was progressing in Washington, almost all other public business came to a standstill. The newspapers, the financial world, and political observers all sought signs of the outcome of the great inquest. At first there seemed to be considerable unanimity in predicting that Johnson's days were numbered. As the vitriolic governor of Tennessee, "Parson" William G. Brownlow, put it, "Wade will be President ad interim while Johnson will be President ad outerim."[37] Thomas Ewing advised his son, the American minister to Holland, to look for a new job, and as late as April 20 ex-Governor Hahn of Louisiana still asserted, "No Republican doubts conviction."[38]

The radicals were especially optimistic. Julian predicted that the trial would be over within one month; Colfax was certain that the hour of deliverance was drawing nigh; and on March 29, Schurz gave Johnson only two or three weeks more. "It will be some weeks before you extract the bad tooth in the White House," Medill wrote to John Sherman. But he did not doubt the outcome.[39]

Even Johnson's supporters believed that the President would be convicted. B. B. French shared the common opinion that the radicals would depose their foe for party reasons alone, no matter what the evidence.[40] The cabinet doubted whether there was any hope, and in Vienna, John Hay counted strongly on Wade's accession even before his letters could reach his friends across the ocean.[41]

Believing Johnson's ouster to be imminent, the press naturally publicized the doings of his putative successor. The newspapers published long stories about Ben Wade's history and family; reporters visited his residence and interviewed him about his program. Would he retain Stanton in his cabinet? Would Sumner be secretary of state? What role would Grant play? The senator was evasive. "O, I don't count my chickens before they are hatched," he said. "I am not calculating on a contingency that may never happen." Should he be called upon to go to the White House, his policy would be to execute the policy of Congress. He would practice economy, protect Unionists in the South, and seek protection for industry and labor. For the time being, unlike the President's

156

son-in-law, he refused to take part in the trial after taking his oath and remained quietly in Washington. Privately, he cursed at the chief justice for his rulings in favor of the defense.[42]

In spite of the impeachers' prevailing optimism, however, from the very beginning there were those who had their doubts. On the day of the impeachment the Boston Republican Samuel Hooper asked Sumner whether the Senate could be relied upon. He feared it would not come up to the action of the House.[43] John Bigelow believed that jealousy of Ben Wade alone would make conviction impossible, and Congressman Dawes heard that impeachment was not as popular back home as was generally thought.[4] By March 16, Johnson received information through intermediaries that his enemies were in trouble, intelligence which seemed to be confirmed at a dinner on April 6. He wished he were on the other side, Butler confessed to Evarts.[45] Increasingly, there were rumors of defection among the senators, and by the time the defense ended its case all of Johnson's attorneys were confident of success.[46]

And the President himself? Confident though he had been when he challenged Congress and brought about his impeachment, he could not know what the outcome of the trial would be. At public dinners he appeared composed and unaffected by the events at the other end of Pennsylvania Avenue.[47] Privately, he sometimes gave the opposite impression. Frank Cowan later wrote that at first Johnson had been pessimistic, but although he told Moore that he had rather be convicted than acquitted by devious means, he continued to deal with the crisis with great prudence. Lorenzo Thomas received orders to desist from any further attempts at the War Department, and within a short time Johnson entered into direct negotiations with the moderates.[48]

It was generally known that Senator Grimes was not happy with his party's course. Although in favor of Congressional Reconstruction, he detested Wade, abhorred financial unorthodoxy, and thought impeachment a mistake.[49] On April 5 he approached Gustavus V. Fox, a close relative of the Blairs who had access to the President. If Johnson were to appoint a secretary of war in whom the country could have confidence, it would be helpful, he said. In addition, Grimes asked for assurances that the President would not do anything rash in case of acquittal.[50]

Johnson responded quickly. Through intermediaries he let Grimes know of his positive reactions. When the senator insisted upon a personal interview, the President complied. At a prearranged dinner party he assured Grimes of his peaceful intentions.[51]

Johnson also followed up Grimes' other advice. On April 21, Evarts met with General John M. Schofield, the moderate commander of the First Military District, at Willard's Hotel. Would he accept the nomination for secretary of war? Schofield wanted to clear the matter with Grant, a suggestion to which Evarts reluctantly agreed. Casually, after dinner, Schofield broached the issue to his commander. Grant was surprised. He had always believed conviction was certain, he said. Should he prove mistaken, he would have no objections to Schofield's acceptance.

That evening Schofield returned to Willard's Hotel. It was clear that the President could not be convicted upon the evidence presented, Evarts told him. If Johnson were to be found guilty, it would be solely on political grounds. But such a verdict would be ruinous to the Republican party as soon as the voters had time to reflect upon it. Because of these considerations, many Republicans were sorry that impeachment had been begun and would now be glad "to get out of the scrape." To be able to do so, however, they first wanted the War Department in a satisfactory condition. Schofield's acceptance would reassure them.

The general, too, wanted guarantees. When on the next day he saw Evarts again, he told him that he could cooperate only if Johnson would cease his irregular methods. Because a personal interview with the President was difficult, he would consider his nomination as an acceptance of his conditions. Evarts agreed. And Johnson, signifying his assent, sent the nomination to the Senate one day later.[52] When he wanted to, the President could be accommodating.

Grimes was not the only moderate with whom Johnson came to some sort of understanding. Both Fessenden and Trumbull seem to have had some knowledge of the Schofield deal. On May

4, Senator Edmund Ross of Kansas, who disliked the secretary of war, suggested through a go-between that the President promptly transmit the new constitutions of South Carolina and Arkansas. Such a move would exert a salutary influence, and he and others would then vote for acquittal. Johnson complied with the proposal on the next day.[53]

This change in tactics was not surprising. Conditions had changed since 1866. Cooperation with moderates at that time seemed impossible to the President because of fundamental differences over Reconstruction. By early 1868, however, radical Reconstruction, such as it was, was a fact. It was no longer necessary to rebuff possible allies. A conservative victory in the impeachment trial would do more to advance Johnson's final aims in the South than further refusals to make concessions.

The close connection between impeachment and Reconstruction remained evident throughout the trial. Speaker after speaker on both sides asserted that neither the dismissal of Stanton nor the appointment of Thomas, but the President's opposition to the radical program in the South, was the reason for the charges against him. The newspapers echoed this analysis. Reconstruction was the overriding issue.[54]

If Republican politicians needed any reminder of the impact of the trial on the South, their Unionist allies in the disaffected section furnished it. "With all other loyal men in this section, [I] am delighted to see that you are all beginning, at last, to mean *business*," a Tennessee Republican wrote to Washburne.

> We have thought for a long time, in this quarter, that the degraded demagogue should have been put aside; and now that the time seems to have come when it will be done, the loyal element of the country, —particularly down south,—rejoices in full sincerity. Whenever we can get a statesman of enlarged views . . . then the rebels will cease to hope for aid and comfort, and reconstruction will begin in earnest.[55]

Similar news came from Texas. "The loyal men are watching with deep interest the progress of the impeachment measure," the

Unionist T. H. Duval commented to Holt. They were hoping that it would be successfully carried out because acquittal would mean the war had been fought for nothing. "The freedmen will be again slaves in fact—loyalty in the South will be crushed out, and treason and traitors will be everywhere triumphant." From Alabama the Republican politician Frank G. Bromberg reported that Southern loyalists were in a state of suspense. "The decisive contest upon which hangs our peace has at length been begun . . . ," he wrote to Sumner. "The impeachment of the President will be the death blow to the rebellion. . . ."[56] Virginia Governor Pierpoint expressed hopes for conviction; in North Carolina, loyalists entertained the same sentiments; Louisiana Republicans counted on Johnson's removal to offset Hancock's influence; and West Virginia Unionists were certain that acquittal would shatter them.[57] General James A. Brisbin, then in Kentucky, summed up the situation for Stanton:

> The rebels are very quiet here and a great deal alarmed about impeachment but, if that measure fails, the Union men will have to leave the state. Here in the South we cannot calmly think of the failure of impeachment and the long train of evils that would follow in its wake.[58]

Fear for the loyalists' future in case of failure to convict was widespread. Imploring senators to expel the President, a Tennessean warned Sumner that otherwise loyal Republicans would not be able to remain in the state.[59] In Mississippi, W. H. Gibbs cautioned Washburne: "If the President is not convicted and removed . . . our efforts here will be defeated, and it will no longer be safe for a white man to advocate the principles of the Republican party in this State except under the immediate protection of federal bayonets. . . . Our only salvation is the removal of the President."[60] In West Virginia, Unionists were afraid acquittal would mean the end of the state.[61] In Alabama they asserted that failure to oust Johnson would crush their hopes, and in Florida the radical wing of the party considered conviction essential for survival. The radical press was not mistaken when it warned that a verdict of guilty was an absolute necessity for Southern Unionists.[62]

The precarious nature of the radicals' position became clear while the trial was in progress. The Republicans won the spring elections in New Hampshire only after unusual exertions. In Connecticut they lost the governorship, although they captured the legislature, which was sure to retire Senator Dixon. And in Michigan the voters rejected a new constitution that included Negro suffrage.[63]

Even more alarming were developments directly affecting the South. Early in March the Supreme Court heard arguments in the McCardle case. Fearing that the tribunal might declare the entire Reconstruction program unconstitutional, the Republicans rushed a measure through Congress to take away the right of appeal in cases under the Habeas Corpus Act of 1867. This hasty action, evidently meant to forestall a decision in the pending case, indicated how insecure the radicals were. The President's veto was easily overridden, and the bill became law on March 26.[64] A few weeks earlier a fourth Reconstruction Act permitting ratification of Southern constitutions by a majority of voters rather than registrants was also passed and Alabama's constitution finally accepted.[65] The President did not even bother to write a veto. Since he did not approve of the entire process of radical Reconstruction, he simply permitted the bill to become law without his signature. His astute defense against the managers' charges was more effective than another futile veto.

Many Southern conservatives appreciated Johnson's efforts. "You are now the only barrier between us and destruction," former Confederate Senator Augustus H. Garland wrote to the President, "and in you the hopes, the last hopes, too, of the friends of the constitution and the government are centered. And they feel that if you are overcome all is lost, and lost forever."[66] Former Confederate officer Edward M. L'Engle agreed. "Our conditions and prospects are bad enough already," he commented, "but they will be much worse if Johnson is overcome." And counsel for

Jefferson Davis was warned that if Wade became President the Confederate leader might well be tried and executed.[67]

In spite of the radicals' growing impatience, the trial continued to drag along, wearying onlookers and heartening the defense. The last weeks of April and the beginning of May were taken up by the closing arguments. Logan led off with an insistence that misdemeanors were impeachable even if they were not statutory crimes. Boutwell then delivered his final speech, an oration which struck Clemenceau as the "longest, weakest and dullest" of the trial. He was followed by T. A. R. Nelson's summing up for the defense, largely a passionate plea for justice based on Johnson's wartime record. A few days later Groesbeck's oration gave proof of his legal skill, especially in his reiteration of the plain truth that differences of opinion did not constitute a crime. On April 27, Thaddeus Stevens addressed the court in a feeble voice. Reviewing the salient facts, he insisted that Grant's appointment in 1867 proved that Stanton was protected by the Tenure of Office Act. He regretted the omission of all references to Reconstruction, and declared that had Johnson been on trial in the Roman senate he would soon have found himself "in the stocks in the middle of the forum." Too weak to finish his speech in person, the Commoner had made his supreme effort.[68]

The other speeches added little that was new. Thomas Williams delivered a partisan harangue. Evarts pointed out once more that the prosecution had no case. It would be offensive to convict a President merely for seeking to raise a question between the Constitution and the law. Stanbery, though still sick, also submitted a closing statement. Pointedly assuring the senators that he knew Johnson would not undertake anything rash if he were acquitted, he also pleaded that the President's desire to seek a court decision about the Tenure of Office Act did not merit conviction. Finally, on May 4, 5, and 6, Bingham closed the case. In a strong attempt once more to justify the indictment, he sought to show that the attempt to test the constitutionality of the Tenure of Office Act was no defense for violation of the law. Appealing to his audience to remember the "great principles of constitutional liberty" for which he professed to be speaking, he asked for conviction of the defendant. At the conclusion of his address, the galleries burst into applause. It was evident that the trial was nearing its end.[69]

In the beginning of May the tension in Washington became all-pervasive. Rumors abounded. Fessenden, Grimes, Henderson, Trumbull, and others were reputed to have decided against conviction; some senators suggested that Ben Wade resign as president of the Senate, and the betting parlors were kept busy.[70] The radicals professed optimism in public. "The removal of the great obstruction to peace and quiet is certain," Butler wired to the New Hampshire Republican convention on May 4. "Wade and prosperity are sure to come with the apple blossoms."[71] In private, however, they were deeply worried. The rumors of corruption, the talk of Republican defections, and other signs of trouble all had their effect. "There is an awful gloom among us this afternoon," Julian confessed to his wife on May 11. "To the surprise and great consternation of everybody on our side the President is likely to be acquitted. It makes me *chilly* and I think I can't write more." On the same day the Chicago *Tribune* expressed its doubts and advised its readers the outcome would make little difference.[72]

May 12 was the day the Senate was expected to vote. But the tremendous number of people who had come to witness the historic event was disappointed. Senator Howard of Michigan had fallen ill; to give him time to return Chandler moved for a postponement until Saturday, May 16. The Senate quickly agreed. Its action was widely interpreted as an admission of the prosecution's weakness.[73]

Thus the President experienced another few days of uncertainty. His counsel assured him the case was won. Almost the entire cabinet agreed, and he himself was fairly optimistic. But he was greatly disturbed by the postponement.[74] One never could tell, and he did not agree with the Chicago *Tribune*. For him, the outcome of the trial was not merely a question of his own fate. He considered it a test of the Constitution and the laws as he understood them. And he was not so wrong. Acquittal would accomplish more than vindicating him. It would greatly further his policies in the South. For this he had labored, for this he had refused to compromise until the very end, and for this he had brought matters to a climax when the Republican party seemed least prepared. He was awaiting the decision in hopes of final justification.

Eleven.

Failure of the Impeachment

Saturday, May 16, 1868, was a beautiful day. The sun was shining, and the public buildings in Washington were enveloped in a soft haze. But the balmy atmosphere was deceptive. The city was in the grip of feverish excitement, for the High Court of Impeachment would meet at noon to decide the fate of the President.

The rush for tickets to the Senate galleries had been tremendous. Long before eleven, all the best seats were taken—a strange contrast to the scarce attendance on the floor when, at 11:30, the Senate was called to order. Slowly the senators drifted in. By noon, the galleries were wholly occupied. The diplomatic box was full, thousands were milling outside the chamber, and the overflow extended to the terraces and streets beyond. Rarely in its history had the capital witnessed such tension.

While the clerk was droning on with the titles of various bills, the spectators eagerly studied the senators. There was Charles Sumner, talking with Stevens, who had arrived long before the rest of the managers. Trumbull was sitting nervously apart. Fessenden looked defiant, while Van Winkle seemed to be occupied with his papers. Fowler, putting on black kid gloves, was restlessly moving about. General Sickles, who together with Joseph Holt and Anthony Trollope had been admitted to the floor, was seen talking to Ross. At twenty minutes to twelve, Roscoe Conkling, still pale from a recent sickness, arrived. He was immediately surrounded by friends. The moment of decision was close at hand.

Precisely at noon the chief justice entered. The usual proclamation was made. The managers and counsel (except for Curtis and Stanbery) appeared at their respective tables. A messenger was sent to notify the House, and reporters busily jotted down every action of the doubtful senators. Here was Thayer addressing Ross. There was Dixon consulting Fessenden, and then hastening to see Anthony. There was Sumner, leaving his seat to talk to Chase. Every little incident seemed portentous.

The first substantial move was to consider Senator Williams' order that the eleventh article—the one most likely to carry—be considered first. It was adopted, 34 to 19, Grimes being absent and Wade voting for the first time. During the balloting, Howard, wrapped in a shawl, tottering and scarcely able to walk, was brought in, supported by Chandler and Drake. Trumbull, seated directly in front of him, turned around and shook his hand. Ross, who opposed the order, was tearing up little bits of paper. His vote was considered one of the most uncertain. Then the House entered. Some further preliminaries occupied a little time, and then Edmunds moved to proceed to the vote. Fessenden asked for delay to permit Grimes to take his seat, as the senator from Iowa was reported to be in the building. Soon Grimes, suffering from a recent paralytic stroke, came in and sank into his seat. The galleries were hushed.[1]

The moment everyone had been waiting for had now arrived. Warning all spectators to preserve proper decorum, the chief justice announced that he would proceed to take the vote on the eleventh article. After the clerk had read it, Chase directed him to call the roll. Senator Anthony was called and rose in his place. "Mr. Senator Anthony," the chief justice asked, "How say you? Is the respondent, Andrew Johnson, President of the United States, guilty or not guilty of a high misdemeanor, as charged in this article?" "Guilty," answered the senator from Rhode Island, and the roll call proceeded.

As each senator rose from his seat, the spectators anxiously counted the votes. Most Republicans, of course, found the defendant guilty, just as all Democrats and conservatives considered him innocent. But there were seven exceptions. Fessenden, Fow-

ler, Grimes, Henderson, Ross, Van Winkle, and Trumbull refused to join their colleagues and voted for acquittal. And when
the letter "R" was reached and Ross rose, tension mounted to a
fever pitch. His negative answer sent a murmur through the
crowd. Only if both West Virginia senators, Van Winkle and
Willey, still voted to convict could Johnson now be found guilty.
But Van Winkle joined the other "recusants," and the final tally
stood 35 to 19, precisely one short of the two-thirds majority
needed for conviction. The court adjourned until May 26, and
Colonel William H. Crook, a member of the President's staff,
hastened to the White House to bring the good news to his chief.
Years later he claimed that he ran all the way.[2]

A great deal has been written about the dramatic nature of the
vote and its narrow margin. The "seven tall men" have been cast
in a heroic light—sterling patriots risking their careers for principle and country. Ross especially has often been described as the
man of the hour—fearless and undaunted in spite of certain political ruin. His vote allegedly turned the tide, and President Kennedy made him one of the principals in his *Profiles in Courage*.
Ben Wade, in contrast, has been accused of the crassest ambition in
voting to convict, and many of his critics have commented upon
his alleged impropriety in participating in a trial in which he had
so large a personal stake.[3] But while these stories are interesting,
they are not entirely accurate.

That the seven "recusants" suffered unrelieved martyrdom as
a result of their stand was disproven conclusively in 1959 by Ralph
J. Roske. While none of them was reelected to Congress, they
continued their varied careers and did not cease their political
activities after 1868. Several even remained active in the inner
councils of the Republican party.[4]

Senator Ross in particular did not play as decisive a role as is
often assumed. His vote was crucial only if that of Van Winkle is
disregarded. It is true that the Kansan had long remained uncommitted, but it is also true that he had fairly consistently voted with
the conservatives in various tests of the powers of the court and
its presiding officer. And although he seemed to be ready to vote

for the eleventh article on the eve of the decision, early next morning he had apparently changed his mind even before he came to the Senate chamber. Consequently, his vote could not have been completely surprising. Peter G. Van Winkle eventually voted for acquittal, but at the moment Ross rose it was not entirely certain how either Van Winkle or his colleague Willey (who finally opted for conviction) would vote. Moreover, within a few weeks Ross was well rewarded for his steadfastness. He received access to the President's patronage.[5]

The case of Ben Wade is slightly different. The propriety of his participating in the trial has long been discussed, and at first it might indeed appear unseemly for the presiding officer of the Senate, as the legal successor of Andrew Johnson, to have cast a vote for the President's removal. Yet it must be remembered that until the morning of the final decision Wade had never participated in any test affecting the trial. When he finally did vote, first for the prior consideration of the eleventh article and then for the article itself, his ballot made little difference. By the time the clerk reached the letter "W" nineteen senators had already voted for acquittal, and Wade's participation changed nothing. The old radical had long since declared that he believed the state of Ohio entitled to two votes; he merely acted accordingly.[6]

In spite of the great tension in the capital, the outcome was not entirely unexpected. Speculation about individual senators' votes had been rife for weeks, and the papers had been filled with rumors of all sorts, especially as the trial drew to a close.[7] By May 12 it was certain that Fessenden, Grimes, Henderson, and Trumbull were lost to the impeachers; they had said so in a closed session of the Senate.[8] On May 11, Horace White of the Chicago *Tribune* had gone so far as to write to Fessenden that he would not hold a not-guilty vote against him, and he encouraged him to show the letter to Grimes.[9] On the next day his paper had virtually given up.[10] Speculation about others had also worried the managers. Frelinghuysen, Anthony, Fowler, Sherman, Sprague, Ross, Willey, and Van Winkle had all been reported as doubtful at one time or another. And while the prosecution attempted to put pressure on the uncommitted senators—the press, public meetings, and communications from constituents were all mobilized for this purpose —the managers could not have been taken totally unaware by the final vote.[11]

The closeness of the balloting in itself may be deceiving. Considerable evidence exists that other senators stood ready to vote for acquittal if their votes had been needed. As early as May 18 the Chicago *Tribune* asserted that the President's friends laid claim to four more votes in case of necessity, and the substance of the story was confirmed shortly after the trial by Samuel Randall, the Democratic congressman from Pennsylvania.[12] On August 3, Johnson himself wrote to Benjamin Truman that Morgan had been one of the Republicans in question.[13] In 1913, Senator Henderson also asserted that Morgan had been the reputed swing voter. Because of the intense pressure, he voted to convict, but would not have done so had his vote made any difference.[14] Some years earlier the Missouri senator told William A. Dunning that Willey had also been ready to switch, a point he later reiterated to Trumbull's biographer, Horace White.[15] He also mentioned Sprague as one of the senators willing to change, and John Bigelow learned that Nye had been another.[16] In short, Johnson's victory was assured long before the vote was taken. A sufficient number of moderate Republicans stood ready to acquit him, come what might.

Whatever their expectations, the managers' consternation at the acquittal was genuine. After the vote Thaddeus Stevens, waving his arms in the air, shouted, "The country is going to the devil."[17] Ben Butler was also outraged. "How does it happen that just enough & no more republican Senators are convinced of the President's innocence . . . ?" he lamented to John Russell Young. "I think we shall be able to show where some of these men got their consciences and how much they are worth."[18] And Butler suspected Ross of out and out bribery. "Tell the d—d scoundrel that if he wants money, there is a bushel of it here to be had!" he said, and induced the House to authorize an investigation of the whole matter.[19] Logan was also dispirited, and Boutwell continued to believe in the justice of his cause long after others had abandoned it.[20] The managers' failure hit them hard.

The investigation in the House verged on the ludicrous. Subpoenaing witnesses and papers, telegrams, letters, and bank statements, the managers even sought to summon the recusant senators in person, only to run into the problem of the independence of the Senate. They eventually arrested a gambler named Charles W. Woolley for contempt, but found nothing. After rendering a preliminary report on May 25, Butler finally submitted another in July which confessed as much. The spectacle made a poor impression on all but his supporters.[21]

The reason for the adjournment of the High Court was the forthcoming Republican convention, scheduled to meet in Chicago on May 18. It was certain that Grant would be nominated. The vice presidency, however, might well affect the final outcome of the impeachment. Wade had been the leading candidate for the honor ever since the beginning of the trial; had he become President, there is little doubt that he would have been able to procure the nomination. Because any number of other Republicans, among them Speaker Colfax, Governor Reuben E. Fenton of New York, and Senator Henry Wilson, were also anxious for the honor, their partisans had been less than anxious for Johnson's conviction prior to the convention.[22]

Grant was nominated as expected, but a spirited contest developed when the convention turned to the selection of his running mate. Wade led on the first few ballots; he had opponents among his own Ohio delegation, however, and the acquittal of the President on the eleventh article proved fatal. On the sixth ballot the convention nominated Schuyler Colfax. Wade had suffered his second disappointment within one week.[23]

On May 26 attention once more centered on Washington. Again the chief justice entered the Senate chamber at noon; again the sergeant-at-arms made his proclamation; and again both counsel and managers took their seats. Once more the members of the

House entered upon special notification. Several attempts to postpone the vote further—Ross suggested September 1—failed. Then Williams of Oregon moved that a vote be taken on the second article, a tactic which had been decided upon because it was known that neither Sherman nor Howe would vote for the first, charging a violation of the Tenure of Office Act in the removal of Stanton. The motion was adopted, and the clerk read the article accusing the President of violating the law in offering an appointment to Thomas without the advice and consent of the Senate.

As he had done ten days earlier, the chief justice once more intoned his formula. Senator after senator rose. "How say you . . . ?" "Guilty" or "not guilty" was the answer, and the vote stood precisely as before: 35 to 19, one short of conviction. Apparently Colfax's nomination for Vice President had not changed any votes.

Williams tried once more. The third article charged the President with actually appointing Thomas in violation of the Tenure of Office Act. Perhaps it might still carry, and the senator from Oregon quickly moved its consideration. The vote was called, but again the result was the same. By a vote of 35 to 19 the President was acquitted.[24]

Williams now gave up. If Johnson could not be convicted for appointing Thomas, he could certainly not be found guilty on the remaining articles, either the first or those accusing him of a conspiracy and various lesser offenses. If every one of the articles were to be voted upon, progressively fewer and fewer senators would vote guilty, and it would be impossible to blame the debacle on the seven recusants alone. Consequently, the radicals decided to call a halt, and Williams moved for an adjournment *sine die*. The motion carried, 34 to 16. The trial was over.

The President and his cabinet had been in session since noon. In communication with the Senate by telegraph, they quickly learned the result. With no outward sign of agitation, calm, dignified, placid, and self-possessed, Johnson received the congratulations of his advisers. His countenance lightened and he permitted himself a pleasant, satisfied smile. When interviewed he said that the result was what he had always expected, that his confidence in the people was undimmed, and that he expected history to vindicate his course.[26]

The President had every reason to be satisfied. His calculated defiance of Congress had succeeded, and his acquittal would doubtless help his cause. On the day the trial ended he received the resignation of the secretary of war. Shortly afterwards, Schofield was confirmed as Stanton's successor. And while the Senate rejected his renomination of Stanbery as attorney general, it accepted his nomination of William M. Evarts instead.[27]

The impeachers' disappointment was evident. The radical press reported the defeat with great bitterness, but this mood did not last long. Within a short time the public's attention turned to other matters. The election of Grant was now the foremost problem confronting the Republican party, which pulled together, moderates joining with radicals to work for victory in November. Consequently, the recusants were neither permanently expelled from the Republican caucus nor censured at Chicago. Every Republican was needed for victory. Thaddeus Stevens might still attempt to frame new charges against the man he hated, suggestions might still be made to try Johnson again once Southern radicals represented their states, but nothing came of these proposals.[28] The President's acquittal was final.

Why was it that a party which had for so long held the President at bay and which for over two years had never lacked a two-thirds majority to override his vetoes now failed to muster the same two-thirds to carry out its goal of ridding itself of the man it considered the chief obstacle to Reconstruction? Why was it that Republican senators who had no love at all for Andrew Johnson came to the conclusion that they had to vote for his acquittal even at the risk of their political careers? The answers to these questions clearly illustrate Johnson's shrewdness. His tactics could not have succeeded had he not assessed correctly the difficulties of the Republican party.

In many ways the considerations which influenced the seven "recusants" to break with the majority were similar to those which had induced the House to reject impeachment in December. All the problems confronting the Republican party and all the weaknesses which had favored the President from the beginning now influenced these senators to vote against conviction—and others to do likewise if necessary. While the excitement in February had momentarily covered up the differences between most moderates and radicals, to some of the former, impeachment had never been appealing. Grimes and Fessenden, for example, refusing to vote when the Senate passed the resolution condemning the ouster of Stanton, had opposed the step from the start. Fowler and Henderson likewise had abstained.[29] Presumably, they never had any reason to change their minds. "I am satisfied that with present lights the thing [impeachment] would never have been begun," Fessenden wrote to his son on May 3. "People now see, as I always told them, that the result would be disastrous anyway."[30]

The weakness of the case was not calculated to impress moderates with the necessity of voting against acquittal. All of the six recusants who filed a final opinion concluded that the secretary of war was not covered by the Tenure of Office Act, and they reasoned that the appointment of an *ad interim* head of the department did not constitute a crime. While the question of impeachment for nonindictable offenses was not conclusively settled, Fessenden undoubtedly spoke for many of his colleagues in his summation. "Granting, for the sake of argument," he stated, "that this latter construction [impeachment for nonindictable offenses] is the true one, . . . it is a power to be exercised with extreme caution, when you once get beyond the line of specific criminal offenses."[31] That caution was lacking. Ross, who did not file an opinion, also stressed the flimsiness of the indictment in his account of the trial.[32]

That some of the remaining senators were unwilling to vote for the first article as well did not strengthen the case. Sherman could not go back on his statement—that it did not cover the cabinet—at the time of the bill's passage. Neither could Howe, who had vainly tried to amend the measure to include the secretaries. "To-day we were informed by the President that he had removed Mr. Stanton," he wrote to his niece on February 21.

Our friends were taken by surprise. I was not. I have only been surprised that he delayed it so long. The Republican press will deny
his authority to remove Mr. Stanton. If so the Republican press will
lie. I struggled for weeks in the Senate to secure an Amendment to
the tenure of office bill which would protect the Secretary of War. . . .
A Committee of Conference . . . reported a clause to which both
Houses agreed and now the dispute is as to whether it protects the
Secretary or not. I know two things about it. 1st. That by its terms it
does *not* protect the Secretary—and 2nd. that when it was reported
to the Senate Mr. Sherman . . . stated that it did not and was not
designed to protect the Secretary of War. . . . I gave them to understand this afternoon they must do their own lying.[33]

In addition to the legal question of the applicability of the
Tenure of Office Act to the secretary of war, the impropriety of
forcing an unwanted confidential adviser upon an unwilling President also affected the judgment of some senators. "The peculiar
relations of the cabinet minister as the organ of the President demands the strictest delicacy and harmony between them," commented Fowler. "And whenever there is the shadow of impaired
confidence every sense of honor, integrity, patriotism and manly
independence demand the prompt and complete resignation of
the cabinet minister." The fact that Stanton himself had held the
Tenure of Office law unconstitutional made the case even more
debatable, as Henderson pointedly remarked.[34]

The conspiracy articles (IV–VII) were even less convincing than
those directly accusing the President of violating the law. As many
senators, even some of those voting for conviction, pointed out, no
evidence whatever was introduced to substantiate charges of unlawful conspiracy between the President and General Thomas.[35]
Article VIII, involving the disbursal of moneys by the War Department, was open to the same objections as the first three. Like
the conspiracy charges, the Emory and Butler articles did not even
convince several of those who joined the majority.[36] The eleventh
article, notwithstanding Stevens' clever wording, caused more difficulty to some of the "recusants." Henderson admitted that it was
the only one upon which he had ever entertained serious doubts,

and Ross at one time seemed likely to give it favorable consideration. But since it did not really add anything, except to tie up
Johnson's alleged denigration of Congress with his action in respect
to the War Department, it too fell because of the weakness of the
case.[37]

The question of intent and the cavalier treatments of its introduction by the managers also influenced a number of "recusants."
The prosecution's efforts to exclude testimony on this topic and
the Senate's partial compliance were extremely damaging. Ross,
Grimes, and Henderson in particular singled out this circum-
stance for their disapprobation. "[The] essential ingredient of
judicial fairness was not shown to Mr. Johnson in this case . . . ,"
Ross commented. "It was difficult to escape the conviction that the
trial was a strictly partisan persecution."[38]

The weakness of the articles was thus manifest. As Trumbull
put it, "To convict and depose the Chief Magistrate of a great
nation, when his guilt was not made palpable by the record, and
for insufficient cause, would be fraught with far greater danger
to the future of the country than can arise from leaving Mr.
Johnson in office. . . ."[39] And Trumbull had originally favored
impeachment.

The other factors which had early given Johnson an advantage
also played their part in procuring his acquittal. Election year
calculations inevitably entered into the trial and its conduct.
While General Grant was totally committed to impeachment and
even used his influence to further it,[40] some of his associates were
less enthusiastic. If Wade were to become President, he might
interfere with their plans. His radicalism would weaken the
ticket, and he might exert an unwanted influence on the incoming
administration.[41] At any rate, Grimes and his associates believed
that they had procured sufficient guarantees to ensure Johnson's
good behavior for the short remainder of his tenure.[42]

That Wade constituted a major stumbling block for the impeachers was widely recognized. His advocacy of women's rights,
high tariffs, the advancement of labor, and—last but not least—
black suffrage had not endeared him to the moderates. As early as

February 28 the New York *Herald* predicted the failure of the trial not merely because of the weakness of the case, but also because of "jealousy of Ben Wade and doubts as to his competency." Other papers agreed, and the pro-Johnson press never wearied of quoting Republican politicians and newspapers in disparagement of the senator from Ohio.[43]

What was known to the journalists was equally known to well-informed politicians. On February 26, John Bigelow told Gideon Welles that many Republicans preferred Johnson to Wade, an analysis that agreed with Senator Morgan's sources of information.[44] Fessenden, who needed no warning, was cautioned that Wade's succession would ensure his nomination as Vice President, a contingency which might cause the defeat of General Grant in at least four states.[45] Atkinson became more and more uneasy about Wade's financial unorthodoxy, and rumors of the selection of E. B. Ward, a Michigan millionaire, as Wade's secretary of the treasury deeply disturbed the business community. Ward was known as an extreme protectionist and unsound on the currency.[46]

Of course the racial question was always in the background. The old radical's commitment to racial equality embarrassed Republicans who were frightened of the issue. " 'The nigger' licked him in Ohio, and in the estimation of most men that inconsiderate act of the African finished his political career," commented the New York *Herald*. "It is not considered desirable to resuscitate 'that grand old man.' "[47]

In addition to general objections to Wade as an extreme radical, certain senators held personal grudges against him. Grimes, Fessenden, and Trumbull, especially since the war years, had clashed with him on political and economic questions. Wade's radicalism was all-inclusive; theirs extended only to the opposition of slavery and related topics. Grimes had opposed Wade's advocacy of high tariffs, greenbacks, higher wages for federal employees, and diminution of the powers of the conservative secretary of the navy.[48] Fessenden had not only been Wade's competitor for president of the Senate, but had long differed with him on confiscation, higher wages, shorter hours, and financial policy.⁴⁹ As for Trumbull, he too had had serious differences with Wade. Conflict about the relative severity of the confiscation bills, the reconstruction of Louisiana, and the proposal to erect a bust in memory of Justice Taney had led to sharp encounters between the two men.⁵⁰ Fowler, who also resented Wade, referred publicly to his aversion to a "few bad, bold conspirators" like Butler and Logan in the House and Wade and Sumner in the Senate.⁵¹ "If Johnson, Wade, and Stanton were in a bag and well shaken," Grimes reputedly remarked, he "would not flip a copper for a choice between them."⁵²

Finally, ever since the Republican convention of 1860, the chief justice had disliked Wade intensely. Believing that his fellow Ohioan's candidacy at that time had ruined his own chances for the presidency, Chase had never forgiven the senator and presumably used his influence to frustrate his rival's ambition.⁵³

The chief justice's precise position was never clear. Chase himself believed that he was merely doing his duty by impartially presiding over the trial. But when he began to insist, with some justification, that the Senate sitting for the impeachment was a court and that ordinary rules of evidence applied, many radicals believed him lost to the cause. This was especially true because of rumors of his angling for the Democratic nomination, later proven to be true, became more and more frequent.⁵⁴ Chase had always been supremely ambitious. He considered impeachment a mistake and sought to make capital of his opinions. If the Democrats nominated him on a platform of universal suffrage, he would accept. Of course the Negrophobe party had no real intention of doing any such thing.⁵⁵

Because of Chase's equivocal position, rumors arose that he was exerting pressure on some senators to vote for acquittal. The most obvious candidate was his son-in-law, Senator Sprague. But since Sprague voted to convict, the chief justice was either unsuccessful or the rumors were not very reliable.⁵⁶ It was also said that Chase had impressed Van Winkle with the necessity of acquitting the President. The story was so persistent that the West Virginian denied it in public, but there may have been some substance to it.[57] At any rate, the chief justice's known antagonism to Wade and his opposition to impeachment played its role in the progress of the trial.[58]

The constitutional issue also affected the outcome of the impeachment. The tripartite system of government was considered fundamental to American institutions, and as early as January 1867, *Harper's Weekly* had pointed out that the removal of a President was not to be undertaken lightly. "If difference with the majority in Congress is an adequate occasion for such a movement," the periodical stated, "it is plain that impeachment of the Executive will become an ordinary party measure, and the independence of the Executive contemplated by the Constitution being thus destroyed the balance of the whole system comes to an end." In the ensuing discussions of the probability of impeachment, the problem was frequently mentioned.[59]

When Johnson was at last impeached, the Democrats in Congress drew up a protest in which they emphasized the importance of the survival of the division of powers in government.[60] In the weeks that followed, the issue was not forgotten, Evarts making it one of the main points of his closing speech.[61] Accordingly, it had its effect upon the "recusants." "Once set an example of impeaching a President for what, when the excitement of the hour shall have subsided, will be regarded as insufficient causes . . . ," Trumbull stated in his final opinion, "and no future President will be safe who happens to differ with the majority of the House and two-thirds of the Senate on any measure deemed by them important. . . . What then becomes of the checks and balances of the Constitution?"[62] Grimes believed that the managers' theory of the case established the complete supremacy of Congress over the other branches of government, a doctrine to which he could not assent. Ross also stressed the problem in his memoirs. That the radicals had at the same time been attacking the Supreme Court seemed to confirm fears about the permanence of the tripartite system.[63]

The political importance of the trial to the party also impressed the waverers. Although at first it seemed absolutely necessary for the good of the party to convict Johnson, as time went on many observers began to feel that Fessenden was right. The outcome would not help the party no matter what it might be. Perhaps the process should never have been begun, and it would be unwise to make a martyr of the obstreperous President.[64] If the result was acquittal, then for better or for worse the party would have to live with it.

Finally, the tactics used by the managers had an adverse effect on many senators. Chief among them was Butler; his effrontery, his brutal cross examinations, his rudeness to counsel, and his insistence on the exclusion of testimony bearing on the President's intent all harmed his case. Nor were rumors of his inclusion in Wade's putative cabinet helpful. Toward the end of the trial his outrageous attempts to browbeat the uncommitted made a bad impression.[65] And neither Boutwell nor Williams was much better.[66] Instead of proceeding in a dignified manner, the managers, by their shenanigans, succeeded only in making the trial ridiculous. Their opponents were the beneficiaries.

So the great trial failed. Johnson's policies of delay and defiance had been successful. It is true that he might have avoided impeachment altogether, but having decided to take a deliberate risk to rid himself of Stanton, he had triumphed. In the end, he had again blocked his radical enemies.

Twelve.

Results of the Acquittal

Andrew Johnson's trial was over on May 26, 1868. The court adjourned *sine die*, and most Republicans gave up all thought of further proceedings against the President. The consequences of his acquittal, however, were not clear. Would it harm the party? Would it retard Reconstruction? Would it have a permanent effect upon the workings of the American government? Or would it remain but a minor incident and soon be forgotten? These and similar questions have long been debated. Whether they can ever be fully answered remains problematical.

In the first shock of defeat, many Republicans were downcast and dispirited. Even moderates had believed that in case of failure to convict, the party would be in serious trouble. "[I]f . . . the President is not removed, I fear the Republican party is well-nigh ship wrecked, the business of the country prostrated, and the cause of liberty and humanity sent shivering," the postmaster of Lawrence warned Banks on May 5.[1] Consequently, the actual news of the verdict struck party leaders with dismay. Party discipline had broken down, conservatives were jubilant, and for a moment the future looked very gloomy indeed. Senator Howe spoke of the "profound humiliation" of the party.[2] George Wilkes was certain that the President had become a virtual monarch, and Joseph Medill worried about Grant's prospects in November. "There is very little enthusiasm for our ticket or cause among the people," he complained. "The failure of impeachment has soured and discontented multitudes of our friends."[3]

But from the very beginning there were those who entertained a contrary opinion. For some time there had been talk that a conviction might be as dangerous for the party as acquittal.[4] Johnson discredited was an asset; Johnson martyred, possibly ousted by a narrow margin with distinguished Republicans dissenting, a liability. "If as we believe, it is better to tolerate wrong, than to punish it by unlawful means," the Toledo *Daily Commercial* asserted, "we think the Republicans may congratulate themselves on the virtue of their Senators, rather than be cast down by their refusal to accept the conviction of the President as their obligation as partisans. Hence, we do not regard this result as damaging to the party."[5] And although E. B. Washburne, like many of his colleagues, was bitterly disappointed, he expressed the conviction that the party was *"not* dead." It would emerge stronger than ever.[6] Some observers even held that the manner of the President's narrow escape, his acquittal by one vote, was fortuitous. It would keep him in bounds and redound to the advantage of the party.[7]

The "recusants" and their friends were naturally convinced that they had rendered a tremendous service. As one admirer wrote to Fowler, the verdict was one the country desired and it would have redounded "to the future prejudice of the Republican party" had it been different.[8] Fessenden was certain that he had saved the party, and Henderson later took great pride in his colleagues' belated respect for him.[9] Because of the "recusants," the Republicans and not the Democrats had saved the President. Thus in the long run the acquittal could not be interpreted as a defeat for the majority.[10] "The Republicans have barely escaped from committing a crime that would have buried them in the fall elections," Gustavus V. Fox commented at the time.[11] And after the Chicago convention, the temporary elevation of Ben Wade would only have embarrassed the party.[12]

After a while, it appeared almost as if the impeachment and its failure would have few important consequences. In his three volume *History of the Rise and Fall of the Slave Power in America,* Henry Wilson came to the conclusion that it did not have a very direct bearing on his subject.[13] In view of the relatively speedy disappearance of the topic from public and private discussion, his analysis may be understandable. But it did not correspond to the truth.

On the surface, it is true, the President's acquittal changed very little. Shortly after the end of the trial all but three Southern states completed the process of Reconstruction. The bill readmitting Arkansas was passed on June 6 and became law on June 22. Alabama, Florida, Georgia, Louisiana, and North and South Carolina were readmitted in an Omnibus Bill on June 25. Finally, on July 20, the Fourteenth Amendment became part of the Constitution. Soon Virginia, Mississippi, and Texas, where Reconstruction was still incomplete, followed suit, so that by 1871 all were once more represented in Congress.[14]

It is also true that Andrew Johnson's course was not materially affected by his narrow escape. Maintaining his position to the last, especially his condemnation of Negro suffrage, he continued his policies of obstruction. Thus he vetoed both the Arkansas and Omnibus bills and reiterated all his objections to Congressional Reconstruction.[15] He issued new proclamations of amnesty, one on July 4 pardoning most remaining Confederates, and one on December 25 encompassing the rest. Finally, in his last annual address, he again lectured Congress about the inviolability of the Union, as well as the impossibility of attempting to place the white population "under the domination of persons of color."[16]

In spite of his espousal of the principles of the Democratic party, Johnson was not able to secure its nomination for the presidency. In fact, it was widely believed that the Democrats would have preferred his ouster and martyrdom to his salvation by Republican votes.[17] Rejecting Johnson, Chase, and Pendleton, the Democrats finally nominated Horatio Seymour of New York and Francis P. Blair, Jr., and adopted a platform which showed that they had neither learned nor forgotten anything. To soothe the President's feelings they passed a resolution of appreciation and tendered him their thanks for his patriotic efforts.[18] But that was all. At heart Johnson might always have been a Democrat, and he might see eye to eye with the Democrats on racial issues, but the minority party kept him at arm's length.

Although the President's isolation was thus clear to all, he still retained his powers as Commander-in-Chief and President. Fearful of further encroachments upon radical Reconstruction, Congress refused to adjourn when the session drew to a close. Instead, as in 1867, it merely recessed until September, subject to recall should the President's behavior make a meeting necessary. But the special session never took place.[19] Johnson was careful not to issue another overt challenge to Congress. He even retained McCulloch in the Treasury Department, no matter how much he distrusted him.[20]

So little had things changed that for a while there was still talk of a revival of impeachment. In addition to Thaddeus Stevens, some of the new Southern members of Congress advocated a new trial, and Boutwell believed that Johnson would again furnish a pretext to bring down the full fury of Congress upon him. But in August, Thaddeus Stevens, Johnson's most implacable foe, died.[21] The President provided no convenient excuse for further proceedings; his term was rapidly drawing to a close. By January, Butler had so thoroughly given up any notions of another impeachment that he appeared in person at Johnson's New Year's reception. Shortly afterward he introduced legislation for the repeal of the Tenure of Office Act.[22]

Nevertheless, the failure of the impeachment trial did have far-reaching effects. It has been repeatedly pointed out that it preserved the American system of the balance of governmental powers. As David M. DeWitt asserted a generation later, the precedent of not convicting Presidents upon partisan grounds alone was not likely to be broken afterward. Michael L. Benedict, insisting on the contrary that it was presidential power that had to be curbed, called impeachment "a dull blade," ineffectual for the removal of Presidents.[23] At any rate, while the process or threat of impeachment was employed several times against Reconstruction governors, tainted federal officials, and controversial justices, until Richard Nixon no President since Andrew Johnson was seriously confronted with this ultimate constitutional weapon.[24] And in Nixon's case, political considerations were not the major issue.

At the time of the acquittal, the trial and its outcome impressed observers with the resilience of the American system. If it could withstand shocks like the impeachment of a President of nearly forty million people without serious violence, it was obviously more viable than generally supposed. American securities quickly recovered on foreign exchanges, and widely held apprehension concerning the future of the trans-Atlantic republic was finally dispelled.[25]

If the prosecution's defeat assured the permanence of the American constitutional system, it also presaged the eventual downfall of the radicals. It was clear at the 1868 Republican convention that the ultras' influence was waning. The rejection of Wade was one indication of their weakness; the suffrage plank adopted by the party was another. Instead of squarely endorsing the right to vote of all citizens, the Republicans merely called for black suffrage in the South.[26] It was a confession of surrender to the counsels of prudence and conservatism.

The radicals' disappointment was evident. With great satisfaction the *Nation* emphasized their weakness, and Thaddeus Stevens expressed regret that he could not speak favorably of the Republican platform. Convinced that the party had sold out in abandoning black enfranchisement, he reaffirmed his belief that the Declaration of Independence treated "every man as a man, and the right of universal suffrage as an *inalienable* right."[27] The *Independent* shared his sentiments.[28]

It was widely known that Grant's candidacy was very popular with moderates and conservatives. The general had long been their favorite, and the "recusants" heartily supported him.[29] But while the radicals were not happy with the choice, they had no place to go. The Democrats were infinitely worse, and party unity had to be maintained. The *Independent* was not entirely mistaken when it accused Trumbull and Fessenden of voting against conviction in order "to seize the helm of the Republican party from the Radicals, and steer the ship themselves."[30]

The radicals' general weakness naturally affected individual ultras. Wade was not the only one to be shelved. Stanton retired from public life, never to return.[31] And Ashley, the mover of the first impeachment resolutions, soon found himself in serious trouble. His old enemies combined against him in his home district, and he was defeated for reelection. The failure of the trial had done him no good.[32]

The party as a whole also suffered some reverses immediately following the President's acquittal. Early in June the Democrats won in Oregon and carried a majority of the wards in Washington, D. C. At the same time, the conservatives in Mississippi defeated the state's radical constitution.[33] Whether these results were directly related to the President's acquittal is difficult to say, but it is certain that the end of the trial did not lift Republican morale.

But the most serious consequence of the failure of impeachment was its effect upon Reconstruction in the South. As soon as the first reports of Johnson's acquittal reached the disaffected section, conservatives went wild with excitement. Cannon boomed, fireworks exploded, and public buildings were illuminated.[34] All over the former Confederacy refractory whites felt great relief. "Allow me to congratulate you from my heart," ex-Senator Garland of Arkansas wrote to the President. "It is a victory of law, constitution, and justice over oppression, misrule and injustice but must be productive of great good to our poor country. We may now safely hope that . . . before another half year our country will be redeemed. . . . And to you almost alone will we be indebted for this blessed victory."[35] Benjamin F. Perry, Johnson's governor of South Carolina, was equally enthusiastic, and Louisiana conservatives expressed the hope that radicalism had received its death blow.[36]

Conservatives in Tennessee, Johnson's home state, were especially pleased with the verdict. "Now that you are strengthened in your position," a Memphis admirer commented, "your friends will expect universal amnesty. We'll fully expect it of you, if it can be made to relieve us of the miserable Negro rule under which we groan in despair of any improvement in affairs." A Tennessean in far-off California sent congratulations in which he lauded the President for having "stood as a breakwater between the Radicals of the North and the South." East Tennessee supporters wanted

Johnson to run for the presidency again, and in the more Democratic sections elsewhere in the state, his popularity rose to un-
precedented proportions. In the eyes of pro-Southern Tennesseans,
the President had redeemed himself.[37]

The conservatives' jubilation was more than matched by the
depression of the Unionists. "It is with sadness that we learn that
the greatest traitor of the century is acquitted," complained Daniel
Richards, the Florida radical. "News of the failure to convict
Johnson will be like Greek fire throughout the entire south. May
God save our country from the consuming conflagration. The eyes
of the rebels sparkle like those of the firey [sic] serpent. They hope
they have found their 'lost cause' and think they see it. I am not
certain but they are right." [38]

South Carolina Unionists were emphatic about their dismay at
the verdict. The failure of the impeachment had hurt them badly,
D. T. Corbin, a federal official in the office of the United States
District Attorney, protested to Senator Justin Morrill. If Congress
were to keep the state out of the Union for three months longer,
the delay was bound to kill the Republican party. The "rebels,"
in great glee, were publicly taking a stand against Reconstruction
as they would not have dared to do prior to acquittal.[39] Charles
Sumner's correspondents confirmed this report. Not only had
Unionists been harmed, but the murder of a Republican legislator-
elect could be attributed directly to the "recusants' " action.[40]

Georgia loyalists also suffered a severe setback. "Our condition
South since the acquittal of Andrew Johnson is a perilous one,"
a black Georgian cautioned Sumner. "Since the election in this
State colored men have been thrown out of employment and driv-
en from their homes. . . . I myself had to be guarded at night by
colored men and finally had to leave the county on account of the
threats against my life. . . ." Unless more adequate protection were
afforded to them, they would be unable to canvass the state for the
next election. Agents of the Freedmen's Bureau bore out these
complaints. The "disunionists" were getting bolder every day.[41]

The adverse effect of the acquittal on Alabama Unionists was
outlined by George E. Spencer, the Tuscaloosa register in bank-

ruptcy who later served as United States senator. "It is impossible to paint in true colors the woeful condition of Union men in the South since the news of the failure of Impeachment," he confided to Washburne. "Our best men both white & black are leaving us & making haste to place them in a condition to be allowed to remain in the country." He thought the state was lost to the Republican party, and although his prediction for the following November proved premature, "redemption" was not long delayed. By 1874 the conservatives were back in control.[42]

In neighboring Mississippi, conditions were even worse. Encouraged by developments in Washington, conservatives refused to ratify the radical constitution of the state so that the whole process of Reconstruction was seriously impeded. "The causes which have led to this result, you doubtless well understand," James L. Alcorn, the well-known former Whig and later governor, wrote to Washburne. "The impeachment failure has revived the spirit of the rebellion. . . ." Asserting that the atmosphere of proscription in 1861 was not as bad as that prevailing in 1868, he warned that the outlook for the Negro was bitter indeed. "Can it be possible," he queried,

> that the northern people have made the negro free, but to be returned, the slave of society, to bear in such slavery the vindictive resentment that the satraps of Davis maintain today towards the people of the north? Better a thousand times for the negro that the government should return him to the custody of his original owner, where he would have a master to look after his well being, than that his neck should be placed under the heel of a society, vindictive towards him because he is free.

To prevent further troubles he pleaded that steps be yet taken to remove Johnson. Otherwise he feared all foes of the Democratic party in Mississippi would fare badly.[43]

In other Southern states, loyalists found themselves in similarly unfavorable circumstances. In Texas, according to one Unionist, conditions were worse than at any time since the surrender.[44] In Louisiana, conservatives were exultant; even before the verdict their opponents had lived in fear of constant terror; their problems would now be simplified.[45] In North Carolina, Albion W. Tourgée, the novelist from New York state who had made the South his home, was in despair, and in Virginia, loyalists were thoroughly disheartened.[46] Undoubtedly, radical Reconstruction had received a serious check throughout the South.

It is true that, in spite of the Unionists' alarm, in the period following the impeachment trial radical Reconstruction was inaugurated in every one of the protesting Southern states. Radical governments were set up, black citizens were given the ballot, and widespread social reforms were finally undertaken. In November 1868, General Grant was elected President. Although there was some dispute whether or not his victory presaged a radical decline,[47] during his administration the Fifteenth Amendment, seeking to bar disfranchisement of blacks, was passed and ratified. Congress placed three Enforcement acts on the statute books, and for a time Grant continued to seek to enforce radical Reconstruction. Because of these developments, Martin E. Mantell has argued that the acquittal constituted somewhat of a Republican victory.[48] But Republican policy did not succeed. As early as 1869, Tennessee returned to conservative rule. Virginia followed suit in 1870, and by 1876 only three Southern states still maintained a semblance of Republican government. Before the end of 1877 all three were also "redeemed," partially as the result of the inauguration of Rutherford B. Hayes. Reconstruction was over. The great experiment of integrating the Negro into American society as a full-fledged citizen had failed.

To what extent did the failure of the impeachment trial contribute to this result? That it afforded a tremendous moral boost for the conservatives is evident. It is also certain that it demoralized the radicals. But had not the real damage already been done? Had not Johnson's policy of delay, his obstruction of all efforts to bring about a real social revolution in the South already enabled Southern conservatives to begin recouping their shattered fortunes?

The answer to all these questions is yes. Nevertheless, the

impeachment marked the last effort to overcome Johnson's perni-
cious influence. Congress might enact ever more radical legislation; it might checkmate the President; but it could never
accomplish its end without cooperation from the executive branch.
Without this assistance the position of the Negro in the South
would remain a subordinate one, reaction would eventually sweep
the land, and sheer terror restore white supremacy. Because of the
lapse of time, not even President Grant was able to stop this trend.
Had Johnson not been as persistent, and had the impeachment
succeeded, it is conceivable that the outcome might have been different. But when the trial failed, as it was bound to do, the consequences were disastrous. As Charles Sumner wrote prophetically
in his final opinion:

> Alas! for all the evil that must break upon the country, especially
> in the suffering south, as it goes forth that this bad man is confirmed
> in the prerogatives he has usurped. . . .
> Alas! for that race so long oppressed, but at last redeemed from
> bondage, now plunged back into another hell of torment. . . .
> Alas! for the Unionists, white and black alike, who have trusted
> our flag. You now offer them as a sacrifice to those persecutors whose
> representative is before you for judgment. May they find in them-
> selves, and in the goodness of an overruling Providence, that rescue
> and protection which the Senate refuses to give.[49]

Sumner's prophecy was fulfilled. In Tennessee, reaction set in as
early as 1869. Ultimately, as if to demonstrate to the world their
gratitude to the man who had made possible the Southern way of
life, the electors of the state recalled the ex-President to the political arena. After rejecting him in 1871 for his old seat in the Senate
and in 1872 for the House, in 1875 they elected him United States
senator and sent him back to Washington.

His reappearance was dramatic. The former President made his
comeback when it was evident that Reconstruction was on the
wane. For the first time since the Civil War the Democrats had
recaptured the House, and the majority of Southern states were
back under conservative rule. With considerable justification, ex-

Senator Doolittle wrote to him, "The broad generous and human attitude which you assumed as President towards the South has been vindicated."[51]

When Johnson died late in July 1875, his work was done. Radical Reconstruction was doomed. It was not surprising, therefore, that Southern newspapers printed laudatory obituaries of the man they had once execrated.[52] The ex-President was buried in his home town with his head resting on a copy of the Constitution. He had indeed preserved the Union *almost* "as it was."

Notes

I: ANDREW JOHNSON AND RECONSTRUCTION

1. Carl Schurz, *The Reminiscences of Carl Schurz* (New York: McClure, 1907–1908), III, 221.

2. Harriet A. Weed and Thurlow Weed Barnes, eds., *Life of Thurlow Weed, Including His Autobiography and a Memoir* (Boston: Houghton Mifflin, 1883–84), I, 630; II, 450; Harrison Grey Otis, "The Causes of Impeachment," *Century Magazine*, 85 (Nov. 1912–April 1913), 192; Claude G. Bowers, *The Tragic Era* (Boston: Houghton Mifflin, 1957), 11.

3. Kenneth M. Stampp, *The Era of Reconstruction, 1865–1877* (New York: Knopf, 1965), 50–82. See also Gaillard Hunt, "The President's Defense: His Side of the Case, As Told by His Correspondence," *Century Magazine*, 85 (Jan. 1913), 426.

4. *Congressional Globe*, 36 Cong., 1 Sess., 117.

5. Lately Thomas, *The First President Johnson* (New York: Morrow, 1968), 279.

6. Charles Nordhoff to W. C. Bryant, Feb. 2, 1867, Bryant-Godwin Collection, NYPL.

7. Benjamin B. French to Johnson, Feb. 8, 1866, Andrew Johnson Papers, LC.

8. W. G. Moore, Short Diary, April 9, 1968 [hereafter cited as Moore Diary]; Johnson to George H. Thomas, Sept. 4, 8, 1865, all in Johnson Papers.

9. Nordhoff to Bryant, Feb. 2, 1867, Bryant-Godwin Collection.

10. Moore Diary, April 9, 1868, Johnson Papers.

11. Frederick Douglass, *Life and Times of Frederick Douglass* (Hartford: Park Publishing, 1881), 371.

12. Roy P. Basler, ed., *The Collected Works of Abraham Lincoln* (New Brunswick, N. J.: Rutgers Univ. Press, 1953), VII, 281; VIII, 399–405.

13. Tyler Dennett, ed., *Lincoln and the Civil War in the Diaries and Letters of John Hay* (New York: Dodd, Mead, 1939), 108; David Donald, *Devils Facing Zionwards*, ed. Grady McWhiney, *Grant, Lee, Lincoln and the Radicals* (Evanston, Ill.: Northwestern Univ. Press, 1964), 72–91.

14. Edward McPherson, *The Political History of the United States of America During the Period of Reconstruction* (Washington: Philp & Solomons, 1871), 58–63.

15. Underwood to Chase, April 28, 1865, Salmon P. Chase Papers, LC. See also Thomas L. Durant to Johnson, May 1, 1865, Carl Schurz Papers, LC. Even Michael Perman, who believes that the Southern conservatives' ob-

stinacy made any sort of meaningful Reconstruction impossible, concedes that, after the surrender, a mandatory system imposed by the army might have succeeded. Michael Perman, *Reunion Without Compromise: The South and Reconstruction, 1865–1868* (Cambridge, Eng.: Cambridge Univ. Press, 1973), 14.

16. George W. Julian, "George W. Julian's Journal—The Assassination of Lincoln," *Indiana Magazine of History*, 11 (Dec. 1915), 334–35.

17. James G. Blaine, *Twenty Years of Congress* (Norwich, Conn.: Henry Bill Publishing, 1884), II, 14.

18. Theodore C. Pease and James G. Randall, eds., *The Diary of Orville Hickman Browning* (Springfield, Ill.: State Historical Library, 1933), II, 22 [hereafter cited as Browning, *Diary*]: Zachariah Chandler to Mrs. Chandler, April 23, 1865, Zachariah Chandler Papers, LC; G. W. Julian to Mrs. Julian, April 21, 1865, George W. Julian Papers, Indiana Historical Society; William Dudley Foulke, *The Life of Oliver P. Morton* (Indianapolis: Bowen-Merrill, 1899), I, 440; Drake to Johnson, April 24, 1865, Johnson Papers. See also James M. McPherson, *The Struggle for Equality* (Princeton: Princeton Univ. Press, 1964), 317.

19. Davis to S. F. DuPont, April 22, 1865, Samuel F. DuPont Papers, Winterthur Collection, Eleutherian Mills Historical Library, Greenville, Del.; Sumner to Francis Lieber, May 2, 1865, Charles Sumner Papers, Harvard Univ.; David Donald, ed., *Inside Lincoln's Cabinet: The Civil War Diaries of Salmon P. Chase* (New York: Longmans, Green, 1954), 270; Schurz to Sumner, May 9, 1865, Schurz Papers. See also Gerald S. Henig, *Henry Winter Davis* (New York: Twayne, 1973), 240.

20. J. M. Ashley to Johnson, April 15, 1865; E. B. Washburne to Johnson, April 15, 1865, Johnson Papers.

21. Stevens to Sumner, June 3, 1865; Loan to Sumner, June 1, 1865, Sumner Papers.

22. Frederick Bancroft, ed., *Speeches, Correspondence and Political Papers of Carl Schurz* (New York: Putnam's, 1913), I, 258–60; Schurz to Johnson, June 6, 1865, Johnson Papers; Boutwell to Sumner, June 12, 1865, Sumner Papers.

23. Stevens to Sumner, June 14, 1865; Winter Davis to Sumner, June 20, 1865; Howard to Sumner, June 22, 1865; Wade to Sumner, July 29, 1865, Sumner Papers; Sumner to Stevens, June 19, 1865, Thaddeus Stevens Papers, LC.

24. Harlan to Washburne, June 12, 1865, Elihu B. Washburne Papers, LC; Harlan to Sumner, June 19, 1865, Sumner Papers.

25. Boutwell to Sumner, June 12, 1865; Welles to Sumner, June 30, 1865, Sumner Papers (copy in Gideon Welles Papers, LC); Sumner to Welles, July 4, 1865, Welles Papers, LC.

26. Walter L. Fleming, ed., *Documentary History of Reconstruction* (Cleveland: A. H. Clark, 1906–1907), I, 177.

27. New York *Tribune*, Sept. 8, 1865; Chicago *Tribune*, Oct. 27, 1865.

28. Chicago *Tribune*, Oct. 13, 1865.

29. Jonathan T. Dorris, *Pardon and Amnesty under Lincoln and Johnson* (Chapel Hill: Univ. of North Carolina Press, 1953), *passim*; Eric L. McKitrick, *Andrew Johnson and Reconstruction* (Chicago: Univ. of Chicago Press, 1960), 142 ff.

30. E. H. Gill to Johnson, Nov. 22, 1865; A. O. P. Nicholson to Johnson, Dec. 1, 1865; W. M. Fishback to Johnson, Dec. 26, 1865; J. Peterkin to Johnson, Jan. 16, 1866; A. H. Stephens to Johnson, April 17, 1866; P. M. Cloud to Johnson, April 21, 1866, Johnson Papers.

31. *New York Times*, Aug. 1, 1865.

32. R. W. Flournoy to Stevens, Nov. 20, 1865, Stevens Papers.

33. LaWanda Cox, "The Promise of Land for the Freedmen," *Mississippi Valley Historical Review*, 45 (Dec. 1958), 428, 429.

34. Selected Series of Records Issued by the Commissioner of the Bureau of Refugees, Freedmen, and Abandoned Lands, 1865–1872, Circular 13, July, 1865, Roll 7, National Archives [hereafter cited as NA]; Oliver Otis Howard, *Autobiography of Oliver Otis Howard* (New York: Baker & Taylor, 1907), II, 231.

35. Howard, *Autobiography*, II, 235–37; Bureau of Refugees, Freedmen, and Abandoned Lands, 1865–1872, Circular 15, Sept. 12, 1865, Roll 7, NA; William S. McFeeley, *Yankee Stepfather: General O. O. Howard and the Freedmen* (New Haven: Yale Univ. Press, 1968), 134; John A. Carpenter, *Sword and the Olive Branch: Oliver Otis Howard* (Pittsburgh: Univ. of Pittsburgh Press, 1964, 108. See also Willie Lee Rose, *Rehearsal for Reconstruction: The Port Royal Experiment* (Indianapolis: Bobbs-Merrill, 1964), 351 ff.

36. Howard, *Autobiography*, II, 238–39.

37. W. G. Snethen to Johnson, July 19, 1865, Johnson Papers; H. W. Davis to Sumner, July 26, 1865, Sumner Papers.

38. Schurz to Stanton, Aug. 29, 1865; Sharkey to Johnson, Aug. 30, 1865; Johnson to Schurz, Aug. 30, 1865, Edwin M. Stanton Papers, LC; Johnson to Slocum, Sept. 3, 1865, Johnson Papers; James E. Sefton, *The United States Army and Reconstruction, 1865–1877* (Baton Rouge: Louisiana State Univ. Press, 1967), 27–28; Bancroft, ed., *Speeches . . . Carl Schurz*, II, 269.

39. John Hope Franklin, *Reconstruction after the Civil War* (Chicago: Univ. of Chicago Press, 1961), 32 ff.

40. McPherson, *Reconstruction*, 64–66; William A. Dunning, "More Light on Andrew Johnson," *American Historical Review*, 11 (April 1906), 574–94, esp. 585.

41. Howard, *Autobiography*, II, 227.

42. A. C. Fuller to Trumbull, Dec. 27, 1865; F. A. Eastman to Trumbull, Jan. 4, 1866, Lyman Trumbull Papers, LC.

43. Howard K. Beale, ed., *Diary of Gideon Welles* (New York: Norton, 1960), II, 434–35 [hereafter cited as Welles, *Diary*].

44. John H. and LaWanda Cox, "Andrew Johnson and His Ghost Writers," *Mississippi Valley Historical Review*, 48 (Dec. 1961), 460–79, esp. 466, 472.

45. McPherson, *Reconstruction*, 52–56.

46. Philip Ripley to Manton Marble, Feb. 8, 1866, Manton Marble Papers, LC. Ripley heard this account from the secretary himself.

47. James D. Richardson, ed., *A Compilation of the Messages and Papers of the Presidents, 1789–1897* (Washington: Government Printing Office, 1896–99), VI, 403–404; Cox and Cox, "Andrew Johnson and His Ghost Writers," 472.

48. Browning, *Diary*, II, 57.

49. Moore Diary, April 18, 1866, Johnson Papers.

50. J. F. Miller to David Patterson, Nov. 10, 1865; J. W. Schaumburg to Johnson, Jan. 21, 1866, Johnson Papers; Dr. H. Schroder to Trumbull, Dec. 23, 1865, Trumbull Papers, LC; Chicago *Tribune*, Feb. 6, 1866; David M. DeWitt, *The Impeachment and Trial of Andrew Johnson* (1903; rpt. Madison: State Historical Society of Wisconsin, 1967), 54.

II: THE RADICALS AND RECONSTRUCTION

1. *Congressional Globe*, 39 Cong., 2 Sess., 251–53.

2. William R. Brock, *An American Crisis: Congress and Reconstruction, 1865–1867* (London: Macmillan, 1963), viii.

3. *Congressional Globe*, 39 Cong., 1 Sess., 40.

4. *Ibid.*, 2 Sess., 163.

5. Bancroft, ed., *Speeches . . . Carl Schurz*, I, 405.

6. Charles Sumner, *The Works of Charles Sumner* (Boston: Lee & Shepard, 1870–83), IX, 206–27, 333–35; Sumner to Francis Lieber, May 14, 1865, Sumner Papers.

7. New York *Tribune*, Nov. 27, 1866; *New York Times*, May 14, 1867.

8. *New York Times*, May 14, 1867; Smith to Johnson, April 19, 1865, Johnson Papers; S. Anderson to Linton Stephens, Sept. 5, 1865, Alexander H. Stephens Papers, LC; Henry Wilson to Johnson, Aug. 14, 1865, March 3, 1866, Johnson Papers; Dorris, *Pardon and Amnesty under Lincoln and Johnson*, 173, 269–70.

9. Blaine, *Twenty Years of Congress*, II, 205; Fawn Brodie, *Thaddeus Stevens: Scourge of the South* (New York: Norton, 1959), 214–15, 305–307.

10. Howard K. Beale, *The Critical Year: A Study of Andrew Johnson and Reconstruction* (1930; rpt. New York: Ungar, 1958), 7–9, 236–99.

11. Stanley Coben, "Northeastern Business and Radical Reconstruction: A Re-Examination," *Mississippi Valley Historical Review*, 46 (June 1959), 67–90; Hans L. Trefousse, *The Radical Republicans: Lincoln's Vanguard for Racial Justice* (New York: Knopf, 1968), 63, 333, 340.

12. Stampp, *Era of Reconstruction*, 55–58.

13. Schurz to Johnson, June 6, 1865, Johnson Papers.

14. Owen to Johnson, June 21, 1865, Johnson Papers.

15. Stevens to Johnson, June 16, 1865, Johnson Papers.

16. Medill to Johnson, Sept. 15, 1865, Johnson Papers.

17. J. Brown to Johnson, Sept. 20, 1865, Johnson Papers.

18. Jessie Ames Marshall, ed., *Private and Official Correspondence of Gen. Benjamin F. Butler during the Period of the Civil War* (Norwood, Mass.: Plimpton, 1917), V, 641; Albert Mordell, ed., *Civil War and Reconstruction: Selected Essays by Gideon Welles* (New York: Twayne, 1959), 214–15.

19. Wilson to Sumner, Sept. 9, 1865, Sumner Papers; George T. Brown to Trumbull, Sept. 8, 1865, Trumbull Papers, LC.

20. Bancroft to Johnson, Dec. 1, 1865, Johnson Papers; Sumner to Lieber, Dec. 3, 1865, Sumner Papers.

21. Boutwell to Butler, Dec. 29, 1865, Benjamin F. Butler Papers, LC.

22. Sumner to Wade, June 9, 1865, Benjamin F. Wade Papers, LC.

23. Stevens to Sumner, June 14, 1865, Sumner Papers.

24. *New York Times*, June 26, 1865; Boston *Commonwealth*, Sept. 9, 1865; Wilson to Sumner, Sept. 9, 1865, Sumner Papers; Simon Cameron to Johnson, Sept. 20, 1865, Johnson Papers; Sherman to Chase, Sept. 24, 1865, Salmon P. Chase Papers, Historical Society of Pennsylvania; New York *Herald*, Oct. 11, 1865; LaWanda Cox and John H. Cox, *Politics, Principle, and Prejudice, 1865–1866* (New York: Free Press of Glencoe, 1963), 81–82, 68 ff.

25. David Donald, *Charles Sumner and the Rights of Man* (New York: Knopf, 1970), 143–45, 152, 156, 248.

26. Hans L. Trefousse, *Benjamin Franklin Wade: Radical Republican from Ohio* (New York: Twayne, 1963), 183, 228–29.

27. Theodore Clarke Smith, *The Life and Letters of James Abram Garfield* (New Haven: Yale Univ. Press, 1925), I, 392; Welles, *Diary*, 239; Hans L. Trefousse, *Ben Butler: The South Called Him Beast* (New York: Twayne, 1957), 169, 174, 187–88.

28. Brodie, *Thaddeus Stevens*, 261.

29. Smith, *Garfield*, I, 392.

30. John Sherman, *John Sherman's Recollections of Forty Years in the House, Senate, and Cabinet* (Chicago: Werner, 1895), I, 365 ff.; George R. Brown, ed., *Reminiscences of Senator William M. Stewart of Nevada* (New York: Neale, 1908), 198; *Congressional Globe*, 39 Cong., 1 Sess., 1760; Welles, *Diary*, II, 447–49.

31. New York *Herald*, Dec. 3, 8, 14, 1865.

32. Hans L. Trefousse, "Ben Wade and the Negro," *Ohio Historical Quarterly*, 68 (April 1959), 161–76; T. O. Howe to Fessenden, Aug. 28, 1864, Timothy O. Howe Papers, Wisconsin Historical Society.

33. William Gillette, *The Right to Vote: Politics and the Passage of the Fifteenth Amendment* (Baltimore: Johns Hopkins Univ. Press, 1965), 25–27. Minnesota rejected black suffrage several times.

34. Simeon Nash to Chase, June 10, 1864, Chase Papers, LC.

35. Chase to Francis Lieber, Feb. 14, 1865, S. L. M. Barlow Papers, Huntington Library.

36. Phelps to Sumner, April 20, 1865, Sumner Papers.

37. Martin Ryerson to Marcus Ward, Aug. 1, 1865, Marcus Ward Papers, New Jersey Historical Society.

38. Taft to Stevens, Dec. 28, 1865, Stevens Papers.

39. Williams to M. P. Deady, June 20, 1866, Matthew P. Deady Papers, Oregon Historical Society.

40. Stevens to W. D. Kelley, Sept. 6, 1866, Stevens Papers.

41. C. H. Ray to Trumbull, Feb. 7, 1866; N. L. Mayo to Trumbull, May 1, 1866, Trumbull Papers, LC.

42. Rachel Sherman Thorndike, ed., *The Sherman Letters: Correspondence between General and Senator Sherman from 1837 to 1891* (New York: Scribner's, 1894), 252, 261–62.

43. Woodman to Stanton, April 24, 1865, Stanton Papers.

44. George W. Julian, *Political Recollections, 1840–1872* (Chicago: Jansen, McClurg, 1884), 264–65.

45. T. W. Egan to Johnson, Oct. 7, 1867, Johnson Papers.

46. Boston *Daily Advertiser*, Sept. 14, 18, 1867; *Harper's Monthly*, 36 (Jan. 1868), 263; Endicott Kinsley to Sumner, Sept. 19, 1867, Sumner Papers; Ellis Paxson Oberholtzer, *Jay Cooke, Financier of the Civil War* (Philadelphia: G. W. Jacobs, 1907), II, 28.

47. Cox and Cox, *Politics, Principle, and Prejudice*, 139–42.

48. Benjamin B. Kendrick, *The Journal of the Joint Committee of Fifteen on Reconstruction* (New York: Columbia Univ. Press, 1914), 39–41.

49. Welles, *Diary*, II, 43.

50. McKitrick, *Andrew Johnson and Reconstruction*, 285–87; Cox and Cox, *Politics, Principle, and Prejudice*, 178–84.

51. C. H. Ray to Montgomery Blair, April 10, 1866, Johnson Papers; *Congressional Globe*, 39 Cong., 1 Sess., 1760; Welles, *Diary*, II, 459, 461, 463.

52. Richardson, ed., *Messages and Papers of the Presidents*, VII, 3603–11.

53. Cowan to Johnson, March 23, 1866, Johnson Papers.

54. Sherman, *Recollections*, 365 ff.

55. *Congressional Globe*, 39 Cong., 1 Sess., 1760; Chicago *Tribune*, March 31, 1866.

56. A. Brandagee to Hawley, January or February, 1866; H. B. Harrison to Hawley, Feb. 23, 1866; Welles to Hawley, March 14, 1866; A. H. Byington to Hawley, March 25, 1866, James R. Hawley Papers, LC; Hawley to Welles, Feb. 28, March 17, March 22, 1866; Welles to W. A. Croffut, March 13, 1866; Welles to Hawley, March 20, 24, 1866, Welles Papers, LC; Welles, *Diary*, II, 452, 474.

57. McPherson, *Reconstruction*, 15–17.

58. Blaine, *Twenty Years of Congress*, II, 192 ff.; Stewart, *Reminiscences*, 215–18; Robert Dale Owen, "Political Results from the Varioloid," *Atlantic Monthly*, 35 (June 1875), 660–70; New York *Herald*, April 26, 30, 1866; Trefousse, *Butler*, 183–85.

59. James A. Brisbin to Chandler, Oct. 5, 1866, Zachariah Chandler Papers, LC; New York *Herald*, June 15, 1866; Chase to Nettie, May 20, 1866, Chase Papers, LC.

60. Welles, *Diary*, II, 521–22.

61. Richardson, ed., *Messages and Papers of the Presidents*, VIII, 3589 ff.

62. *New York Times*, Oct. 24, 1866; Cox and Cox, *Politics, Principle, and Prejudice*, 229.

63. Carpenter, *Sword and Olive Branch*, 118–20; Richardson, ed., *Messages and Papers of the Presidents*, VIII, 3620.

III: THE WIDENING BREACH

1. Cox and Cox, *Politics, Principle, and Prejudice, passim.*
2. William A. Newall to Johnson, April 9, 1866, Johnson Papers.
3. Barlow to James Hughes, Dec. 21, 1865, Johnson Papers.
4. Feb. 21, 1866, Benjamin Brown French MS Diary, LC.
5. *Ibid.*, March 17, 1866.
6. W. W. Holden to Johnson, Dec. 6, 1865, Johnson Papers; *Harper's Weekly*, 10 (Jan. 13, 1866), 18; (March 31, 1866), 194; *National Anti-Slavery Standard*, March 24, 1866; Franklin, *Reconstruction*, 43–45; Daniel Richards to Washburne, June 7, 11, 1866, Washburne Papers; Daniel Richards to Trumbull, June 7, 1866, Trumbull Papers, LC.
7. Memminger to Schurz, April 25, 1871, Schurz Papers.
8. R. W. Flournoy to Stevens, Nov. 20, 1866, Stevens Papers.
9. A. O. P. Nicholson to Johnson, Dec. 1, 1865, Johnson Papers.
10. E. H. Gill to Johnson, Nov. 2, 1865, Johnson Papers.
11. Raleigh *Daily Sentinel*, Jan. 4, 1866.
12. Kenneth Rayner to Johnson, April 10, 1866, Johnson Papers.
13. S. Corley to Stevens, Feb. 6, 1866, Stevens Papers.
14. Jonathan Roberts to Trumbull, April 21, 1866, Trumbull Papers, LC.
15. Chase to Nettie, May 19, 1866, Chase Papers, LC.
16. Elizabeth Van Lew to Doolittle, James R. Doolittle Papers, Wisconsin Historical Society.
17. J. G. Foster to George C. Hartsuff, July 8, 1866; Orrin McFadden to Nathaniel Burbank, July 15, 1866, Philip H. Sheridan Papers, LC; W. L. Mallet to Stevens, May 28, 1866, Stevens Papers; S. G. Burbridge to Joseph Holt, June 26, 1865, Stanton Papers; *New York Times*, Aug. 1, 1865; Boston *Commonwealth*, Feb. 10, 1866; W. W. Boardman to Wade, April 16, 1866, Wade Papers.
18. "Memphis Riots and Massacres," *House Report*, 39 Cong., 1 Sess., no. 101.
19. Richardson, ed., *Messages and Papers of the Presidents*, VIII, 3620, 3611–14.
20. McPherson, *Reconstruction*, 118–19.
21. *National Anti-Slavery Standard*, July 7, 1866.
22. Welles, *Diary*, II, 553, 554, 563; Bowers, *Tragic Era*, 120; McPherson, *Reconstruction*, 101. Alexander W. Randall became the new postmaster general, Orville H. Browning, secretary of the interior, and Henry Stanbery, attorney general.

23. Benjamin P. Thomas and Harold M. Hyman, *Stanton: The Life and Times of Lincoln's Secretary of War* (New York: Knopf, 1962), *passim*.

24. "New Orleans Riots," *House Report*, 39 Cong., 2 Sess., no. 16, 28–34; Philip H. Sheridan, *Personal Memoirs of P. H. Sheridan* (New York: Charles L. Webster, 1888), II, 233–42.

25. "New Orleans Riots," 441.

26. *Ibid.*, 441–42.

27. *Ibid.*, 448; Andrew J. Herron and Albert Voorhees to Johnson, July 28, 1866; Johnson to Albert Voorhees, July 28, 1866; Johnson to Wells, July 28, 1866; Wells to Johnson, July 28, 1866, Johnson Papers.

28. "New Orleans Riots," 443.

29. *Ibid.*, 28–34, 445; Blaine, *Twenty Years of Congress*, 235.

30. *Independent*, Aug. 16, 1866; *Harper's Weekly*, 10 (Aug. 25, 1866), 530; Welles, *Diary*, II, 569–70; Brodie, *Thaddeus Stevens*, 280–82.

31. "New Orleans Riots," 610; Johnson to A. J. Herron, July 30, 1866, Johnson Papers.

32. McPherson, *Reconstruction*, 240–41; Blaine, *Twenty Years of Congress*, II, 220–23; Welles, *Diary*, II, 582.

33. McPherson, *Reconstruction*, 194–96.

34. Toledo *Blade*, Aug. 3, 1866; Fessenden to McCulloch, Aug. 10, 17, 29, 1866, Hugh McCulloch Papers, LC; George W. Ernest to Weed, Oct. 2, 1866; W. S. Lincoln to Weed, Oct. 3, 1866, Thurlow Weed Papers, Univ. of Rochester; H. B. Anthony to Seward, Oct. 3, 1866, William H. Seward Papers, Univ. of Rochester.

35. McPherson, *Reconstruction*, 241–43; Boston *Daily Advertiser*, Sept. 4, 27, 1866.

36. Hugh McCulloch, *Men and Measures of Half a Century* (New York: Scribner's, 1888), 397; McKitrick, *Andrew Johnson and Reconstruction*, 428 ff.

37. *Trial of Andrew Johnson, President of the United States, Before the Senate of the United States, on Impeachment . . .* (Washington: Government Printing Office, 1868), I, 8–9 [hereafter cited as *Impeachment Trial*].

38. *New York Times*, Sept. 10, 1866.

39. *The Pending Canvass, Speech of the Hon. Thaddeus Stevens, delivered at Bedford, Pennsylvania, on Tuesday Evening, September 4, 1866* (Lancaster, Pa., 1866) pamphlet in Stevens Papers.

40. New York *Tribune*, Oct. 9, 1866; Milwaukee *Sentinel*, Oct. 22, 1866 (in Butler Papers); *Independent*, Aug. 30, 1866; Margarit Spalding Gerry, ed., *Through Five Administrations: Reminiscences of Colonel William H. Crook, Body-Guard to President Lincoln* (New York: Harper, 1910), 108–109.

41. Blaine, *Twenty Years of Congress*, II, 241, 383 ff. Because of varying terminology, exact figures on party affiliation are difficult to establish. Republicans had a more than two-thirds majority in both houses, both in the 39th and 40th Congresses. But in the latter, conservative strength diminished. See David Donald, *The Politics of Reconstruction 1863–1867* (Baton Rouge: Louisiana State Univ. Press, 1965), 91 ff.; John L. McCarthy, "Reconstruction

Legislation and Voting Alignments in the House of Representatives," Ph.D. diss., Yale Univ., 1970, 115 ff., 229 ff.

42. Fessenden to McCulloch, Sept. 11, 1866, McCulloch Papers.

43. *Independent*, Nov. 1, 1866.

44. *Ibid.*, Nov. 8, 1866.

45. Bancroft, ed., *Speeches . . . Carl Schurz*, I, 417.

46. Welles, *Diary*, II, 518; *Harper's Weekly*, 10, 738 (Nov. 24, 1866); Grimes to Welles, Oct. 14, 1866, Welles Papers, LC.

47. E. G. Cook to Seward, Oct. 15, 1866, Seward Papers.

48. W. B. Phillips to Johnson, Nov. 8, 1866, Johnson Papers.

49. Hiram Ketchum to Johnson, Nov. 9, 1866, Johnson Papers.

50. Blaine, *Twenty Years of Congress*, II, 241.

51. Beale, *The Critical Year*, 400 ff. Beale believes that the radicals' increased militancy, especially their failure to guarantee the finality of the Fourteenth Amendment, caused him to change his mind. The radicals, however, were by no means agreed on this point. See Trefousse, *Wade*, 278–79; Trefousse, *Radical Republicans*, 350–53.

52. McPherson, *Reconstruction*, 143–47.

53. Wager Swayne to Chase, Dec. 10, 1866, Chase Papers, LC. As late as December 14, Senator Wade for one still considered the amendment's ratification the sole prerequisite for readmission of the seceded states, although others disagreed with him. *Congressional Globe*, 39 Cong., 2 Sess., 124 ff.

54. Johnson to L. E. Parsons, Jan. 17, 1867, Stanton Papers.

55. McPherson, *Reconstruction*, 194.

56. Moore Diary, Jan. 30, 1867, Johnson Papers.

57. McPherson, *Reconstruction*, 154–59.

58. *Congressional Globe*, 39 Cong., 2 Sess., 124 ff.

59. Stanley I. Kutler, *Judicial Power and Reconstruction Politics* (Chicago: Univ. of Chicago Press, 1968), 50 ff.

60. William A. Dunning, *Reconstruction: Political and Economic, 1865–1877* (New York: Harper, 1907), 95.

61. "Impeachment of the President," *House Reports*, 40 Cong., 1 Sess., no. 7, I, 85 [hereafter cited as *Impeachment Investigation*]; Michael Les Benedict, *The Impeachment and Trial of Andrew Johnson* (New York: Norton, 1973), 48 ff.

62. Louis Weichman to Holt, Oct. 23, 1866, Joseph Holt Papers, LC.

63. *Congressional Globe*, 39 Cong., 2 Sess., 2, 382, 547–48.

64. *Ibid.*, 943, 969–70.

65. Dennett, ed., *Diaries of John Hay*, 266–67.

66. *Congressional Globe*, 39 Cong., 2 Sess., 966 ff., 1047, 1514–18. The President's veto was overridden. McPherson, *Reconstruction*, 173–76.

67. George S. Boutwell, "Johnson's Plot and Motives," *North American Review*, 141 (Dec. 1885), 572–73; McPherson, *Reconstruction*, 178. The President contemplated a veto, but finally signed the bill with an appended protest against the sections in question. Moore Diary, March 4, 1867, Johnson Papers.

NOTES TO PAGES 45–51

68. Blaine, *Twenty Years in Congress*, II, 281–82. Johnson continued his pardoning policies afterward. See McPherson, *Reconstruction*, 342–44.
69. U.S., *Statutes at Large*, XIV, 428–29.
70. Washington *Triweekly National Intelligencer*, Feb. 14, 1867.
71. Charles Nordhoff to W. C. Bryant, Feb. 2, 1867, Bryant-Godwin Collection.
72. Moore Diary, Feb. 18, 1867, Johnson Papers. The act did not specifically deprive citizens of the right of habeas corpus.
73. Weed to Seward, Feb. 21, 1867, Seward Papers; H. A. Smythe to Johnson, Feb. 25, 1867; George P. Este to Johnson, Feb. 27, 1867, Johnson Papers.
74. F. P. Blair, Sr. to Johnson, Feb. 24, 1867; Moore Diary, March 2, 1867, Johnson Papers.
75. McPherson, *Reconstruction*, 166–73.

IV: FIRST DEMANDS FOR IMPEACHMENT

1. J. F. Miller to David Patterson, Nov. 10, 1865, Johnson Papers; Dr. H. Schroder to Trumbull, Dec. 23, 1865, Trumbull Papers, LC; New York *Herald*, Oct. 1, 1865.
2. James W. Schaumburg to Johnson, Jan. 21, 1866, Johnson Papers; Chicago *Tribune*, March 31, 1866.
3. *National Anti-Slavery Standard*, Oct. 6, 1866.
4. Trefousse, *Butler*, 1–188.
5. Charles S. Ashley, "Governor Ashley's Biography and Messages," *Contributions to the Historical Society of Montana*, 6 (1907), 143–289; Margaret Ashley (Paddock), "An Ohio Congressman in Reconstruction," M.A. thesis, Columbia Univ., 1916; Robert F. Horowitz, "James M. Ashley: A Biography," Ph.D. diss., City Univ. of New York, 1973; Welles, *Diary*, III, 12; Ben: Perley Poore, *Perley's Reminiscences of Sixty Years in the National Metropolis* (Philadelphia: Hubbard, 1886), 201–203; *Impeachment Investigation*, 1194–99.
6. New York *Herald*, Jan. 8, 1867.
7. E. B. Boutwell to Johnson, Sept. 16, 1866, Johnson Papers; Chandler to J. A. J Cresswell, Oct. 22, 1866, Zachariah Chandler Papers, Burton Collection, Detroit Public Lib.; Toledo *Blade*, Oct. 23, 1866; *National Anti-Slavery Standard*, Dec. 29, 1866; Boston *Commonwealth*, Nov. 17, 1866; *Independent*, Oct. 4, 1866, Jan. 10, 1867; *Wilkes' Spirit of the Times*, Sept. 22, 1866; Robert Schenck to Stevens, Sept. 23, 1866, Stevens Papers.
8. Brodie, *Thaddeus Stevens, passim.*
9. Allen Johnson and Dumas Malone, eds., *Dictionary of American Biography* (New York: Scribner's, 1929–44), I, 390–91; II, 34–37; VII, 563–64; *Register of Debates*, VII, 21 Cong., 2 Sess., 45; *Congressional Globe*, 37 Cong., 2 Sess., 1062; Charles Warren, *The Supreme Court in United States History* (Boston: Little, Brown, 1926), I, 290–95; Irving Brant, *Impeachment: Trials and Errors* (New York: Knopf, 1972), 24–83, 122–32, 297; Benedict, *Impeach-*

ment and Trial of Andrew Johnson, 26 ff.; Raoul Berger, *Impeachment: The Constitutional Problem* (Cambridge, Mass.: Harvard Univ. Press, 1973), 297 ff.

10. H. G. Marquand to Morgan, Jan. 11, 1867; M. G. Leonard to Morgan, Jan. 11, 1867, Edwin D. Morgan Papers, New York State Library; J. S. Morrill to Blaine, Oct. 29, 1866, James G. Blaine Papers, LC; J. W. Shaffer to Butler, Dec. 1, 1866, Butler Papers; Charles Loring to Sumner, Jan. 31, 1867, Sumner Papers; John Bright to Greeley, Nov. 28, 1866, Horace Greeley Papers, NYPL. See also *Independent*, Dec. 13, 1866; Mary Hinsdale, ed., *Garfield-Hinsdale Letters: Correspondence between James Abram Garfield and Burke Aaron Hinsdale* (Ann Arbor: Univ. of Michigan Press, 1945), 83.

11. New York *Herald*, Oct. 5, 1866; *Harper's Weekly*, 10 (Oct. 27, 1866), 627.

12. Chicago *Tribune*, Oct. 8, 1866.

13. Chicago *Tribune*, Oct. 18, 1866; Boston *Daily Advertiser*, Nov. 3, 1866.

14. *Wilkes' Spirit of the Times*, Sept. 22, 1866.

15. Schenck to Stevens, Sept. 23, 1866, Stevens Papers.

16. Toledo *Blade*, Oct. 23, 1866.

17. *Harper's Weekly*, 10 (Oct. 27, 1866), 674; Enclosure in J. F. Kipe to Johnson, Nov. 7, 1866, Johnson Papers; Washington *Daily National Intelligencer*, Nov. 26, 1866.

18. Trefousse, *Radical Republicans*, 336 ff.; Michael Les Benedict, "The Right Way: Congressional Republicans and Reconstruction, 1863–1869," Ph.D. diss., Rice Univ., 1971, 274 ff. and *passim*. The moderate Lyman Trumbull was chairman of the Senate Committee on the Judiciary; the moderate James F. Wilson was his counterpart in the House; and William Pitt Fessenden, another moderate, chaired the Joint Committee of Fifteen on Reconstruction.

19. L. W. Hall to Garfield, Dec. 11, 1866, James A. Garfield Papers, LC; *Harper's Weekly*, 10 (Nov. 3, 1866), 690; (Nov. 17, 1866), 722; Washington *Daily National Intelligencer*, Nov. 26, 1866.

20. New York *Herald*, Dec. 3, 1866.

21. *Ibid.*; McPherson, *Reconstruction*, 187.

22. *New York Times*, Jan. 6, 7, 1867.

23. *Ibid.*, Jan. 8, 1867; Washington *Triweekly National Intelligencer*, Jan. 8, 1867; Toledo *Daily Commercial*, Jan. 10, 1867; New York *Herald*, Jan. 9, 1867; Chicago *Tribune*, Jan. 9, 1867.

24. *Congressional Globe*, 39 Cong., 2 Sess., 319 ff.

25. New York *Herald*, Jan. 9, 1867; Welles, *Diary*, III, 12; Toledo *Daily Commercial*, Jan. 5, 1867; Chicago *Tribune*, Jan. 11, 12, 1867.

26. Washington *Triweekly National Intelligencer*, Jan. 8, 1867.

27. Chicago *Tribune*, Jan. 9, 1867.

28. J. H. Rhodes to Garfield, Jan. 12, 1867, Garfield Papers, LC.

29. Toledo *Daily Commercial*, Jan. 7, 1867.

30. Welles, *Diary*, III, 8, 12.

31. *New York Times*, Jan. 9, 1867.

32. *Harper's Weekly*, 11 (Jan. 26, 1867), 50.

33. Johnson and Malone, eds., *DAB*, XX, 331–33; Donald, *Politics of Reconstruction*, 100–105. Donald calls Wilson an "Independent Radical," Woodbridge a "Moderate," Thomas a "Conservative," and Morris a "Republican not clearly identified with any faction." The point is that all these men fall outside his category of "Ultra Radicals" or "Stevens Radicals."

34. *Impeachment Investigation*, 2–15, 29–33.

35. *Ibid.*, 15–28.

36. *Ibid.*, 1199; New York *Herald*, Dec. 22, 1867.

37. *Congressional Globe*, 39 Cong., 2 Sess., 443–46.

38. *Impeachment Investigation*, 28–29.

39. *Ibid.*, 33–42, 66–84, 149–78, 183–264, 264–71.

40. *Congressional Globe*, 39 Cong., 2 Sess., 1754–55.

41. New York *World*, Jan. 9, 1867.

42. *New York Times*, Jan. 6, 1867.

43. Blair to Johnson, Feb. 24, 1867, Johnson Papers; see draft of this letter in Blair-Lee Family Papers, Princeton Univ.

44. Nordhoff to Bryant, Feb. 2, 1867, Bryant-Godwin Collection.

45. George P. Este to Johnson, n.d., probably Feb. 27, 1867, Johnson Papers.

46. Welles, *Diary*, III, 12, 17.

47. Fox to Mrs. Fox, Feb. 22, 1867, Gustavus V. Fox Papers, New York Historical Society.

48. New York *Herald*, Jan. 12, 1867.

49. *Ibid.*, Jan. 5, 1867; Washington *Triweekly National Intelligencer*, Feb. 2, 1867.

50. Frank Smith to Johnson, Jan. 23, 1867, Johnson Papers.

51. James Ashley to R. K. Scott, Jan. 20, 1867, R. K. Scott Papers, Ohio Historical Society, courtesy of Dr. Robert F. Horowitz. Cf. Horowitz, "James M. Ashley," 299–300.

52. Trefousse, *Butler*, 157. It was believed that Ashley was merely Butler's front man. William Schouler to Dawes, Feb. 5, 1867, Henry L. Dawes Papers, LC.

53. Hinsdale, ed., *Garfield-Hinsdale Letters*, 93–94.

54. Boston *Commonwealth*, Jan. 26, Feb. 16, 1867.

55. Toledo *Daily Commercial*, Feb. 12, 1867; *Wilkes' Spirit of the Times*, Feb. 16, 23, 1867.

56. Toledo *Blade*, Jan. 8, 1867; Oscar Sherwin, *Prophet of Liberty: The Life and Times of Wendell Phillips* (New York: Bookman, 1958), 560.

57. Trefousse, *Wade*, *passim*.

58. Charles A. Jellison, *Fessenden of Maine, Civil War Senator* (Syracuse: Syracuse Univ. Press, 1962), *passim*, esp. 222; Hamilton Gay Howard, *Civil-War Echoes: Character Sketches and State Secrets* (Washington: Howard Publ., 1907), 24.

59. Welles, *Diary*, II, 552.

60. *National Anti-Slavery Standard*, Sept. 1, 1866.

61. John Bigelow, MS Diary, NYPL; Oct. 23, 1866, John Bigelow Papers, NYPL.

62. Forney to Chandler, Nov. 3, 1866, Zachariah Chandler Papers, LC.

63. New York *Herald*, Nov. 29, 1886; Detroit *Post Tribune, Zachariah Chandler: An Outline of His Life and Public Services.*

64. Oberholtzer, *Jay Cooke*, II, 26; Detroit *Post Tribune* (1880), 287. The fear about the Milligan Case was exaggerated because it dealt with wartime problems.

65. Dennett, ed., *Diaries of John Hay*, 263.

66. *Harper's Weekly*, 11 (Feb. 16, 1867), 98; John Bigelow, *Retrospections of a Busy Life* (New York: Baker & Taylor, 1909–13), IV, 40.

67. New York *Tribune*, March 2, 1867; *Congressional Globe*, 39 Cong., 2 Sess., 2003.

68. *Congressional Globe*, 39 Cong., 2 Sess., 2003.

69. New York *Herald*, March 2, 1867.

70. New York *World*, March 2, 1867.

71. Toledo *Blade*, March 12, 1867.

72. McClure, *Recollections of Half A Century*, 65.

73. Bigelow, *Retrospections of a Busy Life*, IV, 40.

74. New York *Herald*, July 8, 1867.

75. Elmer Ellis, "Colorado's First Fight for Statehood, 1865–1868," *Colorado Magazine*, 8 (Jan. 1931), 23–30; McPherson, *Reconstruction*, 81–82; Trefousse, *Wade*, 269–70.

76. Victor Rosewater, "The Political and Constitutional Development of Nebraska," *Nebraska State Historical Society Transactions and Reports*, 5 (1893), 240–66; Trefousse, *Wade*, 269–71.

77. Trefousse, *Wade*, 269–71, 275–81; *Congressional Globe*, 39 Cong., 2 Sess., 36, 122 ff., 145, 162 ff., 184 ff., 215 ff., 247, 484 ff.

78. Doolittle to Johnson, May 7, 1866; Alexander Cummings to Johnson, Jan. 4, 1867; A. P. Hunt to Johnson, Jan. 18, 1867; J. M. Thayer and T. W. Tipton to Johnson, Jan. 19, 1867, Johnson Papers; *Impeachment Investigation*, 18–22.

79. McPherson, *Reconstruction*, 160–66.

80. *Ibid.*, 166.

81. New York *Tribune*, Dec. 11, 1866; *Congressional Globe*, 39 Cong., 1 Sess., 1357–58.

82. *Congressional Globe*, 39 Cong., 2 Sess., 1922 ff.; DeWitt, *Impeachment and Trial of Andrew Johnson*, 177–79. On the next day, the motion to override the veto received fewer than the necessary two-thirds of the votes, being defeated by 29 in favor to 19 against. *Congressional Globe*, 39 Cong., 2 Sess., 1927–28.

83. Trefousse, *Wade*, 287.

84. Lloyd Paul Stryker, *Andrew Johnson, Profile in Courage* (New York: Macmillan, 1929), 399; Robert W. Winston, *Andrew Johnson, Plebeian and Patriot* (New York: Holt, 1926), 411; Robert S. Henry, *The Story of Reconstruction* (Indianapolis: Bobbs-Merrill, 1938), 304.

V: PRESIDENTIAL DEFIANCE

1. For example, see Johnson's speech on receiving the proceedings of the Philadelphia Union Convention; McPherson, *Reconstruction*, 128.

2. Moore Diary, April 7, 1866, 15 ff., Johnson Papers.

3. S. S. Cox to Marble, Oct. 3 or 10, 1866, Marble Papers; Nordhoff to Bryant, Feb. 2, 1867, Bryant-Godwin Collection.

4. P. M. Cloud to Johnson, April 21, 1866, Johnson Papers.

5. J. W. Eldridge to Johnson, April 28, 1866; R. W. Johnson to Johnson, July 23, 1866; A. H. Stephens to Johnson, April 17, 1866, Johnson Papers; D. H. Hooper to Holt, Sept. 10, 1866, Holt Papers; John Forsyth to Manton Marble, March 5, 1867, Marble Papers.

6. Fernando Wood to Johnson, Feb. 24, 1866; P. H. Kerr to Johnson, March 2, 1866; August Belmont to Johnson, March 24, 1866; S. J. Randall to Johnson, Oct. 24, 1866, Aug. 16, 1867, Johnson Papers.

7. *Impeachment Investigation*, 780–82.

8. McPherson, *Reconstruction*, 178–81.

9. Welles, *Diary*, III, 64–65; Thomas and Hyman, *Stanton*, 530.

10. Grant to Sheridan, May 26, 1867, Sheridan Papers; Toledo *Blade*, June 26, 1867; Washington *Triweekly National Intelligencer*, July 25, 1867; *Congressional Globe*, 40 Cong., 1 Sess., 438–41.

11. Washington *Daily National Intelligencer*, April 15, 1867.

12. New York *Herald*, March 9, 1867; Toledo *Daily Commercial*, March 8, 1867.

13. *Congressional Globe*, 40 Cong., 1 Sess., 18–25.

14. New York *Herald*, March 5, 1867.

15. *Impeachment Investigation*, 178–83, 45–51, 368–84, 544 ff., 604–18, 333–45, 417–49, 550–78, 271–73, 276–84, 395–415, 698–700; Moore Diary, n.d., 33; J. S. Black to Johnson, March 23, 1867, Johnson Papers.

16. *Impeachment Investigation*, 84–111, 111 ff., 512–18, 761–76; 280–87, 323–33, 479–92, 532–35, 671–80; 299–306; 345–61, 686–94, 664–71; *Congressional Globe*, 40 Cong., 1 Sess., 446–51.

17. *Congressional Globe*, 40 Cong., 1 Sess., 256–64, 362–64; Trefousse, *Butler*, 191–92.

18. *Congressional Globe*, 40 Cong., 1 Sess., 448–51.

19. *Impeachment Investigation*, 56 ff.

20. Moore Diary, n.d., 33, Johnson Papers; Boutwell to Sumner, April 7, 1867, Sumner Papers; Chicago *Tribune*, June 4, 1867.

21. Chicago *Tribune*, June 4, 1867; Toledo *Daily Commercial*, June 4, 1867. The committee voted to reassemble on June 26.

22. Welles, *Diary*, III, 61; *Congressional Globe*, 40 Cong., 1 Sess., 303, 315 ff., 332 ff., 438–41. For details on the long adjournment struggle see DeWitt, *Impeachment and Trial of Andrew Johnson*, 217–21.

23. Washington *Triweekly National Intelligencer*, May 28, 1867.

24. Welles, *Diary*, III, 105, 107, 109–14; New York *World*, June 17, 1867; Minutes of Cabinet Meeting, June 19, 1867, Johnson Papers.

25. Adam Badeau, *Grant in Peace* (Hartford, Conn.: S. S. Scranton, 1887), 60–61, 85, 102; Grant to Sheridan, April 5, 21, May 26, June 7, 1867, Sheridan Papers; Welles, *Diary*, III, 104–105; Harold M. Hyman, "Johnson, Stanton, and Grant: A Reconsideration of the Army's Role in the Events Leading to Impeachment," *American Historical Review*, 66 (Oct. 1960), 85–100, esp. 85, 96 ff.

26. E. L. Plumb to Sumner, April 23, 1867, Sumner Papers.

27. Badeau, *Grant in Peace*, 68–70; George Fort Milton, *The Age of Hate* (New York: Coward-McCann, 1931), 439; Thomas and Hyman, *Stanton*, 537–39; Sickles to Adjutant General, June 14, 1867, Stanton Papers.

28. Sickles to Adjutant General, June 19, 1867, Stanton Papers; Sickles to Johnson, June 19, 1867, Johnson Papers. Sickles' request was refused. E. D. Townsend to Sickles, June 21, 1867, Johnson Papers; Sheridan to Grant, June 21, 22, July 2, 1867; Grant to Sheridan, June 21, 29, 1867; Adjutant General to Sheridan, June 21, 1867; Sheridan to Adjutant General, June 29, 1867, Johnson Papers (mostly included in Stanton to Johnson, July 3, 1867, Johnson Papers).

29. New York *Herald*, June 23, 1867; Washington *Triweekly National Intelligencer*, June 25, 1867.

30. Toledo *Blade*, June 26, 1867; *Independent*, July 1, 1867; New York *World*, June 1, 1867; Welles, *Diary*, III, 117, 124 ff.

31. Butler to Mrs. Butler, July 4, 1867, Butler Papers.

32. Howe to Grace Howe, July 4, 1867, Howe Papers.

33. *Congressional Globe*, 40 Cong., 1 Sess., 479–80, 481, 492 ff., 498; New York *Herald*, July 5, 1867.

34. Thomas Shankland to Holt, June 25, 1867, Holt Papers; Washington *Triweekly National Intelligencer*, June 18, 1867.

35. *Impeachment Investigation*, 777–819.

36. *Congressional Globe*, 40 Cong., 1 Sess., 565–67.

37. Brodie, *Thaddeus Stevens*, 327.

38. New York *Herald*, July 8, 1867.

39. *Congressional Globe*, 40 Cong., 1 Sess., 565–67, 587–91.

40. *Ibid.*, 697–98, 656, 720.

41. *Ibid.*, 747, 762 ff.

42. *Ibid.*, 515.

43. Trefousse, *Butler*, 192; *New York Times*, Feb. 12, 1867.

44. Washington *Daily National Intelligencer*, July 9, 17, 18, 1867.

45. Thomas and Hyman, *Stanton*, 546.

46. U.S., *Statutes at Large*, XV, 14–16.

47. Richardson, ed., *Messages and Papers of the Presidents*, IX, 3734–43.

48. *Congressional Globe*, 40 Cong., 1 Sess., 743–47, 759 ff., 762–63, 767.

49. New York *Herald*, July 21, 22, 23, 1867; Chicago *Tribune*, July 26, 1867.

50. *Impeachment Investigation*, 825 ff., 861 ff., 1166.

51. *Independent*, July 25, 1867.

52. A. C. Maxwell to Johnson, Aug. 17, 1866, Johnson Papers.

53. F. P. Blair to Johnson, Sept. 20, 1866, Johnson Papers; Welles, *Diary*, II, 580–81.

54. Randall to Johnson, Oct. 24, 1866, Johnson Papers.

55. Welles, *Diary*, III, 4, 22, 45, 49.

56. *Ibid.*, 50–51, 52, 54–55; Thomas and Hyman, *Stanton*, 526; Moore Diary, April 5, May 2, 1867, Johnson Papers.

57. Welles, *Diary*, III, 74, 126; Badeau, *Grant in Peace*, 77.

58. Louis J. Dupre to Seward, July 24, 1867, Seward Papers; W. J. D. Hilton to Weed, July 26, 1867, Weed Papers.

59. Welles, *Diary*, III, 56–57.

60. Hyman, "Johnson, Stanton, and Grant," *passim*.

61. Washington *Triweekly National Intelligencer*, July 25, 1867.

62. Welles, *Diary*, III, 146–47.

63. *Ibid.*, 143–46, 159, 161; Browning, *Diary*, II, 152–53; Charles Dunham to Johnson, July 26, 1867, and enclosures, Johnson Papers. Prior to sending this material to the President, Dunham, alias Conover, had applied to him for a pardon through his radical contacts. A. G. Riddle to Johnson, July 23, 1867, Johnson Papers.

64. W. G. Moore, "Notes of Colonel W. G. Moore, Private Secretary to President Johnson, 1866–1868," *American Historical Review*, 19 (Oct. 1913), 107–108; Grant to Johnson, Aug. 1, 1867, Johnson Papers.

65. Moore, "Notes of Colonel W. G. Moore," 107–108; *New York Times*, Aug. 5, 8, 1867; DeWitt believed this revelation to have been the final issue to convince Johnson of the necessity of removing Stanton: DeWitt, *Impeachment and Trial of Andrew Johnson*, 272–78. Whether Stanton or Judge Advocate General Joseph Holt had been responsible for the incident has never been fully determined.

66. W. Winthrop to Holt, Aug. 12, 1867, Holt Papers; Johnson to Stanton, Aug. 5, 1867; Moore Diary, Aug. 6, 1867, Johnson Papers. The President's letter read: "Sir: Public considerations of a high character constrain me to say, that your resignation as Secretary of War will be accepted."

67. Stanton to Johnson, Aug. 5, 1867, Johnson Papers.

68. Welles, *Diary*, III, 158–59, 162–63, 164–66; W. P. Phillips to Johnson, Aug. 6, 1867; Dixon to Johnson, Aug. 10, 1867, Johnson Papers.

69. Johnson to Stanton, Aug. 12, 1867, Johnson Papers; Moore, "Notes of Colonel W. G. Moore," 109.

70. Moore, "Notes of Colonel W. G. Moore," 109; Stanton to Johnson, Aug. 12, 1867, Johnson Papers.

71. Moore, "Notes of Colonel W. G. Moore," 110; Moore Diary, Dec. 15, 1867; Johnson to Grant, Aug. 17, 19, 1867, Grant to Johnson, Aug. 17, 1867, Johnson Papers.

72. Order in Johnson Papers, Aug. 26, 1867; Moore Diary, Aug. 24, 27, 1867; Johnson to Grant, Aug. 26, 1867, Johnson Papers. Thomas declined for reasons of health. McPherson, *Reconstruction*, 306–308, 342–44, 345.

73. Bigelow, MS Diary, Aug. 16, 1867, Bigelow Papers.

74. Hinsdale, *Garfield-Hinsdale Letters*, 96.

75. R. Hill to Jenckes, Aug. 23, 1867, Thomas A. Jenckes Papers, L. C.

76. G. W. Patterson to Weed, Aug. 21, 1867, Weed Papers.

77. Anthony to Seward, Aug. 27, 1867, Seward Papers.

78. Dixon to Welles, Aug. 29, 1867, Welles Papers, LC; Moore Diary, Dec. 15, 1867, Johnson Papers.

79. Chicago *Tribune*, Aug. 21, 1867; Horace White to Chandler, Aug. 20, 1867, Zachariah Chandler Papers, LC.

80. *National Anti-Slavery Standard*, Aug. 17, 31, 1867; *Wilkes' Spirit of the Times*, Aug. 31, Sept. 7, 1867.

81. A. N. Cole to McCulloch, Aug. 26, 1867, McCulloch Papers.

82. Joseph Schafer, ed., *Intimate Letters of Carl Schurz, 1841–1869*, Publications of the State Historical Society of Wisconsin Collections, 30 (Madison: State Historical Society of Wisconsin, 1928), 391; Fessenden to McCulloch, Sept. 2, 1867, McCulloch Papers; Colfax to Garfield, Sept. 11, 1867, Garfield Papers, LC.

VI: THE ELECTION OF 1867

1. McPherson, *Reconstruction*, 57, 61, 62.

2. *Ibid.*, 128, 129, 140–41.

3. *Ibid.*, 143.

4. Milton, *The Age of Hate*, 434; J. F. Babcock to Welles, Feb. 14, 1867, Welles Papers, LC.

5. Welles, *Diary*, III, 77–78.

6. Dixon to Welles, Sept. 8, 1868, Welles Papers, LC.

7. Georges Clemenceau, *American Reconstruction, 1865–1870*, ed. Fernand Baldensperger (New York: Da Capo, 1969), 131.

8. New York *Herald*, Sept. 5, 1867.

9. Clifford H. Moore, "Ohio in National Politics, 1865–1896," *Ohio State Archaeological and Historical Quarterly*, 37 (April–July 1928), 247.

10. Trefousse, *Wade*, 289.

11. *Ibid.*; P. B. Cole to Sherman, June 16, 1867, John Sherman Papers, LC; Cincinnati *Gazette*, June 20, 1867.

12. Trefousse, *Wade*, 68, 79, 111–13, 119, 124, 129.

13. *New York Times*, June 20, 1867.

14. New York *Herald*, June 27, 1867; *New York Times*, June 20, 1867; Washington *Daily National Intelligencer*, June 29, 1867.

15. *New York Times*, July 1, 1867; Cincinnati *Daily Gazette*, July 9, 1867; William F. Zornow, " 'Bluff Ben' Wade in Lawrence, Kansas: The Issue of Class Conflict," *Ohio Historical Quarterly*, 65 (Jan. 1956), 44–52; Hans L. Trefousse, "Ben Wade and the Failure of the Impeachment of Johnson," *Historical and Philosophical Society of Ohio Bulletin*, 18 (Oct. 1960), 245–46.

16. John Sherman to Colfax, Oct. 20, 1867, Schuyler Colfax Collection, Univ. of Rochester; *New York Times*, Aug. 20, 1867; James Ford Rhodes, *History of the United States from the Compromise of 1850 to the McKinley-*

Bryan Campaign of 1896 (New York: Macmillan, 1920), VI, 160. Pendleton reversed himself completely during the year; in the spring, he did not yet favor his Ohio idea. McKitrick, *Andrew Johnson and Reconstruction*, 373–74; Benedict, "The Right Way," 411–12.

17. Colfax to Garfield, Sept. 11, 1867, Garfield Papers, LC; W. H. P. Denny to Wade, Aug. 6, 1867, Wade Papers; New York *World*, Sept. 7, 1867.

18. *New York Times*, Aug. 14, 1867. He repeated the argument elsewhere. *Ibid.*, Sept. 2, 1867.

19. *New York Times*, Aug. 22, Sept. 2, 1867; *Independent*, Oct. 10, 1867.

20. Cincinnati *Daily Gazette*, Aug. 21, 1867; Trefousse, "Ben Wade and the Negro," *Ohio Historical Quarterly*, 68 (April 1959), 162–76.

21. *Independent*, Oct. 10, 1867; New York *World*, Sept. 7, 10, 13, Oct. 9, 10, 1867.

22. New York *World*, Aug. 12, Oct. 9, 10, 11, 1867.

23. New York *World*, Nov. 7, 1867; *New York Times*, Nov. 6, 1867.

24. Clemenceau, *American Reconstruction*, 117; New York *World*, Oct. 10, 1867; Washington *Triweekly National Intelligencer*, Oct. 16, 1867.

25. Dixon to Welles, Oct. 14, 1867, Welles Papers, LC.

26. Babcock to Welles, Oct. 8, 1867, Gideon Welles Papers, NYPL; Campbell to Johnson, Oct. 12, 1867, Johnson Papers.

27. John A. McClernand to Johnson, Oct. 11, 1867; Amos Layman to Johnson, Oct. 12, 1867; Seymour to Johnson, Nov. 9, 1867, Johnson Papers.

28. A. S. Paddock to F. W. Seward, Oct. 19, 1867, Seward Papers.

29. Campbell to Johnson, Oct. 12, 1867; Ewing to Johnson, Oct. 12, 1867, Johnson Papers.

30. Parsons to Sumner, Oct. 10, 1867, Sumner Papers.

31. Sherman to Colfax, Oct. 20, 1867, Colfax Papers, Univ. of Rochester.

32. *New York Times*, Nov. 8, 1867.

33. T. B. Shannon to Washburne, Oct. 20, 1867, Washburne Papers.

34. M. Ralph Thayer to Washburne, Oct. 10, 1867, Washburne Papers; John Birney to Colfax, Nov. 2, 1867, William Pitt Fessenden Papers, LC; Washington *Triweekly National Intelligencer*, Nov. 2, 1867; William B. Lynn to Strong, Nov. 4, 1867, John D. Strong Papers, Illinois State Historical Society; Bigelow to W. H. Huntington, Nov. 4, 1867, Bigelow Papers; New York *World*, Sept. 7, 10, 1867.

35. William B. Lynn to Strong, Nov. 4, 1867, Strong Papers; New York *World*, Aug. 16, Sept. 7, 1867; *Harper's Weekly*, 11 (Sept. 28, Oct. 26, Nov. 23, 30, 1867), 610–11, 674–75, 738, 755.

36. See above, note 16. See also Wade to Chandler, Oct. 10, 1867, Zachariah Chandler Papers, LC.

37. Thomas Ewing to Hugh Ewing, Oct. 16, 1867, Thomas Ewing Papers, LC; *New York Times*, Oct. 12, 1867; Oberholtzer, *Jay Cooke*, II, 28.

38. Sherman to Colfax, Oct. 20, 1867, Colfax Papers, Univ. of Rochester; *Wilkes' Spirit of the Times*, Oct. 26, Nov. 9, 1867; *National Anti-Slavery Standard*, Oct. 12, 1867; Charles B. Rice to Henry Dawes, March 6, 1868, Dawes Papers; New York *Herald*, Oct. 10, 1867.

39. J. Bowles to Shellabarger, Oct. 11, 1867, Washburne Papers.
40. Richmond *Whig*, Oct. 11, 1867.
41. J. Henly Smith to Alexander H. Stephens, Oct. 17, 1867, Stephens Papers.
42. *Independent*, Nov. 14, 1867; L. D. Evans to Johnson, Nov. 4, 1867, Johnson Papers; Toledo *Daily Commercial*, Nov. 15, 1867; J. Glancey Jones to Stephens, Nov. 26, 1867, Stephens Papers; H. R. Linderman to McCulloch, Oct. 9, 1867, McCulloch Papers.
43. Parsons to Sumner, Oct. 10, 1867, Sumner Papers.
44. Schafer, ed., *Intimate Letters of Carl Schurz*, 406.
45. *Wilkes' Spirit of the Times*, Oct. 26, 1867; *New York Times*, Nov. 8, 1867; Toledo *Daily Commercial*, Nov. 15, 1867; French MS Diary, Nov. 28, 1867; Washington *Triweekly National Intelligencer*, Oct. 3, 1867.
46. Grow to Washburne, Oct. 13, 1867; Charles A. Page to Washburne, Oct. 12, 1867; Samuel Purviance to Washburne, Oct. 12, 1867; Blaine to Washburne, Oct. 22, 1867; Galloway to Washburne, Nov. 5, 1867, Washburne Papers; John Bigelow to W. H. Huntington, Nov. 4, 1867, Bigelow Papers.
47. Clemenceau, *American Reconstruction*, 123–24.
48. *Independent*, Nov. 14, 1867; Clemenceau, *American Reconstruction*, 124.
49. Cox to Garfield, Nov. 27, 1867, Garfield Papers, LC; Michael Les Benedict, "The Rout of Radicalism: Republicans and the Election of 1867," *Civil War History*, 18 (Dec. 1972), 334–44.
50. *New York Times*, Nov. 14, 1867.
51. French MS Diary, Dec. 5, 1867.
52. Richardson, ed., *Messages and Papers of the Presidents*, VIII, 3762–64.

VII: FAILURE OF THE FIRST IMPEACHMENT

1. New York *Herald*, Sept. 4, 22, Oct. 18, 21, 1867; Chicago *Tribune*, Aug. 20, 21, Sept. 18, 1867; Hinsdale, ed., *Garfield-Hinsdale Letters*, 96, 99; Schafer, ed., *Intimate Letters of Carl Schurz*, 388, 390, 391; Fessenden to McCulloch, Sept. 2, 1867; A. N. Cole to McCulloch, Aug. 26, 1867, McCulloch Papers; Colfax to Garfield, Sept. 11, 1867, Garfield Papers, LC; Dixon to Welles, Sept. 12, 1867, Welles Papers, LC.
2. William Lawrence, "The Law of Impeachment," *American Law Register*, 6 (Sept. 1867), 641–80; Chicago *Tribune*, Sept. 18, 1867; *Wilkes' Spirit of the Times*, Aug. 31, Sept. 2, 7, 1867; *Independent*, Aug. 15, Sept. 12, 19, 1867; New York *Herald*, Oct. 24, 25, 1867; Washington *Daily Morning Chronicle*, Aug. 13, 1867.
3. Welles, *Diary*, III, 165.
4. That Johnson was not the rash politician many believed him to be was underlined by Seward when Benjamin B. French characterized the President as a man who spoke without much preparation. The secretary of state contradicted this analysis and pointed out that he had often been surprised to

find how much Johnson relied on his previous reading and study for what appeared to be extemporaneous speaking. French MS Diary, July 23, 1867.

5. Francis P. Blair, Jr. to Francis P. Blair, Sr., Aug. 2, 1867, Blair-Lee Papers; J. M. Edmunds to Sprague, July 11, 1867, William Sprague Papers, Columbia Univ.; Bigelow MS Diary, July 13, 1867; L. J. Dupre to Seward, July 24, 1867, Seward Papers; W. J. D. Hilton to Weed, July 26, 1867, Weed Papers; Welles, *Diary*, III, 167; Hyman, "Johnson, Stanton, and Grant," *American Historical Review*, 66 (Oct. 1960), 98; Milton Lomask, *Andrew Johnson: President on Trial* (New York: Farrar, Straus, 1960), 254.

6. McPherson, *Reconstruction*, 261, 262; Badeau, *Grant in Peace*, 91–94; Babcock to Washburne, Aug. 13, 1867, Washburne Papers.

7. Trefousse, *Butler*, 193; *New York Times*, Aug. 11, 1867.

8. Welles, *Diary*, III, 167, 169; F. P. Blair, Jr. to Montgomery Blair, Aug. 22, [1867], Blair-Lee Papers.

9. J. M. Shankland to Holt, Aug. 13, 1867, Holt Papers; Horace White to Washburne, Aug. 13, 1867, Washburne Papers.

10. Moore, "Notes of Col. W. G. Moore," 110; Johnson to Grant, Aug. 17, 1867; Grant to Johnson, Aug. 17, 1867, Johnson Papers.

11. Badeau, *Grant in Peace*, 104; J. W. Forsyth to Sheridan, Aug. 12, 14, 1867, Sheridan Papers.

12. Johnson to Grant, Aug. 19, 1867, Johnson Papers.

13. Moore, "Notes of Col. W. G. Moore," 110–11; Moore Diary, Aug. 19, 1867, Johnson Papers.

14. Moore Diary, Aug. 24, 1867, Johnson Papers.

15. Moore, "Notes of Col. W. G. Moore," 111.

16. *Ibid.*, 111–12; Moore Diary, Aug. 24, 1867, Johnson Papers.

17. Welles, *Diary*, III, 185–87.

18. *Ibid.*, 182, 185–88; Sefton, *United States Army and Reconstruction*, 158–60; William A. Swanberg, *Sickles the Incredible* (New York: Ace Books, 1956), 237–38.

19. Moore, "Notes of Col. W. G. Moore," 111–12.

20. *Ibid.*; Johnson to Grant, Aug. 27, 1867, Johnson Papers.

21. Moore Diary, Aug. 27, 28, 1867; Grant to Johnson, Aug. 28, 1867; Johnson to Grant, Aug. 28, 1867, Johnson Papers.

22. Grant to Sheridan, Sept. 8, 1867, Sheridan Papers.

23. *New York Times*, Sept. 24, 25, 1867; Thomas and Hyman, *Stanton*, 558; Welles, *Diary*, III, 207; Sickles to Adjutant General, Sept. 11, 1867 (with Grant's endorsement), Johnson Papers.

24. Sherman, *John Sherman's Recollections of Forty Years*, I, 414–15; Welles, *Diary*, III, 221–22.

25. Welles, *Diary*, III, 254–55.

26. *New York Times*, Nov. 14, 1867.

27. Atkinson to McCulloch, Aug. 7, Sept. 3, 1867, McCulloch Papers; Grimes to Atkinson, Sept. 15, 1867, Edward Atkinson Papers, Massachusetts Historical Society; T. W. Egan to Johnson, Oct. 7, 1867, Johnson Papers;

R. H. McClellan to Washburne, Nov. 27, 1867, Washburne Papers; Oberholtzer, *Jay Cooke*, II, 28.

28. McCulloch to Greeley, July 22, 1867, Greeley Papers; Moore Diary, Aug. 14, 1867; McCulloch to Johnson, Aug. 19, 1867; E. G. White to Johnson, Oct. 12, 1867; J. B. Stoll to Johnson, Nov. 19, 1867, Johnson Papers; J. K. Myers to McCulloch, Aug. 20, 1867; C. H. Van Dyke to McCulloch, Aug. 16, 1867; P. F. Kelly to McCulloch, Aug. 28, 1867; C. F. Coffin to McCulloch, Aug. 29, 1867; Moses Bates to McCulloch, Sept. 11, 1867, McCulloch Papers.

29. Richardson, ed., *Messages and Papers of the Presidents*, VIII, 3765.

30. Welles, *Diary*, III, 152.

31. New York *Herald*, Oct. 18, 21, Nov. 25, 1867; Chicago *Tribune*, Oct. 25, 1867.

32. *Impeachment Investigation*, 1166–94.

33. *Ibid.*, 1194–1208.

34. G. V. Moody to Johnson, April 13, 1866; E. A. Allen to Johnson, Oct. 20, 1866; F. H. DeRolette to Johnson, Nov. 24, 1866; O. C. Richardson to Johnson, Dec. 3, 1866; Thomas Powell to Johnson, Jan. 5, 1867; F. P. Blair, Sr. to Johnson, Aug. 17, 1867; W. C. Jewett to Johnson, Nov. 3, 1867; John Tyler to Johnson, Nov. 26, 1867, Johnson Papers.

35. New York *Herald*, Nov. 19, 1866; Nashville *Daily Press and Times*, Sept. 4, 1867, Johnson Papers; Toledo *Daily Commercial*, Oct. 6, 1867; Clemenceau, *American Reconstruction*, 110–11, 120–21; R. S. Holt to Joseph Holt, Sept. 12, 1866, Holt Papers; Greeley to Morgan, Feb. 5, 1867, Morgan Papers; Schafer, ed., *Intimate Letters of Carl Schurz*, 392; John Binney to Colfax, Sept. 9, 1867, John A. Andrew Papers, Massachusetts Historical Society; James W. Ogden to Holt, Oct. 22, 1867, Holt Papers. See also William A. Russ, "Was There Danger of a Second Civil War during Reconstruction?" *Mississippi Valley Historical Review*, 25 (June 1938), 39–58.

36. *Congressional Globe*, 40 Cong., 1 Sess., 791 ff.

37. *Ibid.*; *Impeachment Investigation*, 1–111. For a discussion of the problem of impeachment for offenses not covered by statute, see Benedict, *Impeachment and Trial of Andrew Johnson*, 27 ff., 79; Berger, *Impeachment*, 43 ff., 271; and for a more conservative view, Brant, *Impeachment*, 20 ff.

38. Chicago *Tribune*, Nov. 24, 25, 26, 27, Dec. 6, 7, 8, 1867; *Independent*, Nov. 8, 1867; Washington *Triweekly National Intelligencer*, Dec. 3, 1867; French MS Diary, Nov. 28, 1867.

39. Moore Diary, Nov. 21, 1867, Johnson Papers.

40. New York *Herald*, Oct. 15, 26, Nov. 19, 24, 1867; Memorandum of Cabinet Meeting, Nov. 30, 1867, Johnson Papers; Browning, *Diary*, II, 167–68.

41. Moore Diary, Nov. 30, 1867, Johnson Papers.

42. *New York Times*, Nov. 23, 1867.

43. Fogg to Washburne, Nov. 20, 1867, Washburne Papers.

44. Emory Washburne to Dawes, Dec. 5, 1867, Dawes Papers; John Binney to Fessenden, Nov. 15, 1867, Fessenden Papers, LC.

45. Grimes to Atkinson, Sept. 15, Oct. 14, 1867, Atkinson Papers; Atkinson to McCulloch, Sept. 3, 1867, McCulloch Papers.

46. Emory Washburne to Dawes, Dec. 5, 1867, Dawes Papers; Grimes to Atkinson, Sept. 15, 1867, Atkinson Papers; W. C. Jewett to Johnson, Nov. 3, 1867; Wm. Thorpe to Johnson, Dec. 5, 1867, Johnson Papers.

47. Emory Washburne to Dawes, Dec. 5, 1867, Dawes papers.

48. F. Smith to Johnson, Nov. 30, 1867, Johnson Papers.

49. Hinsdale, ed., *Garfield-Hinsdale Letters*, 117.

50. Schurz to Pastorius, Dec. 5, 1867, Schurz Papers ["da der Majoritäts-anriss so gänzlich in den Dreck gerfallen war"].

51. The majority report was a good indication of this attitude. See especially *Impeachment Investigation*, 2; Cincinnati *Daily Gazette*, Sept. 11, 1867; *New York Times*, Nov. 8, 1867.

52. Washington *Triweekly National Intelligencer*, Nov. 19, 1867.

53. *Ibid.*, Dec. 7, 1867.

54. W. H. Gibbs to Washburne, Sept. 30, 1867, Washburne Papers; A. Jervis to Sumner, Dec. 3, 1867, Sumner Papers; C. W. Clarke to Covode, Aug. 31, 1867, John Covode Papers, Historical Society of Western Pennsylvania; A. N. Cole to Morgan, Nov. 28, 1867, Morgan Papers.

55. Cohen to Stephens, Aug. 12, 1867, Stephens Papers.

56. John W. Overall to Johnson, Sept. 5, 1867, Johnson Papers.

57. *National Anti-Slavery Standard*, Aug. 31, 1867.

58. *Congressional Globe*, 40 Cong., 2 Sess., 61, 65; Chicago *Tribune*, Dec. 6, 7, 1867.

59. *Congressional Globe*, 40 Cong., 2 Sess., Ap., 54–62.

60. *Ibid.*, 62–65.

61. *Ibid.*, 67; *New York Times*, Dec. 8, 1867.

62. *Wilkes' Spirit of the Times*, Dec. 14, 1867.

63. Chicago *Tribune*, Dec. 8, 1867.

64. *New York Times*, Dec. 8, 1867; *Harper's Weekly*, 11, 786, 802–803 (Dec. 14, 21, 1867).

65. Julian to Mrs. Julian, Dec. 8, 1867, Julian Papers.

66. New York *Herald*, Dec. 14, 1867.

67. *National Anti-Slavery Standard*, Dec. 28, 1867; Theodore McCurran to McPherson, Dec. 17, 1867, Edward McPherson Papers, LC.

68. Clemenceau, *American Reconstruction*, 136–37. The Fourteenth Amendment was certainly not passed in the form the radicals desired; see Joseph P. James, *The Framing of the Fourteenth Amendment* (Urbana: Univ. of Illinois Press, 1965), 151.

69. Washington *Triweekly National Intelligencer*, Dec. 10, 1867.

70. French MS Diary, Dec. 8, 1867.

71. Richmond *Whig*, Dec. 31, 1867; Richmond *Enquirer*, Jan. 10, 1868.

72. S. Horton to Henry Edwards, Jan. 1, 1868; J. L. Dunning to Sumner, Dec. 29, 1867, Sumner Papers; C. H. Hopkins to Stevens, Jan. 3, 1868, Stevens Papers.

73. New York *World*, Sept. 25, 1867.

74. *Congressional Globe*, 40 Cong., 2 Sess., 172 ff.

75. Charles Halpine to Johnson, Jan. 4, 1868, Johnson Papers.
76. Welles, *Diary*, III, 240.

VIII. RENEWED PRESIDENTIAL DEFIANCE

1. McPherson, *Reconstruction*, 324.
2. Moore Diary, Nov. 30, Dec. 15, 1867, Johnson Papers; Welles, *Diary*, III, 241, 242; Richardson, ed., *Messages and Papers of the Presidents*, IX, 3793–94; *Congressional Globe*, 40 Cong., 2 Sess., 264, 402; Clemenceau, *American Reconstruction*, 139.
3. Moore Diary, Dec. 15, 1867, Johnson Papers.
4. John Forsyth to Manton Marble, Dec. 19, 1867, Marble Papers; John Jones to Pope, Dec. 21, 1867; Thomas Ewing to Johnson, Dec. 24, 1867; Pope to Grant, Dec. 26, 27, 1867; M. M. Cooke to Johnson, Dec. 27, 1867; John Forsyth to Johnson, Dec. 12, 1867, Johnson Papers; Wager Swayne to Chase, June 27, 1867, Chase Papers, LC; Sefton, *United States Army in Reconstruction*, 160–69.
5. Thomas and Hyman, *Stanton*, 558; Welles, *Diary*, III, 245, 249.
6. Welles, *Diary*, III, 242–44, 251; McPherson, *Reconstruction*, 345–46.
7. *New York Times*, Dec. 12, 1867.
8. Moore, "Notes of Col. W. G. Moore," 113–14; Richardson, ed., *Messages and Papers of the Presidents*, IX, 3781–92 (the President had originally prepared a shorter message, but sent in the longer one upon Stanbery's suggestion); Welles, *Diary*, III, 240–41.
9. *New York Times*, Dec. 17, 1867; Chicago *Tribune*, Dec. 18, 1867.
10. A. W. Cole to Morgan, Dec. 4, 1867, Morgan Papers; J. L. Dunning to Sumner, Dec. 29, 1867, Sumner Papers; Foster Blodgett to Fessenden, Dec. 30, 1867, Fessenden Papers, LC; Foster Blodgett to John Sherman, Dec. 30, 1867, Sherman Papers; W. M. Lowry to Johnson, Dec. 30, 1867; R. A. Alatin to Johnson, Jan. 3, 1868; A. H. Stephens to Johnson, Jan. 6, 1868, Johnson Papers; Henry, *Story of Reconstruction*, 266–67, 284–86; John Hope Franklin, ed., *Reminiscences of an Active Life, The Autobiography of John Roy Lynch* (Chicago: Univ. of Chicago Press, 1970), 48–51; Clara M. Thompson, *Reconstruction in Georgia* (New York: Columbia Univ. Press, 1915), 199; William W. Davis, *The Civil War and Reconstruction in Florida* (New York: Columbia Univ. Press, 1913), 492, 497; Francis B. Simkins and Robert H. Woody, *South Carolina during Reconstruction* (Chapel Hill: Univ. of North Carolina Press, 1932), 86–87; Hamilton, *Reconstruction in North Carolina*, 251–52; Jack P. Maddex, Jr., *The Virginia Conservatives* (Chapel Hill: Univ. of North Carolina Press, 1970), 55; Franklin, *Reconstruction*, 83.
11. Franklin, *Reconstruction*, 116–17; Bowers, *The Tragic Era*, 218–19; Simkins and Woody, *South Carolina during Reconstruction*, 83–84.
12. Henry S. Fitch to Johnson, Dec. 1, 1867, Johnson Papers; *Impeachment Trial*, I, 375–76, 708–15, 719–26.

13. Underwood to Greeley, Nov. 27, 1867, Greeley Papers; Underwood to Washburne, Dec. 9, 1867, Washburne Papers.

14. C. W. Buckley to Washburne, Jan. 9, 1868, Washburne Papers.

15. Foster Blodgett to John Sherman, Dec. 30, 1867, Sherman Papers; W. H. Gibbs to Washburne, Jan. 18, 1868, Washburne Papers. A. H. Stephens was so delighted that Johnson had removed Pope that he wrote him a congratulatory letter: A. H. Stephens to Johnson, Jan. 6, 1868, Johnson Papers.

16. C. H. Hopkins to Stevens, Jan. 3, 1868, Stevens Papers.

17. Washburne to Underwood, Dec. 7, 1867, John C. Underwood Papers, LC.

18. Underwood to Washburne, Dec. 9, 16, 1867, Washburne Papers; Colfax to Underwood, Jan. 7, 1868, Underwood Papers.

19. W. H. Gibbs to Washburne, Jan. 16, 1868, Washburne Papers; Edmund G. Ross, *History of the Impeachment of Andrew Johnson* (Santa Fe: New Mexico Printing Co., 1896), 49; Clemenceau, *American Reconstruction*, 75.

20. Schouler to Dawes, Sept. 12, 1867, Dawes Papers.

21. Hassaurek to Sherman, Jan. 27, 1868, Sherman Papers.

22. J. R. Young to Washburne, Nov. 26, 1867; R. H. McClellan to Washburne, Nov. 27, 1867; W. W. Murphy to Washburne, Jan. 30, 1868, Washburne Papers; L. W. Hall to Garfield, Dec. 28, 1867, Garfield Papers, LC.

23. General Sherman told Johnson in October to cooperate with the moderates and advised his brother of the conversation. Sherman, *John Sherman's Recollections of Forty Years*, I, 415.

24. Clemenceau, *American Reconstruction*, 138; Edward McPherson MS biography of Stevens, Stevens Papers, 55322–23; Julian, *Political Recollections*, 361; Brodie, *Thaddeus Stevens*, 260, 292–93, 322 ff.; Kendrick, *Journal of the Joint Committee of Fifteen on Reconstruction*, 137; *Independent*, Dec. 26, 1867.

25. Poore, *Perley's Reminiscences of Sixty Years in the National Metropolis*, 202–203; *Independent*, Jan. 10, 1867; Kutler, *Judicial Power and Reconstruction Politics*, 64 ff., 102; Warren, *The Supreme Court in United States History*, 455–66; Harold M. Hyman, *A More Perfect Union: The Impact of the Civil War and Reconstruction on the Constitution* (New York: Knopf, 1973), 473.

26. *Congressional Globe*, 40 Cong., 2 Sess., 19, 477–89; Kutler, *Judicial Power and Reconstruction Politics*, 76–77.

27. *New York Times*, Jan. 14, 24, 1868; Chicago *Tribune*, Jan. 15, 18, 11, 1868; John Binney to Fessenden, Jan. 22, 1868, Fessenden Papers, LC. Cf. McCardle case, 122, 161.

28. *Congressional Globe*, 40 Cong., 2 Sess., 19, 51, 53, 132, 218, 264, 267–68, 331, 384, 476, 517, 664, 722 ff.; McPherson, *Reconstruction*, 338–39, 336–37.

29. *Congressional Globe*, 40 Cong., 2 Sess., 332–33.

30. Resolution, Senate Executive Sess., Jan. 13, 1868, Johnson Papers; *New York Times*, Jan. 8, 10, 1868.

31. Moore Diary, Jan. 7, 1868, Johnson Papers; Washington *Triweekly National Intelligencer*, Jan. 14, 1868.

32. J. S. Rollins to Blair, Sept. 16, 1867, Blair-Lee Papers; Welles, *Diary*, III, 234, 240.

33. Welles, *Diary*, III, 242: Frank Blair, Jr. to Montgomery Blair, Dec. 18, 1867, Blair-Lee Papers; Doolittle to Marble, Dec. 21, 1867, Marble Papers; *Independent*, Jan. 2, 1868.

34. Sherman, *John Sherman's Recollections of Forty Years*, I, 414.

35. Welles, *Diary*, III, 254; Badeau, *Grant in Peace*, 125.

36. Badeau, *Grant in Peace*, 125–26; 110 ff.; McPherson, *Reconstruction*, 283, 285, 286, 290–91; Moore, "Notes of Col. W. G. Moore," 115.

37. Badeau, *Grant in Peace*, 110–15; Sherman to Grant, Jan. 27, 1868, Blaine Papers; Ewing to Johnson, n.d. [prior to Senate's vote on Stanton, possibly December 1867], Johnson Papers.

38. Badeau, *Grant in Peace*, 110–15; McPherson, *Reconstruction*, 283–86; Grant to Johnson, Jan. 14, 1868; Moore Diary, Jan. 14, Feb. 4, 1868, Johnson Papers. Johnson was also incensed at Grant for having upheld General Meade, who, contrary to Johnson's wishes, had removed the governor of Georgia in a continuation of the dispute with Pope: Moore Diary, Jan. 14, Feb. 4, 1868; Charles J. Jenkins to John Bigby, Dec. 28, 1867; Meade to Charles J. Jenkins, Jan. 7, 1868, Johnson Papers; McPherson, *Reconstruction*, 320.

39. Sherman to Grant, Jan. 27, 1868, Blaine Papers; Moore Diary, Feb. 3, 1868, Johnson Papers.

40. Moore Diary, Jan. 15, 1868, Johnson Papers; Sherman to Grant, Jan. 27, 1868, Blaine Papers; McPherson, *Reconstruction*, 285–86.

41. Memorandum, W. T. Sherman, Jan. 18, Johnson Papers; McPherson, *Reconstruction*, 283, 285, 286–87.

42. McPherson, *Reconstruction*, 283; Grant to Johnson, Jan. 24, 1868, Johnson Papers.

43. Moore Diary, Jan. 26, 1868; Grant to Johnson, Jan. 28, 1868, Johnson Papers; also in McPherson, *Reconstruction*, 283.

44. Moore Diary, Jan. 28, 29, 1868; endorsement in Johnson Papers, Jan. 29, 1868.

45. Memorandum of Cabinet Meeting, Jan. 17, 1868, Johnson Papers.

46. Johnson to Grant, Jan. 31, 1868, Johnson Papers; also in McPherson, *Reconstruction*, 284–86. Grant further defied the President by informing him that he would continue to obey the secretary of war as long as there were no orders limiting his authority. McPherson, *Reconstruction*, 284 (Jan. 30, 1868).

47. McPherson, *Reconstruction*, 286–92; Chicago*Tribune*, Feb. 6, 1868; *New York Times*, Feb. 6, 1868; Toledo *Daily Commercial*, Feb. 6, 1868. General John A. Rawlins advised Grant to make the correspondence more personal than Grant had originally intended. William B. Hesseltine, *Ulysses S. Grant, Politician* (New York: Dodd, Mead, 1935), 109–10.

48. Hesseltine, *Ulysses S. Grant*, 112; *Congressional Globe*, 40 Cong., 2 Sess., 977; *Independent*, Feb. 13, 1868.

49. Moore, "Notes of Col. W. G. Moore," 116–17; Moore Diary, Feb. 3, 1868; Sherman to Johnson, Jan. 31, 1868, Johnson Papers; *Impeachment Trial*, I, 521, 529. During the impeachment trial the defense made much of Johnson's alleged effort to test the constitutionality of the Tenure of Office Act in the courts. Thomas and Hyman have questioned this thesis on the grounds that Johnson sought to oust Stanton, not test his right to office. *Impeachment Trial*, II, 387; Thomas and Hyman, *Stanton*, 589–90.

50. Moore Diary, Feb. 3, 1868; W. T. Sherman to Johnson, Jan. 31, 1868, Johnson Papers.

51. Moore Diary, Feb. 17, 1868; W. T. Sherman to Johnson, Feb. 14, 1868, Johnson Papers; Sherman, *John Sherman's Recollections of Forty Years*, I, 418–20; Moore, "Notes of Col. W. G. Moore," 119–20; Lloyd Lewis, *Sherman: Fighting Prophet* (New York: Harcourt, Brace, 1932), 591–93.

52. *Congressional Globe*, 40 Cong., 2 Sess., 1087; Cincinnati *Daily Gazette*, Feb. 8, 10, 13, 1868; Browning, *Diary*, II, 102.

53. Chicago *Tribune*, Feb. 13, 14, 1868; Clemenceau, *American Reconstruction*, 148–49.

54. Washington *Triweekly National Intelligencer*, Feb. 15, 1868; Chicago *Tribune*, Feb. 14, 1868.

IX: IMPEACHMENT OF THE PRESIDENT

1. McPherson, *Reconstruction*, 292–93; Welles, *Diary*, III, 280; Sherman to Grant, Jan. 27, 1868, Blaine Papers.

2. Moore Diary, Jan. 28, Feb. 16, 1868, Johnson Papers; Frank Cowan, *Andrew Johnson, President of the United States. Reminiscences of His Private Life and Character* (2nd ed., Greensburgh, Pa.: Oliver Publishing, 1894), 11–12; Lomask, *Andrew Johnson*, 305.

3. John P. Gaskin to Johnson, Jan. 16, 1868; Stephens to Johnson, Jan. 6, 1868; J. A. Stewart to Johnson, Jan. 10, 1868; W. M. Lowry to Johnson, Dec. 30, 1867, Johnson Papers.

4. Moore Diary, Feb. 17, 1868, Johnson Papers.

5. Welles, *Diary*, III, 279; E. D. Townsend, *Anecdotes of the Civil War in the United States* (New York: Appleton, 1884), 79–82, 124–25; Thomas and Hyman, *Stanton*, 581–82, 159; Johnson and Malone, eds., *DAB*, XVIII, 441–42.

6. Johnson and Malone, eds., *DAB*, XVIII, 441–42; Moore Diary, Feb. 19, 1868, Johnson Papers.

7. Ewing to W. T. Sherman, Jan. 25, 1868, Johnson Papers.

8. H. H. Haight to Johnson, Jan. 18, 1868, Johnson Papers.

9. Browning, *Diary*, II, 102; Moore Diary, Feb. 20, 1868, Johnson Papers; Bigelow MS Diary, Feb. 23, 1868 [misdated April]; French MS Diary, Feb. 23, 1868.

10. Moore, "Notes of Col. W. G. Moore," 120–21.

11. *Ibid.*; Welles, *Diary*, III, 285; Lomask, *Andrew Johnson*, 265 ff.; Milton, *Age of Hate*, 504.

12. Milton, *Age of Hate*, 503–504; Richmond *Enquirer*, Feb. 24, 1868; McPherson, *Reconstruction*, 262–63; Frank Abial Flower, *Edwin McMasters Stanton* (Akron: Saalfield, 1905), 334; George C. Gorham, *Life and Public Services of Edwin M. Stanton* (Boston: Houghton Mifflin, 1899), 438. The effort to court George H. Thomas failed; he wrote a letter to Senator Wade asking not to be promoted. Wade took the letter to the War Department, where the assembled politicians gave three cheers for Thomas. New York *Tribune*, Feb. 24, 1868. According to the *Tribune*, the general had rejected Johnson's bribe.

13. *Congressional Globe*, 40 Cong., 2 Sess., 1326 ff.; Clemenceau, *American Reconstruction*, 153–54; Bigelow MS Diary, Feb. 21, 1868, Bigelow Papers.

14. Thomas and Hyman, *Stanton*, 586–87; New York *Tribune*, Feb. 24, 1868; Welles to John Welles, March 1, 1868, Welles Papers, LC; Mrs. John A. Logan, *Reminiscences of a Soldier's Wife* (New York: Scribner's, 1913), 154 ff.; Gorham, *Stanton*, 442–44. Stanton stayed in the building for several weeks; afterward, he went home late at night.

15. Moore Diary, Feb. 22, 1868, Johnson Papers; *Impeachment Trial*, I, 210, 220–21, 429. Stanton again refused to yield to Thomas on Feb. 24. Gorham, *Stanton*, 443.

16. Moore, "Notes of Col. W. G. Moore," 121; Moore Diary, Feb. 22, 1868, Johnson Papers; *Impeachment Trial*, I, 428; Welles, *Diary*, III, 286; Thomas and Hyman, *Stanton*, 589–90; McPherson, *Reconstruction*, 289–91.

17. Moore Diary, Feb. 22, 1868, Johnson Papers.

18. Chicago *Tribune*, Feb. 23, 1868; Clemenceau, *American Reconstruction*, 152.

19. Gaillard Hunt, "The President's Defense," 429; Milan Donan to Johnson, Feb. 22, 1868; M. H. Beaumont to Johnson, Feb. 23, 1868; William Lordan et al. to Johnson, Feb. 21, 1868; Daniel Crowley to Johnson, Feb. 24, 1868, Moore Diary, Feb. 22, 1868, Johnson Papers. On Feb. 24, Johnson sent a reply to the Senate censure, again insisting that he was within his rights as the Tenure of Office Act did not cover Stanton. Richardson, ed., *Messages and Papers of the Presidents*, IX, 3820–25, dated Feb. 22, 1868; Moore, "Notes of Col. W. G. Moore," 122.

20. Moore Diary, Feb. 22, 1868, Johnson Papers; Bigelow MS Diary, Feb. 23, 1868, Bigelow Papers; *Congressional Globe*, 40 Cong., 2 Sess., 1330, 1331 ff. 1400–1402; McPherson, *Reconstruction*, 266; Samuel S. Cox, *Three Decades of Federal Legislation, 1855 to 1885* (Providence: J. A. & R. A. Reid, 1885), 585; DeWitt, *Impeachment and Trial of Andrew Johnson*, 358–74; Chicago *Tribune*, Feb. 25, 1868.

21. Chicago *Tribune*, Feb. 25, 1868; New York *Herald*, Feb. 26, 1868; Moore Diary, Feb. 26, 1868, Johnson Papers.

22. Chicago *Tribune*, Feb. 25, 27, 29, March 1, 1868; *Congressional Globe*, 40 Cong., 2 Sess., 1542–67; 1604 ff.

23. *Harper's Weekly*, 12 (March 14, 1868), 161–64; Julian, *Political Recollections*, 313.

24. Stevens to Butler, Feb. 28, 1868, Butler Papers; Trefousse, *Butler*, 194–95.

25. *Congressional Globe*, 40 Cong., 2 Sess., 1604 ff., 1640 ff., 1618–19; Fragment of "Journal of the proceedings of the Honorable Managers of the House of Representatives in the matter of the impeachment of Andrew Johnson . . . March 3, 1868," Butler Papers; New York *Tribune*, March 5, 1868.

26. *Impeachment Trial*, I, 210, 221; Benedict, *Impeachment and Trial of Andrew Johnson*, 102 ff.

27. Chicago *Tribune*, Dec. 8, 1867.

28. Washington *Triweekly National Intelligencer*, Jan. 14, 1868; Clemenceau, *American Reconstruction*, 139–40. On Jan. 13, Senator George F. Edmunds of Vermont introduced a resolution instructing the Judiciary Committee to examine the expediency of establishing rules for an impeachment trial.

29. DeWitt, *Impeachment and Trial of Andrew Johnson, passim*. McKitrick describes it as "a great act of ill-directed passion . . . an immense balloon filled with foul air, the most noisome elements of which were those most active." McKitrick, *Andrew Johnson and Reconstruction*, 506.

30. Avery Craven, *Reconstruction: The Ending of the Civil War* (New York: Holt, 1969), 213; Bowers, *Tragic Era*, 116–17; Patrick, *Reconstructing the Nation*, 131; Brock, *An American Crisis*, 260; Lomask, *Andrew Johnson*, 235 ff. Hodding Carter called it a "political lynching." Hodding Carter, *The Angry Scar: The Story of Reconstruction* (Garden City, N.Y.: Doubleday, 1959), 136; Benedict, *Impeachment and Trial of Andrew Johnson*, 172 ff.; Michael Les Benedict, "A New Look at the Impeachment of Andrew Johnson," *Political Science Quarterly*, 88 (Sept. 1973), 357–58; Hyman, *A More Perfect Union*, 502 ff.

31. David Donald has stressed this point in his articles, "Why They Impeached Andrew Johnson," *American Heritage*, 8 (Dec. 1956), 20–26, 102–103. He writes: "Joining with the northern Copperheads, the Southerners could easily regain at the next presidential election all that had been lost on the battlefield. It was this political exigency . . . which united Republicans in opposition to the President." See Martin E. Mantell, *Johnson, Grant, and the Politics of Reconstruction* (New York: Columbia Univ. Press, 1973), 4. For contemporary evidence, see Colfax to K. G. Shyrock, March 7, 1868, Schuyler Colfax Papers, Chicago Historical Society; C. P. Markle to Covode, Feb. 27, 1868, John Covode Papers, LC; T. H. Duval to Holt, March 8, 1868, Holt Papers; James Brisbin to Stanton, March 20, 1868, Stanton Papers; Washington *Triweekly National Intelligencer*, Feb. 25, 1868; *Independent*, March 5, 1868; Chicago *Tribune*, March 5, 1868; Welles, *Diary*, III, 314.

32. A. T. Maupin to Willey, July 8, 1867, Waitman T. Willey Papers, Univ. of West Virginia; C. W. Clarke to Covode, Aug. 31, 1867, Covode Papers, LC.

33. W. H. Gibbs to Washburne, Sept. 30, 1867; W. H. Gibbs to Washburne, Jan. 18, 29, Feb. 3, 21, 1868; F. W. Kellogg to Washburne, Jan. 9, 1868; D.

Richards to Washburne, Jan. 13, Feb. 2, 1868; George Ely to Washburne, Feb. 8, 1868, Washburne Papers.

34. S. Horton to Henry Edwards, Jan. 1, 1868, Sumner Papers.

35. C. H. Hopkins to Stevens, Jan. 3, 1868, Stevens Papers.

36. J. L. Dunning to Sumner, Dec. 29, 1867, Sumner Papers.

37. Pierpoint to Willey, Sept. 11, 1867, Willey Papers.

38. Cincinnati *Gazette*, Feb. 11, 1868; L. S. Berry et al. to Stevens, Feb. 14, 1868, Stevens Papers; George Ely to Yates, Feb. 12, 1868, Richard Yates Papers, Illinois State Historical Library; William A. Dunning, *Reconstruction: Political and Economic, 1865–1877* (New York: Harper, 1907), 118.

39. Welles, *Diary*, III, 277–78; Glenn Tucker, *Hancock the Superb* (Indianapolis: Bobbs-Merrill, 1960), 286. Grant countermanded the order. Rawlins to Hancock, Feb. 21, 1868, Johnson Papers.

40. D. Richards to Washburne, Feb. 2, 11, 1868, Washburne Papers; W. P. Dockray to Sumner, Feb. 22, 1868, Sumner Papers; Davis, *Civil War and Reconstruction in Florida*, 509–11; Ross, *History of the Impeachment*, 49.

41. A. E. Burr to Welles, Feb. 7, April 1, 1868, Welles Papers, NYPL; Chandler to Washburne, Feb. 12, 1868, Washburne Papers; W. E. Chandler to Weed, Feb. 27, 1868, Weed Papers.

42. L. W. Hall to Garfield, Jan. 4, 1868, Garfield Papers, LC; Trefousse, *Radical Republicans*, 379–80.

43. Donald, "Why They Impeached Johnson," 20–26, 102–103; DeWitt Linn to Kate Linn, March 1, 1868, Henry W. Sage Papers, Cornell Univ.; New York *World*, Feb. 25, 1868; Rep. C. A. Newcomb of Missouri said in the House (Feb. 22, 1868): "If the people faltered in the last elections . . . it was because Congress had faltered and failed to do its duty the previous spring, and they intended to rebuke their unworthy Representatives." *Congressional Globe*, 40 Cong., 2 Sess., App., 189; John B. Henderson, "Emancipation and Impeachment," *Century Magazine*, 85 (Dec. 1912), 202.

44. Oglesby to Colfax, Feb. 22, 1868, Richard Oglesby Papers, Illinois State Historical Library; New York *Herald*, Feb. 26, 1868; J. H. Rhodes to Garfield, Feb. 28, 1868, Garfield Papers, LC; James Fishback to Logan, Feb. 23, 1868, John A. Logan Papers, LC; E. R. Tinker to Dawes, March 2, 1868, Dawes Papers; W. Dennison to Sherman, March 2, 1868, Sherman Papers.

45. J. M. Hagans to Willey, Feb. 21, 1868, Willey Papers.

46. Welles, *Diary*, III, 295–96.

47. L. W. Hall to Garfield, Jan. 4, 1868; J. H. Rhodes to Garfield, Feb. 28, 1868, Garfield Papers, LC.

48. Blaine, *Twenty Years of Congress*, II, 358; Sherman, *John Sherman's Recollections of Forty Years*, I, 422–23.

49. Shelby M. Cullom, *Fifty Years of Public Service* (Chicago: McClurg, 1911), 154.

50. Medill to Logan, March 5, 1868, Logan Papers.

51. Moore, "Notes of Col. W. G. Moore," 122; Browning, *Diary*, II, 182–83; French MS Diary, Feb. 22, 23, 25, March 1, 1868; S. P. Lee to Col. J. G. Gantt, Feb. 24, 1868, Letterbooks, Blair-Lee Papers.

52. Chicago *Tribune*, Feb. 23, 1868.
53. Moore Diary, Feb. 24, 1868, Johnson Papers.

X: THE PRESIDENT'S TRIAL

1. Richmond *Enquirer*, Jan. 22, Feb. 27, 1868; Chicago *Tribune*, Feb. 23, 1868.
2. In 1926 the Supreme Court seemed to uphold the President's contention. (*Myers* v. *United States*, 272 U.S. 52); Berger, *Impeachment*, 280. In 1935, in *Humphrey's Executor* v. *United States*, 295 U.S. 602, it modified that opinion in the case of independent commissions. See James G. Randall and David Donald, *The Civil War and Reconstruction* (2nd ed. rev., Lexington, Mass.: Heath, 1969), 616–17.
3. *Impeachment Trial*, I, 694; III, 196 ff.; I, 381 ff.
4. *Ibid.*, III, 48, 77, 93, 142.
5. *Harper's Weekly*, 12 (March 21, 1868), 179.
6. Medill to Logan, March 5, 1868, Logan Papers; Chicago *Tribune*, March 5, 1868; *New York Times*, March 4, 1868; Toledo *Daily Commercial*, March 7, 1868.
7. William Goddard to Jenckes, March 5, 1868, Jenckes Papers.
8. Washington *Triweekly National Intelligencer*, Feb. 15, 1868; Greeley to Chandler, Aug. 25, 1868, Zachariah Chandler Papers, LC; William Dennison to Greeley, Jan. 23, 1868, Greeley Papers; *New York Times*, Nov. 8, 1867; L. W. Hall to Garfield, Dec. 28, 1867, Garfield Papers, LC; David Donald, *Charles Sumner and the Rights of Man* (New York: Knopf, 1970), 338–39; John Barr to Butler, March 6, 1868; Butler to Wilson, March 10, 1868, Butler Papers.
9. J. W. Schuckers, *The Life and Public Services of Salmon P. Chase* (New York: Appleton, 1874), 548.
10. T .W. Egan to Johnson, Oct. 7, 1867; J. C. Kennedy to Johnson, Feb. 22, 1868, Johnson Papers.
11. Horace White saw this as early as Aug. 1867. White to Washburne, Aug. 13, 1867, Washburne Papers. See New York *Herald*, May 2, 1868; New York *World*, May 4, 1868.
12. Trefousse, *Wade*, 305–10; Noah Sanborn to Sumner, April 30, 1868, Sumner Papers; Ari Hoogenboom, *Outlawing the Spoils: A History of the Civil Service Reform Movement, 1865–1883* (Urbana: Univ. of Illinois Press, 1961), 31.
13. H. D. Moore to Washburne, Dec. 7, 1867; J. A. Putnam to Washburne, Jan. 29, 1868, Washburne Papers; Emory Washburne to Dawes, Dec. 5, 1867; William Schouler to Dawes, Dec. 12, 1867, Dawes Papers; B. P. Poore to Clapp, January 31, 1868, William Warland Clapp Papers, LC.
14. Washington *Triweekly National Intelligencer*, Feb. 25, 1868.

15. Atkinson to Sumner, Feb. 25, 1868, Sumner Papers; Atkinson to Norton, Feb. 26, 1868, Charles Eliot Norton Papers, Harvard Univ.; Trefousse, "Ben Wade and the Failure of the Impeachment of Johnson," 245.

16. Trefousse, "Ben Wade and the Failure of the Impeachment of Johnson," 249; J. C. Kennedy to Johnson, Feb. 22, 1868, Johnson Papers; Thomas Graham Belden and Marva Robins Belden, *So Fell the Angels* (Boston: Little, Brown, 1956), 185 ff.; William Goddard to Jenckes, March 12, 1868, Jenckes Papers.

17. Chicago *Tribune*, Feb. 23, 1868; Clemenceau, *American Reconstruction*, 52. Some thought that the President was seeking impeachment to become a martyr, or that he deliberately challenged Congress in order to curry favor with the Democrats, whose Executive Committee was then meeting in Washington.

18. Washington *Daily National Intelligencer*, May 5, 1868.

19. Moore Diary, Feb. 28, 1868; R. W. Latham to Johnson, Feb. 28, March 11, 1868; T. W. Egan to Johnson, March 16, 1868, Johnson Papers; McCulloch to Greeley, March 5, 1868, Greeley Papers.

20. Welles, *Diary*, III, 307–308; Browning, *Diary*, II, 183–84; Chester L. Barrows, *William M. Evarts* (Chapel Hill: Univ. of North Carolina Press, 1941), 138 ff.; Blaine, *Twenty Years of Congress*, II, 363–65.

21. Blaine, *Twenty Years of Congress*, II, 365; William Norwood Brigance, "Jeremiah Black and Andrew Johnson," *Mississippi Valley Historical Review*, 19 (Sept. 1932), 205–18; Hunt, "The President's Defense," 430–32; John Niven, *Gideon Welles: Lincoln's Secretary of the Navy* (New York: Oxford Univ. Press, 1973), 562.

22. Welles, *Diary*, III, 311.

23. Moore, "Notes of Col. W. G. Moore," 123, 127, 230; Moore, Long Diary, March 22, 30, April 8, 15, 23, 1868, Johnson Papers; fragment of speech in Butler Papers.

24. Browning, *Diary*, II, 187; B. R. Curtis to George Ticknor, March 26, 1868, in Benjamin R. Curtis, Jr., ed., *A Memoir of Benjamin Robbins Curtis* (Boston: Little, Brown, 1879), I, 415–16. For the approach to the moderates, see below, 157ff.

25. Benjamin F. Butler, *Butler's Book* (Boston: A. M. Thayer, 1892), 529; New York *Tribune*, March 5, 6, 14, 24, 1868; Richmond *Enquirer*, March 31, 1868; Crook, *Through Five Administrations*, 125; Lomask, *Andrew Johnson*, 285 ff.

26. *Impeachment Trial*, I, 5; *Harper's Weekly*, 12 (March 14, 1868), 161–64.

27. *Impeachment Trial*, I, 6–10, 11–16; III, 361–401; *Congressional Globe*, 40 Cong., 2 Sess., 1568–1603, 1486–87, 1516–35.

28. George S. Boutwell, *Reminiscences of Sixty Years in Public Affairs* (New York: McClure, Phillips, 1902), II, 119–21; Butler, *Butler's Book*, 927–30.

29. *Impeachment Trial*, I, 16; the summons, dated March 7, 1868, is in the Johnson Papers.

30. Chicago *Tribune*, March 14, 1868; Boston *Daily Advertiser*, April 8, 1868, describing Butler's appearance at a different occasion; *Impeachment Trial*, I, 17–34.

31. *Impeachment Trial*, I, 34–83.

32. *Ibid.*, 87–147; *New York Times*, March 31, 1868; Trefousse, *Butler*, 196–98.

33. *Impeachment Trial*, I, 157–377; Chicago *Tribune*, April 2, 3, 1868; Richmond *Enquirer* quoting Baltimore *Sun*, April 4, 1868.

34. *Impeachment Trial*, I, 377–414; Butler, *Butler's Book*, 930.

35. *Impeachment Trial*, I, 460 ff., 481 ff., 498 ff., 517–31; 663 ff., 674 ff., 693 ff., 700–704.

36. *Ibid.*, 532–33, 628–31, 632–717.

37. E. Merton Coulter, *William G. Brownlow: Fighting Parson of the Southern Highlands* (Chapel Hill: Univ. of North Carolina Press, 1937; rpt. Knoxville: Univ. of Tennessee Press, 1971), 350.

38. Thomas Ewing to Hugh Ewing, Feb. 26, 1868, Ewing Papers; Hahn to Warmoth, April 20, 1868, Henry Clay Warmoth Papers, Univ. of North Carolina.

39. Julian to Mrs. Julian, Feb. 29, 1868, Julian Papers; Colfax to Oglesby, March 20, 1868, Oglesby Papers; Schafer, ed., *Intimate Letters of Carl Schurz*, 531; Medill to Sherman, March 9, 1868, Sherman Papers.

40. New York *Herald*, March 11, April 3, 1868; Richmond *Daily Whig*, March 10, 1868; French MS Diary, Feb. 27, March 15, 1868.

41. Welles, *Diary*, III, 324; Hay to Bigelow, Feb. 27, 1868, John Hay Papers, Brown Univ.

42. Cincinnati *Daily Gazette*, March 3, 6, 11, 13, 18, 1868; New York *Herald*, Feb. 25, 1868; Alexander K. McClure, *Recollections of Half a Century* (Salem, Mass.: Salem Press, 1902), 67; Trefousse, *Wade*, 294–95, 299–300.

43. Hooper to Sumner, Feb. 24, 1868, Sumner Papers.

44. Welles, *Diary*, III, 292–93; Charles Rice to Dawes, March 6, 1868, Dawes Papers.

45. T. W. Egan to Johnson, March 16, 1868, Johnson Papers; Barrows, *Evarts*, 157. Evarts politely replied that he, too, would like to change sides.

46. *Independent*, March 26, April 2, 1868; Chicago *Tribune*, April 9, 15, May 6, 7, 11, 1868; Moore, "Notes of Col. W. G. Moore," 127; Moore, Long Diary, March 21, April 24, 1868, Johnson Papers; Curtis to Evarts, May 4, 1868, William M. Evarts Papers, LC. Counsel had been optimistic from the beginning.

47. French MS Diary, Feb. 27, 1868; Thomas, *The First President Johnson*, 581.

48. Cowan, *Andrew Johnson*, 11–12; Moore, Long Diary, March 27, 1868, Johnson Papers; Browning, *Diary*, II, 187.

49. New York *Herald*, April 18, 1868; William Salter, *The Life of James W. Grimes* (New York: Appleton, 1876), 268 ff.; New York *Tribune*, May 1, 1868; Grimes to Atkinson, Sept. 4, 15, 1867, Atkinson Papers; Edmunds, "Ex-Senator Edmunds on Reconstruction and Impeachment," 862–63.

50. Fox MS Diary, April 5, 1868, Fox Papers; Welles, *Diary*, III, 338–39.
51. Flower, *Stanton*, 342. Additional contacts between the President and Grimes are mentioned in Cox, *Three Decades of Federal Legislation*, 392–94.
52. Schofield's Memorandum, May 1868, Box 82, Schofield Papers; Moore, Long Diary, April 23, 1868, Johnson Papers.
53. Schofield's Memorandum, May 1868, Box 82, Schofield Papers; Browning, *Diary*, II, 195; Welles, *Diary*, III, 347; Washington *Triweekly National Intelligencer*, Jan. 16, 1868. Ross refused to vote for Stanton's reinstatment, allegedly because of a personal quarrel with the secretary.
54. *Congressional Globe*, 40 Cong., 2 Sess., 1331 ff., 1340 ff., 1391 ff., 1360 ff., 1382 ff., 1399 ff., App. 191, 196 ff., 206–208; Richmond *Enquirer*, Feb. 24, 1868; *Independent*, March 5, 1868; Chicago *Tribune*, March 5, 1868; New York *Herald*, April 25, 1868.
55. W. R. Moore to Washburne, Feb. 29, 1868, Washburne Papers.
56. T. H. Duval to Holt, March 8, 1868, Holt Papers; F. G. Bromberg to Sumner, March 5, 1868, Sumner Papers.
57. Pierpoint to Willey, March 6, 1868, J. O. Addison to Willey, April 10, 1868, Willey Papers; J. T. Simpson to Sumner, April 15, 1868, Sumner Papers; L. A. Sheldon to Garfield, April 22, 1868, Garfield Papers, LC.
58. Brisbin to Stanton, March 20, 1868, Stanton Papers.
59. T. A. Hamilton to Sumner, March 23, 1868, Sumner Papers.
60. W. H. Gibbs to Washburne, April 11, 1868, Washburne Papers.
61. A. B. Schuyler to Willey, April 21, 1868, Willey Papers.
62. G. Horton to Sumner, April 23, 1868, Sumner Papers; D. Richards to Washburne, May 6, 1868, Washburne Papers; Washington *Daily Morning Chronicle*, April 19, 22, 1868; Toledo *Blade*, May 1, 1868; *National Anti-Slavery Standard*, May 9, 1868.
63. Poore to Clapp, March 6, 1868, Clapp Papers; A. E. Burr to Welles, Feb. 7, 1868, Welles Papers, NYPL; *Independent*, March 19, 1868; Cincinnati *Gazette*, April 11, 1868; Gillette, *The Right to Vote*, 26.
64. *Independent*, March 5, 1868; *Congressional Globe*, 40 Cong., 2 Sess., 1807, 1808, 1847, 1859 ff., 1881 ff., 1883, 2128, 2165–70; Kutler, *Judicial Power and Reconstruction Politics*, 100 ff.
65. McPherson, *Reconstruction*, 336–37; Patrick, *Reconstruction of the Nation*, 114. Professor Kutler has shown that the older interpretation of a supine court is not warranted. Kutler, *Judicial Power and Reconstruction Policies*, 100–108.
66. A. H. Garland to Johnson, March 15, 1868, Johnson Papers.
67. E. M. L'Engle to Mrs. Plane, March 5, 1868, Edward M. L'Engle Papers, Univ. of North Carolina; William B. Reed to Robert Ould, April 2, 1868, Isaac Howell Carrington Papers, Duke Univ.
68. *Impeachment Trial*, II, 14–249; Clemenceau, *American Reconstruction*, 176–78; Chicago *Tribune*, April 21, 1868; *Independent*, April 30, 1868. Upset by the length of the trial, on April 17 Charles Sumner suggested that the court sit daily from morning to night. His proposition was rejected, but a motion to meet at 11 A.M. was adopted. It was rescinded five days later when

the starting time was fixed at noon. *Impeachment Trial*, I, 632–33; II, 141.

69. *Impeachment Trial*, II, 249–469.

70. Chicago *Tribune*, May 7, 9, 1868; *New York Times*, May 9, 1868. Earlier in the trial the question of Wade's eligibility for the presidency had been debated in the newspapers. His opponents alleged that the Constitution provided for Congress to declare what "officer" should act as President in the absence of a Vice President, and they maintained that no senator was an "officer" within the meaning of the term. Washington *Daily National Intelligencer*, April 2, 24, 1868.

71. *New York Times*, May 6, 1868.

72. John R. Young to Stanton, May 6, 1868, Stanton Papers; John C. Hamilton to Chandler, May 6, 1868, Zachariah Chandler Papers, LC; Julian to Mrs. Julian, May 11, 1868, Julian Papers; Chicago *Tribune*, May 11, 1868.

73. *Impeachment Trial*, II, 482–84; New York *Tribune*, May 13, 1868; French MS Diary, May 14, 1868.

74. Browning, *Diary*, II, 196–97; Welles, *Diary*, III, 349, 350, 352–53; Bigelow to Hay, May 15, 1868, Hay Papers; French MS Diary, May 11, 1868.

XI: FAILURE OF THE IMPEACHMENT

1. *New York Times*, May 17, 1868; New York *Tribune*, May 18, 1868; New York *World*, May 17, 1868; French MS Diary, May 16, 1868. In a caucus on May 15 at Senator Pomeroy's rooms, the conferees agreed that Article XI stood the best chance for conviction. Welles, *Diary*, III, 357.

2. *Impeachment Trial*, II, 484–89; *New York Times*, May 17, 1868; New York *Tribune*, May 18, 1868; William H. Crook, *Memories of the White House*, ed. Henry Rood (Boston: Little, Brown, 1911), 16; Crook, *Through Five Administrations*, 133.

3. Rhodes, *History of the United States*, VI, 156; Lomask, *Andrew Johnson*, 332–35; Stryker, *Johnson*, 723, 732–34; Carter, *The Angry Scar*, 143; John F. Kennedy, *Profiles in Courage* (New York: Pocket Books, 1957), 107–28; Edward Bumgardner, *The Life of Edmund G. Ross* (Kansas City: Fielding-Turner, 1949), 71; Washington *Daily National Intelligencer*, May 18, 1868; Trefousse, *Wade*, 304.

4. Ralph J. Roske, "The Seven Martyrs?" *American Historical Review*, 64 (Jan. 1959), 323–30.

5. Colfax to J. R. Young, April 16, 1868, John Russell Young Papers, LC; Ottawa *Western Home Journal*, April 30, 1868, Edmund G. Ross Papers, Kansas State Historical Society; *New York Times*, May 17, 1868; Joseph Fowler, undated MS in Joseph S. Fowler Papers, Univ. of North Carolina, 18 [hereafter cited as Fowler MS]; New York *Tribune*, May 16, 18, 1868; Clemenceau, *American Reconstruction*, 180; Cameron to Young, May 13, 1868, Young Papers; Evert F. Whitner, "Peter Godwin Van Winkle," M.A. thesis, Univ. of West Virginia, 1946, p. 36; Ross to Johnson, June 6, 1868, Johnson Papers; Jellison, *Fessenden*, 153–55. On May 15, Ross attended a meeting of the

"recusants" at Trumbull's house, but his exact intentions were not known to the radicals. Fowler MS, 18, Fowler Papers; Theodore Tilton to Butler, April 7, 1886, Butler Papers.

6. Trefousse, *Wade*, 302–304.

7. A. N. Cole to Morgan, April 18, 1868, Morgan Papers; W. S. King to Washburne, May 12, 1868, Washburne Papers; Forney to Sumner, May 13, 1868, Sumner Papers; G. H. Halsey to Ward, May 14, 1868, Ward Papers; S. P. Lee to Mr. and Mrs. Blair, May 12, 1868, Letterbooks, Blair-Lee Papers; Chicago *Tribune*, May 7, 9, 10, 12, 13, 1868; New York *Tribune*, May 16, 1868; *New York Times*, May 12, 13, 1868.

8. Cincinnati *Daily Gazette*, May 12, 1868; Ross, *History of the Impeachment*, 129.

9. White to Fessenden, May 10, 1868, Charles F. Heartman Collection, New York Historical Society.

10. Chicago *Tribune*, May 11, 1868. According to Trumbull's most recent biographer, this fact made things easier for the senator from Illinois. Mark M. Krug, *Lyman Trumbull: Conservative Radical* (New York: A. S. Barnes, 1965), 268.

11. Colfax to J. R. Young, April 16, 1868, Young Papers; Chicago *Tribune*, May 7, 1868; Francis Fessenden, *Life and Public Services of William Pitt Fessenden* . . . (Boston: Houghton Mifflin, 1907), II, 165; DeWitt, *Impeachment and Trial of Andrew Johnson*, 548–49; Ross, *History of the Impeachment*, 143.

12. Chicago *Tribune*, May 18, 1868; William S. Hawley to Tilden, May 22, 1868, Samuel J. Tilden Papers, NYPL.

13. Benjamin C. Truman, "Anecdotes of Andrew Johnson," *Century Magazine*, 85 (Jan. 1913), 435–40, esp. 438.

14. Henderson, "Emancipation and Impeachment," 207; James A. Rawley, *Edwin D. Morgan* (New York: Columbia Univ. Press, 1955), 228–29.

15. Dunning, *Reconstruction*, 107; R. W. Bayless, "Peter G. Van Winkle and Waitman T. Willey in the Impeachment Trial of Andrew Johnson," *West Virginia History*, 13 (Jan. 1952), 75–80, esp. 80; Horace White, *The Life of Lyman Trumbull* (Boston: Houghton Mifflin, 1913), 321.

16. Dunning, *Reconstruction*, 107; Bigelow MS Diary, Sept. 23, 1868, Bigelow Papers.

17. Crook, *Through Five Administrations*, 133.

18. Butler to J. R. Young, May 16, 1868, Young Papers.

19. Ross, *History of the Impeachment*, 153; "Impeachment Managers' Investigation," *House Report* No. 44, 40 Cong., 2 Sess.

20. Logan to Mrs. Logan, May 26, 1868, Logan Papers; George S. Boutwell, "The Impeachment of Andrew Johnson from the Standpoint of One of the Managers of the Impeachment Trial," *McClure's Magazine*, 14 (Nov. 1899–April 1900), 182.

21. "Impeachment Managers' Investigation," *House Report* No. 44, 40 Cong., 2 Sess.; "Raising Money to Be Used in Impeachment," *House Report* No. 75, 40 Cong., 2 Sess.; Boston *Daily Advertiser*, May 19, 26, 27, July 1, 1868;

Henderson to Managers, May 19, 1868, Butler Papers. The managers lodged Woolley in a room in the basement of the Capitol, from which quarters they first evicted the sculptress Vinnie Ream who had friendly relations with Ross. Lomask, *Andrew Johnson*, 326–27, 333. Stevens later saw to it that the room was restored to her. Bowers, *Tragic Era*, 197, 220. The Senate started an investigation of its own. New York *Tribune*, May 29, 1868.

22. B. G. Brown to Wade, March 26, 1868, Wade Papers; Colfax to Morrill, May 1, 1868, Justin Morrill Papers, LC; W. E. Webster to Sumner, May 22, 1868, Sumner Papers; New York *World*, May 13, 1868; Richmond *Whig*, April 28, May 5, 1868; Blaine, *Twenty Years of Congress*, II, 389–90.

23. Cincinnati *Daily Gazette*, May 19, 22, 1868; *Proceedings of the National Union Republican Convention Held at Chicago, May 20 and 21, 1868* (Chicago, 1868), 118; Bigelow, *Retrospections of an Active Life*, IV, 182.

24. *Wilkes' Spirit of the Times*, May 23, 1868; Ross, *History of the Impeachment*, 148; *Impeachment Trial*, II, 489–96; Chicago *Tribune*, May 27, 1868.

25. *Impeachment Trial*, II, 496–98; *New York Times*, May 27, 1868.

26. *New York Times*, May 27, 1868; Welles, *Diary*, III, 367–68; Browning, *Diary*, II, 199.

27. Townsend, *Anecdotes of the Civil War in the United States*, 132–36; Thomas, *The First President Johnson*, 607.

28. Milton, *Age of Hate*, 625; Roske, "The Seven Martyrs?" 326; McKitrick, *Andrew Johnson and Reconstruction*, 508–509; *National Anti-Slavery Standard*, May 23, 30, 1868; Washington *Daily Morning Chronicle*, May 29, 30, 1868; Chicago *Tribune*, May 20, 1868; Atkinson to Sumner, June 1, 1868, Sumner Papers; Fessenden to Grimes, June 17, 1868, William Pitt Fessenden Papers, Bowdoin College; J. G. Whittier to Greeley, May 16, 1868, Greeley Papers; Clemenceau, *American Reconstruction*, 207–208. The sudden disappearance of all references to impeachment in the private correspondence of most Republicans is remarkable.

29. McPherson, *Reconstruction*, 263; Fessenden to E. F. Warriner, Feb. 21, 1868, Fessenden Papers, Bowdoin College.

30. Fessenden to William Fessenden, May 3, 1868, Fessenden Papers, Bowdoin College.

31. *Impeachment Trial*, III, 16 ff., 29–30, 193–204, 328–34, 294–304; 319–27, 147–50. Henderson stressed the fact that Stanton was still physically in possession of his office. *Ibid.*, 304.

32. Ross, *History of the Impeachment*, 148 ff.

33. Howe to Grace Howe, Feb. 21, 1868; Howe to Rublee, May 28, 1868, Howe Papers.

34. Fowler MS, 16, Fowler Papers; *Impeachment Trial*, III, 304.

35. *Impeachment Trial*, III, 12, 26, 92, 140, 147, 204–205, 305, 316, 327, 334–35. Sherman, Edmunds, Morrill of Vermont, and Patterson of New Hampshire found either all the conspiracy articles or Article IV unsubstantiated by the evidence.

36. *Ibid.*, 26, 93, 150, 304, 327, 335; 15, 26–28, 48, 77, 93, 142, 150, 192, 205,

305, 316, 327, 335; 15, 93, 142, 150, 205–206, 305–306, 317, 327, 338. Edmunds, Sherman, Howard, Howe, Morrill of Vermont, Tipton, and Patterson of New Hampshire would have acquitted the President on Article IX; Edmunds, Sherman, Morrill of Vermont, and Patterson of New Hampshire also on Article X.

37. *Ibid.*, 307 ff.; Schuckers, *Chase*, 68. Some hope was also entertained that Van Winkle might vote for the article. New York *Tribune*, May 13, 1868; W. S. King to Washburne, May 12, 1868, Washburne Papers.

38. Ross, *History of the Impeachment*, 155 ff., esp. 164; *Impeachment Trial*, III, 336, 303–304.

39. *Impeachment Trial*, III, 328.

40. Badeau, *Grant in Peace*, 136.

41. John W. Frazier to Fessenden, March 4, 1868, Heartman Collection; Noah Sanborne to Sumner, April 30, 1868, Sumner Papers; Horace White to Washburne, May 1, 1868, Washburne Papers; New York *Herald*, May 4, 1868; Ashtabula *Sentinel*, April 15, 1868; Washington *Daily National Intelligencer*, May 6, 1868; McCulloch, *Men and Measures of Half a Century*, 400.

42. A. H. Bull to Morgan, March 2, 1868, Morgan Papers; McClure, *Recollections of Half a Century*, 65–66; *New York Times*, May 8, 1868; Edmunds, "Ex-Senator Edmunds on Reconstruction and Impeachment," 862–63; Flower, *Stanton*, 342.

43. New York *Herald*, Feb. 28, March 2, 17, May 6, 1868; New York *World*, April 3, May 4, 1868; Cincinnati *Daily Gazette*, April 14, 16, 1868; Washington *Daily National Intelligencer*, May 1, 9, 1868.

44. Welles, *Diary*, III, 292; A. H. Bull to Morgan, March 2, 1868, Morgan Papers.

45. John W. Frazier to Fessenden, March 4, 1868, Heartman Collection.

46. Atkinson to Sumner, Feb. 25, May 1, 4, 1868; George Walker to Sumner, Feb. 27, 1868 Sumner Papers.

47. New York *Herald*, March 2, 1868.

48. Trefousse, "Ben Wade and the Failure of the Impeachment of Johnson," 244–49; Salter, *Grimes*, 268, 272, 305; *Congressional Globe*, 39 Cong., 2 Sess., 1150; Grimes to Atkinson, Sept. 15, 1867, Atkinson Papers.

49. Fessenden, *Life*, I, 275, 332–34, II, 127; *Congressional Globe*, 39 Cong., 2 Sess., 1150; New York *Tribune*, May 12, 1868.

50. *Congressional Globe*, 37 Cong., 2 Sess., 2170; 38 Cong., 2 Sess., 559–60, 580 ff., 1128, 1012. Both Trumbull and Ross were present when Wade delivered his intemperate speech in Kansas. His remarks probably did not win their approval. Zornow, " 'Bluff Ben' Wade in Lawrence, Kansas: The Issue of Class Conflict," 51.

51. New York *Tribune*, June 13, 1868.

52. New York *Tribune*, May 12, 1868. Because of the widespread uneasiness about Wade, shortly before the crucial vote it was rumored that Henry Wilson had urged him to resign to make Colfax President. In return, Wilson allegedly promised support for Wade's vice presidential ambitions. But no arrangement was ever consummated, and Wade was already giving serious thought to the selection of his cabinet. Chicago *Tribune*, May 7, 1868; Cincin-

nati *Daily Gazette*, May 7, 1868. On the cabinet, see Badeau, *Grant in Peace*, 136–37; Schuckers, *Chase*, 559.

53. Washington *Daily Morning Chronicle*, May 13, 1868; Trefousse, *Wade*, 308; W. E. B. DuBois, *Black Reconstruction in America* (New York: S. A. Russell, 1935), 375.

54. Chase Statement, May 18, 1868, in reply to George Wilkes, Chase Papers, LC; Cincinnati *Daily Gazette*, March 9, April 4, 9, 17, 1868; *Independent*, April 30, 1868; Toledo *Daily Commercial*, March 16, 1868; Chase to Halstead, March 16, 1868, Salmon P. Chase Papers, New York Historical Society; H. O. Wagoner to Washburne, April 2, 1868, Washburne Papers; T. W. Higginson to Sumner, April 7, 1868, Sumner Papers; Smith, *Life and Letters of James Abram Garfield*, I, 426; Schuckers, *Chase*, 560 ff.

55. Schuckers, *Chase*, 577–78; Chase to "My dear friend," April 19, 1868, Chase Papers, Series II, LC; Chase to Greeley, May 25, 1868, Greeley Papers; William Goddard to Jenckes, March 12, 1868, Jenckes Papers; Barney to Chase, May 28, 1868, J. W. Schuckers to Chase, June 3, 1868, Chase Papers, LC; Chase to Barney, May 29, 1868, Chase to John Van Buren, June 25, 1868, Chase Papers, Historical Society of Pennsylvania.

56. E. D. Fogg to Jenckes, March 23, 1868, Jenckes Papers. It is true that Sprague might have changed his vote had it been needed. See 169 above.

57. Chicago *Tribune*, May 26, 1868, quoting a letter from Willey to the Wheeling *Intelligencer*, May 19, 1868. Willey wrote that it was untrue to charge Chase with changing Van Winkle's vote after a personal interview, but that the chief justice's statement in the Senate concerning the form of Article XI (in effect, his explanation of the charge) changed Van Winkle's opinion. For rumors of Chase's influence on others, see *Wilkes' Spirit of the Times*, May 16, 1868.

58. Nevertheless, Chase, who doubted the constitutional competency of the President *pro tem* of the Senate to act as President, had prepared an oath of office which he would have administered on May 16 had Johnson been convicted. "I Benjamin F. Wade, President *pro tempore* of the Senate of the United States," it read, "do solemnly swear that I will, well and faithfully, to the best of my ability act as President of the United States until a President shall have been elected." Memorandum, May 27, 1868, Chase Papers, Historical Society of Pennsylvania.

59. *Harper's Weekly*, 11 (Jan. 26, 1867), 50; Chicago *Tribune*, Jan. 18, July 2, 1867; New York *Herald*, March 2, 1867; Hinsdale, ed., *Garfield-Hinsdale Letters*, 107–108; George Fogg to Washburne, Dec. 10, 1867, Washburne Papers.

60. Protest of the Democrats, March 2, 1868, Johnson Papers.

61. Washington *Triweekly National Intelligencer*, March 17, 1868; New York *Herald*, April 29, 1868; *Impeachment Trial*, II, 270 ff.

62. *Impeachment Trial*, III, 328.

63. *Ibid.*, 338; Ross, *History of the Impeachment*, 135, 169; Chase to Marble, May 30, 1868, Marble Papers; *New York Times*, Jan. 14, 1868; Ed-

mund G. Ross, "Historic Moments: The Impeachment Trial," *Scribner's Magazine*, 11 (Jan.–June 1892), 520; New York *Herald*, April 15, 29, 1868. See also Berger, *Impeachment*, 295.

64. Hinsdale, ed., *Garfield-Hinsdale Letters*, 133–35, 136–37; Toledo *Daily Commercial*, April 25, 1868; B. F. Potts to Sumner, April 30, 1868; Chicago *Tribune*, May 7, 1868; *New York Times*, May 14, 1868; New York *Herald*, March 19, 1868; Schofield Memorandum, May 1868, Schofield Papers; Fessenden to Samuel Fessenden, March 8, 1868; Fessenden to E. F. Warriner, March 21, 1868, Fessenden Papers, Bowdoin College; Medill to Logan, March 5, 1868, Logan Papers; S. L. M. Barlow to Chandler, Feb. 26, 1868, William E. Chandler Papers, LC; A. Campbell to Garfield, March 14, 1868, Garfield Papers, LC.

65. Charles B. Rice to Dawes, March 6, 1868, Dawes Papers, J. M. Barr to W. G. Moore, April 21, 1868, Johnson Papers; Chicago *Tribune*, April 11, 18, May 26, 1868; *New York Times*, March 4, 1868; *Harper's Weekly*, 12 (May 23, 1868) 330; M. A. DeWolfe Howe, *Portrait of an Independent: Moorfield Storey, 1845–1929* (Boston: Houghton Mifflin, 1932), 93, 99; Ross, *History of the Impeachment*, 143; Rhodes, *History of the United States*, VI, 135; Ellis P. Oberholtzer, *History of the United States Since the Civil War* (New York: Macmillan, 1917–37), II, 96 f.; F. E. Hutchins to Garfield, May 16, 1868, Garfield Papers, LC; H. C. Bowditch to Sumner, May 18, 1868, Sumner Papers.

66. C. H. Hill to Garfield, March 17, 1868, Garfield Papers, LC; DeWitt, *Impeachment and Trial of Andrew Johnson*, 483–85; Berger, *Impeachment*, 270–72.

XII: RESULTS OF THE ACQUITTAL

1. George S. Merrill to Banks, May 5, 1868, Nathaniel P. Banks Papers, LC.
2. Howe to Grace Howe, May 27, 1868, Howe Papers.
3. Medill to Washburne, June 16, 1868, Washburne Papers.
4. Richmond *Whig*, April 29, 1868; *New York Times*, May 8, 1868.
5. Toledo *Daily Commercial*, May 18, 1868.
6. Washburne to Dawes, May 17, 1868, Dawes Papers.
7. Blaine, *Twenty Years of Congress*, II, 376.
8. W. R. Fleming to Fowler, June 1, 1868, Fowler Papers.
9. Fessenden, *Life*, II, 232; Henderson, "Emancipation and Impeachment," 196.
10. Sherman, *John Sherman's Recollections of Forty Years*, I, 432. Sherman wrote that he felt bound to vote guilty, "but was entirely satisfied with the result of the vote, brought about by the action of several Republican Senators." See M. C. Verplanck to Caverly, May 1868, Gulian Verplanck Papers, New York Historical Society.
11. Fox to Welles, May 24, 1868, Welles Papers, LC.

12. John Jay to Morgan, May 25, 1868, Morgan Papers.

13. Wilson, *History of the Rise and Fall of the Slave Power*, III, 733. See also Note 28, Ch. XI, above.

14. McPherson, *Reconstruction*, 337 ff.; Randall and Donald, *Civil War and Reconstruction*, 618–22, 634–35.

15. Richardson, ed., *Messages and Papers of the Presidents*, VIII, 3846–49.

16. *Ibid.*, 3853, 3906, 3870.

17. S. J. Anderson to Johnson, March 31, 1868; J. B. Bingham to Johnson, May 23, 1868, Johnson Papers; W. H. H. to Marble, n.d., Marble Papers; Welles, *Diary*, III, 319.

18. McPherson, *Reconstruction*, 367–68.

19. *Harper's Weekly*, 12 (Aug. 8, 1868), 498–99; *Congressional Globe*, 40 Cong., 2 Sess., 4518, 4500. Both Houses met in September, October, and November, only to adjourn immediately. *Ibid.*, 4518 ff.

20. G. G. Glavis to Johnson, May 21, 1868, Johnson Papers; Welles, *Diary*, II, 390.

21. Welles, *Diary*, III, 388, 391; Clemenceau, *American Reconstruction*, 207–208, 224–25; New York *Herald*, July 24, 28, 1868; *Independent*, July 30, Aug. 6, 1868.

22. Trefousse, *Butler*, 208.

23. DeWitt, *Impeachment and Trial of Andrew Johnson*, 578–79; Berger, *Impeachment*, 295; Benedict, *Impeachment and Trial of Andrew Johnson*, 180.

24. Brant, *Impeachment*, 155 ff.; Cortez A. Ewing, "Two Reconstruction Impeachments," *North Carolina Historical Review*, 15 (July 1938), 204–30; Ewing, "Florida Reconstruction Impeachments," *Florida Historical Quarterly*, 36 (April 1958), 299–318; Blanche Butler Ames, ed., *Chronicles from the Nineteenth Century: Family Letters of Blanche Butler and Adelbert Ames* (Clinton, Mass.: Colonial Press, 1957), II, 285 ff.

25. Henry S. Sandford to Weed, May 17, 1868, Weed Papers; Schurz, *Reminiscences*, III, 281–82.

26. McPherson, *Reconstruction*, 364; Hans L. Trefousse, "The Acquittal of Andrew Johnson and the Decline of the Radicals," *Civil War History*, 14 (June 1968), 148–61.

27. *Nation*, 6 (May 28, 1868), 421; Stevens to C. S. Spence, June 24, 1868 (draft), Stevens Papers.

28. *Independent*, June 18, July 16, 1868.

29. Charles H. Coleman, *The Election of 1868: The Democratic Effort to Regain Control* (New York: Columbia Univ. Press, 1933), 375; Roske, "The Seven Martyrs?" 326.

30. *Independent*, May 21, 1868.

31. Grant appointed him to the Supreme Court, but he died before he could serve. Henry Dawes, "Recollections of Stanton under Johnson," *American Mercury*, 84 (Dec. 1894), 503–505; Thomas and Hyman, *Stanton*, 634 ff.

32. Margaret Ashley (Paddock), "An Ohio Congressman in Reconstruction," 65.

33. Johnson to J. W. Nesmith, June 30, 1868; Johnson to W. Davidson, June 8, 1868, Johnson Papers; Richmond *Daily Whig*, June 11, 1868; Welles, *Diary*, III, 375; James H. Whyte, *The Uncivil War: Washington during the Reconstruction, 1865–1878* (New York: Twayne, 1958), 66–67.

34. Richmond *Daily Whig*, May 28, 1868; Joshua Nye to Fessenden, May 20, 1868, William Pitt Fessenden Papers, Duke Univ.; A. L. Hill to Willey, May 29, 1868, Willey Papers.

35. A. H. Garland to Johnson, May 27, 1868, Johnson Papers.

36. B. F. Perry to Johnson, May 20, 1868; R. King Cutler to Johnson, May 25, 1868, Johnson Papers.

37. W. B. Miller to Johnson, May 28, 1868; I. H. Harris to Johnson, June 1, 1868; A. A. Kyle to Johnson, May 29, 1868; J. B. Bingham to Johnson, May 23, 1868, Johnson Papers.

38. Richards to Washburne, May 18, 1868, Washburne Papers.

39. D. T. Corbin to Morrill, May 29, 1868, Morrill Papers.

40. J. H. Feriter to Sumner, June 6, 1868, Sumner Papers.

41. Edwin Belcher to Sumner, June 23, 1868, Sumner Papers; J. Mc-Whorter to J. J. Knox, June 7, 1868; Archives of Bureau of Refugees and Freedmen, Georgia, Letters Received 1867–1868, Box No. 5, NA.

42. George E. Spencer to Washburne, May 23, 1868, Washburne Papers.

43. Alcorn to Washburne, June 29, 1868, Washburne Papers.

44. T. W. Duval to Holt, July 23, 1868, Holt Papers.

45. S. B. Packard to Grant, May 14, 1868; R. King Cutler to Johnson, May 27, 1868, Johnson Papers.

46. Tourgée to Mrs. Tourgée, May 17, 1868, Albion Winegar Tourgée Papers, Chautauqua County Historical Society; A. L. Hill to Willey, May 29, 1868, Willey Papers.

47. Trefousse, *Radical Republicans*, 410, 413–14.

48. Mantell, *Johnson, Grant, and the Politics of Reconstruction*, 4.

49. *Impeachment Trial*, III, 281.

50. Stryker, *Johnson*, 830 ff.

51. Doolittle to Johnson, Jan. 26, 1875, Johnson Papers.

52. Mobile *Daily Register*, Aug. 1, 1875; New Orleans *Daily Picayune*, Aug. 1, 1875.

Bibliography

MANUSCRIPT COLLECTIONS

John A. Andrew Papers, Massachusetts Historical Society, Boston.
Edward Atkinson Papers, Massachusetts Historical Society.
Nathaniel P. Banks Papers, Library of Congress, Washington, D.C.
S. L. M. Barlow Papers, Huntington Library, San Marino, Calif.
John Bigelow Papers and MS Diary, New York Public Library.
John A. Bingham Papers, Ohio Historical Society, Columbus.
Jeremiah S. Black Papers, Library of Congress.
James G. Blaine Papers, Library of Congress.
Blair-Lee Family Papers, Princeton University.
Robert Bonner Papers, New York Public Library.
Bryant-Godwin Collection, New York Public Library.
Bureau of Refugees and Freedmen, Selected Series of Records, National
   Archives, Washington, D.C.
Bureau of Refugees and Freedmen, Georgia, Letters Received, National
   Archives.
Benjamin F. Butler Papers, Library of Congress.
Isaac Howell Carrington Papers, Duke University.
William E. Chandler Papers, Library of Congress.
Zachariah Chandler Papers, Burton Collection, Detroit Public Library.
Zachariah Chandler Papers, Library of Congress.
Salmon P. Chase Papers, Historical Society of Pennsylvania, Philadelphia.
Salmon P. Chase Papers, Library of Congress.
Salmon P. Chase Papers, New York Historical Society, New York.
William Warland Clapp Papers, Library of Congress.
William J. Clarke Papers, University of North Carolina.
Schuyler Colfax Papers, Chicago Historical Society.
Schuyler Colfax Papers, University of Rochester.
John Covode Papers, Historical Society of Western Pennsylvania, Pittsburgh.
John Covode Papers, Library of Congress.
Samuel S. Cox Papers, Brown University.
Henry L. Dawes Papers, Library of Congress.
Matthew P. Deady Papers, Oregon Historical Society, Portland.
James R. Doolittle Papers, Wisconsin Historical Society, Madison.
Samuel F. DuPont Papers, Winterthur Collection, Eleutherian Mills Histori-
   cal Library, Greenville, Del.
William Evarts Papers, Library of Congress.

232

Thomas Ewing Papers, Library of Congress.
William Pitt Fessenden Papers, Bowdoin College.
William Pitt Fessenden Papers, Duke University.
William Pitt Fessenden Papers, Library of Congress.
Joseph S. Fowler Papers, University of North Carolina.
Gustavus V. Fox Papers, New York Historical Society.
Benjamin Brown French Papers and MS Diary, Library of Congress.
James A. Garfield Papers, Library of Congress.
James A. Garfield Papers, Ohio Historical Society.
U. S. Grant Papers, Library of Congress.
Horace Greeley Papers, New York Public Library.
James R. Hawley Papers, Library of Congress.
John Hay Papers, Brown University.
Charles F. Heartman Collection, New York Historical Society.
Joseph Holt Papers, Library of Congress.
Jacob Howard Papers, Burton Collection, Detroit Public Library.
Timothy O. Howe Papers, Wisconsin Historical Society.
Thomas A. Jenckes Papers, Library of Congress.
Andrew Johnson Papers, Library of Congress.
Reverdy Johnson Papers, Maryland Historical Society, Baltimore.
George W. Julian Papers, Indiana Historical Society, Indianapolis.
Edward M. L'Engle Papers, University of North Carolina.
John A. Logan Papers, Library of Congress.
Hugh McCulloch Papers, Library of Congress.
Edward McPherson Papers, Library of Congress.
Manton Marble Papers, Library of Congress.
William G. Moore Short and Long Diaries, Johnson Papers, Library of Congress.
Edwin D. Morgan Papers, New York State Library, Albany.
Justin Morrill Papers, Library of Congress.
T. A. R. Nelson Papers, Lawson McGhee Library, Knoxville, Tenn.
Charles Eliot Norton Papers, Harvard University.
Richard Oglesby Papers, Illinois State Historical Library, Springfield.
Edmund G. Ross Papers, Kansas State Historical Society, Topeka.
Henry W. Sage Papers, Cornell University.
John M. Schofield Papers, Library of Congress.
Carl Schurz Papers, Library of Congress.
R. K. Scott Papers, Ohio Historical Society.
William H. Seward Papers, University of Rochester.
Philip H. Sheridan Papers, Library of Congress.
John Sherman Papers, Library of Congress.
William Sprague Papers, Columbia University.
Edwin M. Stanton Papers, Library of Congress.
Alexander H. Stephens Papers, Library of Congress.
Thaddeus Stevens Papers, Library of Congress.
John D. Strong Papers, Illinois State Historical Library.
Charles Sumner Papers, Harvard University.

Samuel J. Tilden Papers, New York Public Library.
Albion Winegar Tourgée Papers, Chautauqua County Historical Society, Westfield, N.Y.
Lyman Trumbull Papers, Illinois State Historical Library.
Lyman Trumbull Papers, Library of Congress.
John C. Underwood Papers, Library of Congress.
Gulian Verplanck Papers, New York Historical Society.
Benjamin F. Wade Papers, Library of Congress.
Marcus Ward Papers, New Jersey Historical Society, Newark.
Henry Clay Warmoth Papers, University of North Carolina.
Elihu B. Washburne Papers, Library of Congress.
Thurlow Weed Papers, University of Rochester.
Gideon Welles Papers, Library of Congress.
Gideon Welles Papers, New York Public Library.
Waitman T. Willey Papers, University of West Virginia.
Richard Yates Papers, Illinois State Historical Library.
John Russell Young Papers, Library of Congress.

GOVERNMENT DOCUMENTS

Congressional Globe.
"Assassination of Abraham Lincoln," *House Reports,* 39 Cong., 1 Sess., no. 104.
"Impeachment of the President," House of Representatives, *Rep. Com.* 7, 40 Cong., 1 Sess.
"Impeachment Managers' Investigation," *House Reports,* 40 Cong., 2 Sess., no. 7.
"Memphis Riot and Massacres," *House Reports,* 39 Cong., 1 Sess., no. 101.
"New Orleans Riots," *House Reports,* 39 Cong., 2 Sess., no. 16.
"Raising Money to be Used in Impeachment," *House Reports,* 40 Cong., 2 Sess., no. 75.
Trial of Andrew Johnson, President of the United States, Before the Senate of the United States, on Impeachment by the House of Representatives for High Crimes and Misdemeanors, Washington: Government Printing Office, 1868.
U.S., *Statutes at Large*

NEWSPAPERS AND PERIODICALS

Ashtabula *Sentinel.*
Boston *Commonwealth.*
Boston *Daily Advertiser.*
Chicago *Tribune.*
Cincinnati *Daily Gazette.*
Harper's Monthly.

Harper's Weekly.
The Independent.
Mobile *Daily Register.*
The Nation.
National Anti-Slavery Standard.
New Orleans *Daily Picayune.*
New York *Evening Post.*
New York *Herald.*
New York Times.
New York *Tribune.*
New York *World.*
Raleigh *Daily Sentinel.*
Richmond *Daily Enquirer.*
Richmond *Whig.*
Toledo *Blade.*
Toledo *Daily Commercial.*
Washington *Daily Morning Chronicle.*
Washington *Daily National Intelligencer.*
Washington *Triweekly National Intelligencer.*
Wilkes' Spirit of the Times.

OTHER PUBLICATIONS

Ames, Blanche Butler, ed. *Chronicles from the Nineteenth Century: Family Letters of Blanche Butler and Adelbert Ames.* Clinton, Mass.: Colonial Press, 1957.

Ashley, Charles S. "Governor Ashley's Biography and Messages." *Contributions to the Historical Society of Montana,* 6 (1907), 143–289.

Ashley, Margaret (Paddock). "An Ohio Congressman in Reconstruction." M. A. thesis, Columbia Univ., 1916.

Badeau, Adam. *Grant in Peace: From Appomattox to Mount McGregor.* Hartford, Conn.: S. S. Scranton, 1887.

Baldensperger, Fernand. See Clemenceau, Georges.

Bancroft, Frank. See Schurz, Carl.

Barrow, Chester L. *William M. Evarts: Lawyer, Diplomat, Statesman.* Chapel Hill: Univ. of North Carolina Press, 1941.

Basler, Roy P., ed. *The Collected Works of Abraham Lincoln.* New Brunswick, N.J.: Rutgers Univ. Press, 1953. 9 vols.

Bayless, R. W. "Peter G. Van Winkle and Waitman T. Willey in the Impeachment Trial of Andrew Johnson." *West Virginia History,* 13 (Jan. 1952), 75–89.

Beale, Howard K. *The Critical Year: A Study of Andrew Johnson and Reconstruction.* 1930; rpt. New York: Ungar, 1958.

Beale, Howard K. See Welles, Gideon.

Belden, Thomas Graham, and Marva Robins Belden. *So Fell the Angels.* Boston: Little, Brown, 1956.

Benedict, Michael Les. *The Impeachment and Trial of Andrew Johnson* New York: Norton, 1973.

———. "The Right Way: Congressional Republicans and Reconstruction, 1863–1869." Ph.D. diss., Rice Univ., 1971.

———. "A New Look at the Impeachment of Andrew Johnson." *Political Science Quarterly,* 88 (Sept. 1973), 349–67.

———. "The Rout of Radicalism: Republicans and the Election of 1867." *Civil War History,* 18 (Dec. 1972), 334–44.

Berger, Raoul. *Impeachment: The Constitutional Problems.* Cambridge, Mass.: Harvard Univ. Press, 1973.

Bigelow, John. *Retrospections of an Active Life.* New York: Baker and Taylor, 1909–17. 5 vols.

Blaine, James G. *Twenty Years of Congress.* Norwich, Conn.: Henry Bill Publishing, 1884. 2 vols.

Boutwell, George S. *Reminiscences of Sixty Years in Public Affairs.* New York: McClure, Phillips, 1902. 2 vols.

———. "The Impeachment of Andrew Johnson from the Standpoint of One of the Managers of the Impeachment Trial." *McClure's Magazine,* 14 (Nov. 1899–April 1900), 171–82.

———. "Johnson's Plot and Motives." *North American Review,* 141 (Dec. 1885), 570–79.

Bowers, Claude G. *The Tragic Era: The Revolution after Lincoln.* Boston: Houghton Mifflin, 1929; rpt. 1957.

Brant, Irving. *Impeachment: Trials and Errors.* New York: Knopf, 1972.

Brigance, William Norwood. "Jeremiah Black and Andrew Johnson." *Mississippi Valley Historical Review,* 19 (Sept. 1932), 205–18.

Brock, William R. *An American Crisis: Congress and Reconstruction, 1865–1867.* London: Macmillan, 1963.

Brodie, Fawn. *Thaddeus Stevens: Scourge of the South.* New York: Norton, 1959.

Brown, George Rothwell. See Stewart, William M.

Browning, Orville Hickman. *The Diary of Orville Hickman Browning.* Theodore C. Pease and James G. Randall, eds. *Illinois Historical Collections,* 20, 22. Springfield: State Historical Library, 1927–33. 2 vols.

Bumgardner, Edward. *Life of Edmund G. Ross, the Man Whose Vote Saved a President.* Kansas City: Fielding-Turner, 1949.

Butler, Benjamin F. *Butler's Book.* Boston: A. M. Thayer, 1892.

———. *Private and Official Correspondence of Gen. Benjamin F. Butler During the Period of the Civil War.* Jessie Ames Marshall, ed. Norwood, Mass.: Plimpton, 1917. 5 vols.

Carpenter, John A. *Sword and the Olive Branch: Oliver Otis Howard.* Pittsburgh: Univ. of Pittsburgh Press, 1964.

Carter, Hodding. *The Angry Scar: The Story of Reconstruction.* Garden City, N.Y.: Doubleday, 1959.

Chase, Salmon P. *Inside Lincoln's Cabinet: The Civil War Diaries of Salmon P. Chase.* David Donald, ed. New York: Longmans, Green, 1954.

Clemenceau, Georges. *American Reconstruction, 1865–1870.* Fernand Baldensperger, ed., New York: Da Capo, 1969.

Coben, Stanley. "Northeastern Business and Radical Reconstruction: A Re-Examination." *Mississippi Valley Historical Review,* 46 (June 1959), 67–70.

Coleman, Charles H. *The Election of 1868: The Democratic Effort to Regain Control.* New York: Columbia Univ. Press, 1933.

Corson, Louis D. *The Legal Career of Waitman T. Willey.* M.A. thesis, Univ. of West Virginia, 1942.

Coulter, E. Merton. *William G. Brownlow: Fighting Parson of the Southern Highlands.* Chapel Hill: Univ. of North Carolina Press, 1937; rpt. Knoxville: Univ. of Tennessee Press, 1971.

Cowan, Frank. *Andrew Johnson, President of the United States. Reminiscences of His Private Life and Character.* 2nd ed. Greensburgh, Pa.: Oliver Publishing, 1894.

Cox, LaWanda. "The Promise of Land for the Freedmen." *Mississippi Valley Historical Review,* 45 (Dec. 1958), 413–14.

Cox, LaWanda, and John H. Cox. *Politics, Principle, and Prejudice, 1865–1866: Dilemma of Reconstruction America.* New York: Free Press, Glencoe, 1963.

———. "Andrew Johnson and His Ghost Writers." *Mississippi Valley Historical Review,* 48 (Dec. 1961), 460–79.

Cox, Samuel S. *Three Decades of Federal Legislation, 1855 to 1885.* Providence: J. A. & R. A. Reid, 1885.

Craven, Avery. *Reconstruction: The Ending of the Civil War.* New York: Holt, 1969.

Crook, William Henry. *Memories of the White House: The Home Life of Our Presidents from Lincoln to Roosevelt.* Henry Rood, ed. Boston: Little, Brown, 1911.

———. *Through Five Administrations. Reminiscences of Colonel William H. Crook, Body-Guard to President Lincoln.* Margarit Spalding Gerry, ed. New York: Harper, 1910.

Cullom, Shelby M. *Fifty Years of Public Service.* Chicago: McClurg, 1911.

Current, Richard Nelson. *Old Thad Stevens: A Story of Ambition.* Madison: Univ. of Wisconsin Press, 1942.

Curtis, Benjamin R. Jr., ed. *A Memoir of Benjamin Robbins Curtis, LL.D., With Some of His Professional and Miscellaneous Writings.* Boston: Little, Brown, 1879. 2 vols.

Davis, William W. *The Civil War and Reconstruction in Florida.* New York: Columbia Univ. Press, 1913.

Dawes, Henry. "Recollections of Stanton under Johnson." *Atlantic Monthly,* 74 (Dec. 1894), 494–564.

Dennett, Tyler, ed., *Lincoln and the Civil War in the Diaries and Letters of John Hay.* New York: Dodd, Mead, 1939.

Detroit *Post Tribune. Zachariah Chandler: An Outline Sketch of His Life and Public Services.* Detroit, 1880.

DeWitt, David Miller. *The Impeachment and Trial of Andrew Johnson.* 1903; rpt. Madison: State Historical Society of Wisconsin, 1967.

Donald, David. *Charles Sumner and the Rights of Man.* New York: Knopf, 1970.

————. *Devils Facing Zionwards,* in Grady McWhiney, ed., *Grant, Lee, Lincoln and the Radicals.* Evanston, Ill.: Northwestern Univ. Press, 1964.

————. *The Politics of Reconstruction, 1863–1867.* Baton Rouge: Louisiana State Univ. Press, 1965.

————, ed. See Chase, Salmon P.

————. "Why They Impeached Andrew Johnson." *American Heritage,* 8 (Dec. 1956), 20–26, 102–103.

Dorris, Jonathan. *Pardon and Amnesty under Lincoln and Johnson.* Chapel Hill: Univ. of North Carolina Press, 1953.

Douglass, Frederick. *Life and Times of Frederick Douglass.* Hartford: Park Publishing, 1881.

DuBois, W. E. B. *Black Reconstruction in America.* New York: S. A. Russell, 1935.

Dunning, William A. *Reconstruction: Political and Economic, 1865–1877.* New York: Harper, 1907.

————. "More Light on Andrew Johnson." *American Historical Review,* 11 (April 1906), 574–94.

Edmunds, George. "Ex-Senator Edmunds or Reconstruction and Impeachment." *Century Magazine,* 85 (April 1913), 862–64.

Ellis, Elmer, "Colorado's First Fight For Statehood, 1865–1868." *Colorado Magazine,* 8 (Jan. 1931), 23–30.

Ewing, Cortez A. "Florida Reconstruction Impeachments." *Florida Historical Quarterly,* 36 (April 1958), 298–319.

————. "Two Reconstruction Impeachments." *North Carolina Historical Review,* 15 (July 1938), 204–30.

Fessenden, Francis. *Life and Public Services of William Pitt Fessenden.* Boston: Houghton Mifflin, 1907, 2 vols.

Fleming, Walter Lynwood, ed. *Documentary History of Reconstruction.* Cleveland: A. H. Clark, 1906–1907. 2 vols.

Flower, Frank Abial. *Edwin McMasters Stanton, The Autocrat of Rebellion, Emancipation, and Reconstruction.* Akron: Saalfield, 1905.

Foster, G. Allen. *Impeached. The President Who Almost Lost His Job.* New York: Criterion Books, 1964.

Foulke, William Dudley. *Life of Oliver P. Morton.* Indianapolis: Bowen-Merrill Co., 1899. 2 vols.

Franklin, John Hope. *Reconstruction after the Civil War.* Chicago: Univ. of Chicago Press, 1961.

————, ed. See Lynch, John Roy.

Gary, Margarit Spalding. See Crook, William H.

Gillette, William. *The Right to Vote: Politics and the Passage of the Fifteenth Amendment.* Baltimore: Johns Hopkins Univ. Press, 1965.

Gorham, George C. *Life and Public Services of Edwin M. Stanton.* Boston: Houghton Mifflin, 1899. 2 vols.

Hamilton, J. G. de Roulhac. *Reconstruction in North Carolina.* New York: Columbia Univ. Press, 1914.

Henderson, John B. "Emancipation and Impeachment." *Century Illustrated Magazine,* 85 (Nov. 1912–April 1913), 196–209.

Henig, Gerald S. *Henry Winter Davis.* New York: Twayne, 1973.

Henry, Robert S. *The Story of Reconstruction.* Indianapolis: Bobbs-Merrill, 1938.

Hesseltine, William B. *Ulysses S. Grant, Politician.* New York: Dodd, Mead, 1935.

Hinsdale, Mary, ed. *Garfield-Hinsdale Letters: Correspondence between James Abram Garfield and Burke Aaron Hinsdale.* Ann Arbor: Univ. of Michigan Press, 1945.

Hoogenboom, Ari. *Outlawing the Spoils: A History of the Civil Service Reform Movement, 1865–1883.* Urbana: Univ. of Illinois Press, 1961.

Horowitz, Robert F. "James M. Ashley: A Biography." Ph.D. diss. City University of New York, 1973.

Howard, Hamilton Gay. *Civil-War Echoes: Character Sketches and State Secrets.* Washington: Howard Publ., 1907.

Howard, Oliver Otis. *Autobiography of Oliver Otis Howard, Major General, United States Army.* New York: Baker & Taylor, 1907. 2 vols.

Howe, M. A. DeWolfe. *Portrait of an Independent: Moorfield Storey, 1845–1929.* Boston: Houghton Mifflin, 1932.

Hughes, Sarah, ed. *Letters and Recollections of John Murray Forbes.* Boston: Houghton Mifflin, 1899. 2 vols.

Hunt, Gaillard. "The President's Defense: His Side of the Case, As Told by His Correspondence." *Century Magazine* 85 (Jan. 1913), 423–34.

Hyman, Harold M. *A More Perfect Union: The Impact of the Civil War and Reconstruction on the Constitution.* New York: Knopf, 1973.

————. "Johnson, Stanton, and Grant: A Reconsideration of the Army's Role in the Events Leading to Impeachment." *American Historical Review,* 66 (Oct. 1960), 85–100.

James, Joseph P. *The Framing of the Fourteenth Amendment.* Urbana: Univ. of Illinois Press, 1965.

Jellison, Charles A. *Fessenden of Maine, Civil War Senator.* Syracuse: Syracuse Univ. Press, 1962.

————. "The Ross Impeachment Vote: A Need for Reappraisal." *Southwestern Social Science Quarterly,* 41 (Sept. 1960), 150–55.

Julian, George W. *Political Recollections, 1840–1872.* Chicago: Jansen, McClurg, 1884.

————. "George W. Julian's Journal—The Assassination of Lincoln." *Indiana Magazine of History,* 11 (Dec. 1915), 324–37.

Kendrick, Benjamin B. *The Journal of the Joint Committee of Fifteen on*

Reconstruction, 39th Congress, 1865–1867. New York: Columbia Univ. Press, 1914.

Kennedy, John F. *Profiles in Courage*. New York: Pocket Books, 1957.

Konkle, Burton Alva. *The Life and Speeches of Thomas Williams, Orator, Statesman and Jurist, 1806–1872*. Philadelphia: Campion, 1905. 2 vols.

Krug, Mark M. *Lyman Trumbull: Conservative Radical*. New York: A. S. Barnes, 1965.

Kutler, Stanley I. *Judicial Power and Reconstruction Politics*. Chicago: Univ. of Chicago Press, 1968.

Lawrence, William. "The Law of Impeachment." *The American Law Register*, 6 (Sept. 1867), 641–80.

Lewis, Lloyd. *Sherman: Fighting Prophet*. New York: Harcourt, Brace, 1932.

Logan, Mrs. John A. *Reminiscences of a Soldier's Wife*. New York: Scribner's, 1913.

Lomask, Milton. *Andrew Johnson: President on Trial*. New York: Farrar, Straus, 1960.

Lonn, Ella. *Reconstruction in Louisiana After 1868*. New York: Putnam's, 1918.

Lynch, John Roy. *Reminiscences of an Active Life, The Autobiography of John Roy Lynch*. John Hope Franklin, ed. Chicago: Univ. of Chicago Press, 1970.

McCarthy, John Lockhart. "Reconstruction Legislation and Voting Alignments in the House of Representatives, 1863–1869." Ph.D. diss., Yale Univ., 1970.

McClure, Alexander K. *Recollections of Half a Century*. Salem, Mass.: Salem Press, 1902.

McCulloch, Hugh. *Men and Measures of Half a Century: Sketches and Comments*. New York: Scribner's, 1888.

McFeeley, William S. *Yankee Stepfather: General O. O. Howard and the Freedmen*. New Haven: Yale Univ. Press, 1968.

McKitrick, Eric L. *Andrew Johnson and Reconstruction*. Chicago: Univ of Chicago Press, 1960.

McPherson, Edward. *The Political History of the United States of America During the Period of Reconstruction, 1865–1870*. Washington: Philp & Solomons, 1871.

McPherson, James M. *The Struggle for Equality: Abolitionists and the Negro in the Civil War and Reconstruction*. Princeton: Princeton Univ. Press, 1964.

McWhiney, Grady. See Donald, David.

Maddex, Jack P. Jr. *The Virginia Conservatives: A Study in Reconstruction Politics*. Chapel Hill: Univ. of North Carolina Press, 1970.

Mantell, Martin E. *Johnson, Grant, and the Politics of Reconstruction*. New York: Columbia Univ. Press, 1973.

Marshall, Jessie Ames. See Butler, Benjamin F.

Milton, George Fort. *The Age of Hate: Andrew Johnson and the Radicals*. New York: Coward-McCann, 1931.

Montgomery, David. *Beyond Equality: Labor and the Radical Republicans 1862–1872.* New York: Knopf, 1967.

Moore, Clifford H. "Ohio in National Politics, 1865–1896." *Ohio State Archaeological and Historical Quarterly,* 37 (April–July 1928), 220–447.

Moore, W. G. "Notes of Colonel W. G. Moore, Private Secretary to President Johnson, 1866–1868." *American Historical Review,* 19 (Oct. 1913), 98–132.

Mordell, Albert. See Welles, Gideon.

Niven, John. *Gideon Welles: Lincoln's Secretary of the Navy.* New York: Oxford Univ. Press, 1973.

Oberholtzer, Ellis Paxson. *A History of the United States since the Civil War.* New York: Macmillan, 1917–37. 5 vols.

———. *Jay Cooke, Financier of the Civil War.* Philadelphia: G. W. Jacobs, 1907. 2 vols.

Otis, Harrison Grey. "The Causes of Impeachment." *Century Magazine,* 85 (Dec. 1912), 186–95.

Owen, Robert Dale. "Political Results from the Varioloid." *Atlantic Monthly,* 35 (June 1875), 660–70.

Patrick, Rembert W. *The Reconstruction of the Nation.* New York: Oxford Univ. Press, 1967.

Pease, Theodore C. See Browning, Orville H.

Perman, Michael. *Reunion Without Compromise: The South and Reconstruction, 1865–1868.* Cambridge, Eng.: Cambridge Univ. Press, 1973.

Poore, Ben: Perley. *Perley's Reminiscences of Sixty Years in the National Metropolis.* Philadelphia: Hubbard, 1886.

Proceedings of the National Union Republican Convention Held at Chicago, May 20 and 21, 1868. Chicago, 1868.

Randall, James G., and David Donald. *The Civil War and Reconstruction.* 2d ed. rev. Lexington, Mass.: Heath, 1969.

Rawley, James A. *Edwin D. Morgan: Merchant in Politics.* New York: Columbia Univ. Press, 1955.

Raymond, Henry J. "Extracts from the Journal of Henry J. Raymond, The Philadelphia Convention of 1866." *Scribner's Monthly,* 10 (1880), 275–80.

Rhodes, James Ford. *History of the United States from the Compromise of 1850 to the McKinley-Bryan Campaign of 1896.* New York: Macmillan, 1893–1920. 7 vols.

Richardson, James D., ed. *A Compilation of the Messages and Papers of the Presidents, 1789–1897.* Washington: Government Printing Office, 1896–99. 10 vols.

Rood, Henry. See Crook, William H.

Rose, Willie Lee. *Rehearsal for Reconstruction: The Port Royal Experiment.* Indianapolis: Bobbs-Merrill, 1964.

Rosewater, Victor. "The Political and Constitutional Development of Ne- (1893), 240–66.
braska." *Nebraska State Historical Society Transactions and Reports,* 5

Roske, Ralph J. "The Seven Martyrs?" *American Historical Review,* 64 (Jan. 1959), 323–30.

Ross, Edmund G. *History of the Impeachment of Andrew Johnson.* Santa Fe: New Mexico Printing Co., 1896.

———. "Historical Moments: The Impeachment Trial." *Scribner's Magazine,* 11 (Jan.–June 1892), 519–24.

———. "A Previous Era of Popular Madness and Its Lessons. *Forum,* 19 (1895), 595–605.

Russ, William A. "Was There Danger of a Second Civil War during Reconstruction?" *Mississippi Valley Historical Review,* 25 (June 1938), 39–58.

Salter, William. *The Life of James W. Grimes.* New York: Appleton, 1876.

Schafer, Joseph, ed. *Intimate Letters of Carl Schurz, 1841–1869.* Publications of the State Historical Society of Wisconsin Collections, 30. Madison: State Historical Society of Wisconsin, 1928.

Schuckers, J. W. *The Life and Public Services of Salmon P. Chase.* New York: Appleton, 1874.

Schurz, Carl. *The Reminiscences of Carl Schurz.* New York: McClure, 1907–1908. 3 vols.

———. *Speeches, Correspondence and Political Papers of Carl Schurz.* Frederick Bancroft, ed. New York: Putnam's, 1913. 6 vols.

Sefton, James E. *The United States Army and Reconstruction, 1865–1877.* Baton Rouge: Louisiana State Univ. Press, 1967.

Seward, Frederick W. *Seward at Washington as Senator and Secretary of State: A Memoir of His Life, with Selections from His Letters, 1861–1872.* New York: Derby and Miller, 1891.

Sheridan, Philip H. *Personal Memoirs of P. H. Sheridan.* New York: Charles L. Webster, 1888. 2 vols.

Sherman, John. *John Sherman's Recollections of Forty Years in the House, Senate, and Cabinet.* Chicago: Werner, 1895. 2 vols.

Sherwin, Oscar. *Prophet of Liberty: The Life and Times of Wendell Phillips.* New York, Bookman, 1958.

Simkins, Francis B., and Robert H. Woody. *South Carolina during Reconstruction.* Chapel Hill: Univ. of North Carolina Press, 1932.

Smith, Theodore Clarke. *The Life and Letters of James Abram Garfield.* New Haven: Yale Univ. Press, 1925. 2 vols.

Stampp, Kenneth M. *The Era of Reconstruction, 1865–1877.* New York: Knopf, 1965.

Stewart, William M. *Reminiscences of Senator William M. Stewart of Nevada.* George Rothwell Brown, ed. New York: Neale, 1908.

Stryker, Lloyd Paul. *Andrew Johnson, Profile in Courage.* New York: Macmillan, 1929.

Sumner, Charles. *The Works of Charles Sumner.* Boston: Lee & Shepard, 1870–83. 20 vols.

Swanberg, William A. *Sickles the Incredible.* New York: Scribner's, 1956; rpt. Ace Books, 1956.

Thomas, Benjamin P., and Harold M. Hyman. *Stanton: The Life and Times of Lincoln's Secretary of War.* New York: Knopf, 1962.

Thomas, Lately. *The First President Johnson: The Three Lives of the Seventeenth President of the United States.* New York: Morrow, 1968.

Thompson, Clara M. *Reconstruction in Georgia, Economic, Social, Political, 1865–1872.* New York: Columbia Univ. Press, 1915.

Thorndike, Rachel Sherman, ed. *The Sherman Letters: Correspondence between General and Senator Sherman from 1837 to 1891.* New York: Scribner's, 1894.

Townsend, E. D. *Anecdotes of the Civil War in the United States.* New York: Appleton, 1884.

Trefousse, Hans Louis. *Ben Butler: The South Called Him Beast.* New York: Twayne, 1957.

————. *Benjamin Franklin Wade: Radical Republican from Ohio.* New York: Twayne, 1963.

————. *The Radical Republicans: Lincoln's Vanguard for Racial Justice.* New York: Knopf, 1968.

————. "The Acquittal of Andrew Johnson and the Decline of the Radicals." *Civil War History*, 14 (June 1968), 148–61.

————. "Ben Wade and the Failure of the Impeachment of Johnson." *Historical and Philosophical Society of Ohio Bulletin*, 18 (Oct. 1960), 241–52.

————. "Ben Wade and the Negro." *Ohio Historical Quarterly*, 68 (April 1959), 161–76.

Truman, Benjamin C. "Anecdotes of Andrew Johnson." *Century Magazine*, 85 (Jan. 1913), 435–40.

Tucker, Glenn. *Hancock the Superb.* Indianapolis: Bobbs-Merrill, 1960.

Warren, Charles. *The Supreme Court in United States History.* Boston: Little, Brown, 1926. 2 vols.

Weed, Thurlow. *Life of Thurlow Weed Including His Autobiography and a Memoir.* Harriet A. Weed and Thurlow Weed Barnes, eds. Boston: Houghton Mifflin, 1883–84. 2 vols.

Welles, Gideon. *Diary of Gideon Welles.* Howard K. Beale, ed. New York: Norton, 1960. 3 vols.

————. *Civil War and Reconstruction: Selected Essays by Gideon Welles.* Albert Mordell, ed. New York: Twayne, 1959.

White, Horace. *The Life of Lyman Trumbull.* Boston: Houghton Mifflin, 1913.

Whitner, Evert F. "Peter Godwin Van Winkle." M.A. thesis, Univ. of West Virginia, 1946.

Whyte, James H. *The Uncivil War: Washington during the Reconstruction, 1865–1878.* New York: Twayne, 1958.

Wilson, Henry. *History of the Rise and Fall of the Slave Power in America.* Boston: James R. Osgood, 1877. 3 vols.

Winston, Robert Watson. *Andrew Johnson, Plebeian and Patriot.* New York: Holt, 1926.

Zornow, William F. " 'Bluff Ben' Wade in Lawrence, Kansas: The Issue of Class Conflict." *Ohio Historical Quarterly*, 65 (Jan. 1956), 44–52.

Index

Adjournment problem, 72, 183, 204 n. 22
Alabama, 69; and XIV Amendment, 42; conservatives in, 116–17, 119, 143; and impeachment, 142–43, 160; defeat of constitution in, 143; and Fourth Reconstruction Act, 161; readmission of, 182; effect of Johnson's acquittal on, 186–87.
Alta Vela, 150
Amnesty: Johnson's proclamations of, 9, 82, 111, 117, 182
Anthony, Henry B., 83, 135, 166, 168
Arkansas: massacre of Negroes in, 34; Reconstruction in, 69, 116; 1868 constitution of, 159; readmission of, 182
Ashley, James M., 83, 91, 110, 202 n. 52; career and character of, 49–50; impeachment efforts of, 54, 55, 56, 57, 59, 60; and judiciary committee investigation, 70, 71, 74, 106; and Conover, 76, 80; defeat of, 184–85

Babcock, James F., 86, 91
Badeau, Adam, 125
Baird, Absalom, 37
Baker, Lafayette C., 57, 105
Banks, N. P., 180
Barlow, S. M. L., 31
Beale, Howard K., 19, 199 n. 51
Benedict, Michael Les, x, 140, 183
Berger, Raoul, x
Bigelow, John, 61, 63, 82, 157, 169, 176
Bingham, John A.: and early demands for impeachment, 53; clashes with Butler, 71; and second impeachment, 129; and final impeachment, 135, 137, 138, 139, 151; one of managers, 139, 152, 162
Black, Jeremiah S., 46, 71, 150
Black codes, 13, 34
Blaine, James G., 40, 41, 72, 75

Blair, Francis P., Sr., 46, 58, 78, 79, 100, 124
Blair, Francis P., Jr., 99, 100, 124, 182
Blodgett, Foster, 118–19
Blount, William, 51
Booth, John Wilkes, 57, 71
Boutwell, George S., 9, 21; colleagues' assessment of, 22; on Reconstruction Committee, 25; and Johnson, 45, 50, 53; and first impeachment, 54, 57, 72, 75, 78; and veto of Third Reconstruction Act, 77–78; impeachment report of, 107–108, 110, 112; and second impeachment attempt, 129; and final impeachment, 138, 183; as manager, 139, 152, 162, 179; and acquittal, 170
Brant, Irving, x
Breckinridge, John C., 5
Brisbin, James A., 28, 160
Brock, William R., 18
Brodie, Fawn, 75
Bromberg, Frank G., 160
Brooks, James, 129
Browning, Orville H., 8, 16, 116, 136; on XIV Amendment, 29, 129; and removal of generals, 117; and second impeachment attempt, 129; appointment of, 197 n. 22
Brownlow, William G., 156
Bryant, William C., 58
Butler, Benjamin F., 55, 78, 83, 93, 99, 154, 176, 202 n. 52; and financial questions, 19, 25, 59, 105, 109, 149; suggested for Johnson's cabinet, 20; moderates and, 2; suggested amendment by, 28; at Pittsburgh, 39; and Negroes, 40, 49; and Grant, 49, 71, 79, 100, 148; early impeacher, 48, 52; characterization of, 48–49; continued advocacy of impeachment by, 60, 70, 71–72, 75; and

Butler, Benjamin F. (*cont.*)
summer session, 72, 74; and Conover, 76, 80; and assassination investigation, 76; and articles of impeachment, 138, 147; as manager, 139, 152, 153, 154, 155, 157, 179, 222 n. 30; optimism of, 163; and acquittal, 169–70, 183

Cabinet: Tenure of Office Act and, 44–45, 132, 145; and impeachment, 55, 56, 154, 156, 163, 171; testimony of, 70–71; and removal of Stanton and Sheridan, 81, 82, 83, 116; and Grant, 103, 127
California: election of 1867 in, 90, 93
Cameron, Simon, 53
Cameron, Stephen F., 76
Campbell, Lewis, 92
Canby, E. R. S., 103, 104
Cartter, David K., 136
Chandler, Zachariah, 61; and economic questions, 19; advocacy of impeachment by, 50, 53, 60, 163, 166; and Wade, 61–62
Chase, Salmon P.: visits Johnson, 8; and economic questions, 19; and Negro suffrage, 23; on Southern Unionists, 34; and elections of 1867, 87, 90, 95; and impeachment, 148, 149–50, 152, 165–66, 170, 171, 177, 228 n. 57; and Wade, 177–78, 228 n. 58; and Democrats, 177, 182
Chicago: Republican convention at, 170, 181, 184
Chivington massacre, 64
Churchill, John C., 70, 72, 107, 108, 111
Civil Rights Bill (1866), 24, 26; veto of, 26, 27, 48
Clemenceau, Georges, 87, 95, 113, 140, 162
Cleveland: Johnson convention at, 39
Cobb, Lucy, 71
Cohen, J. Barrett, 111
Colfax, Schuyler, 84, 95, 120, 135, 156; nominated vice president, 170, 171; possible successor of Wade, 227–28 n. 52
Colorado: question of admission of, 35, 57, 63–64, 65, 79, 203 n. 82
Columbia, District of: Negro suffrage in, 23, 43, 79
"Command of the Army" Act, 45, 68, 138, 199 n. 67
Comstock, Cyrus B., 125
Connecticut: Negro suffrage in, 23; 1866 elections in, 27; 1867 elections in, 86–87; 1868 elections in, 143, 161
Conness, John, 5
Conover, Sanford, 76, 80, 106, 206 n. 63
Cook, Burton C., 57, 70
Cook, E. G., 41

Cooke, Henry, 62
Cooper, Edmund, 108
Corbin, D. T., 186
Couch, Darius, 38
Covode, John, 70, 76, 140; impeachment resolution of, 135, 137, 139, 144, 145
Cowan, Edgar, 27, 44
Cowan, Frank, 157
Cox, James D., 95, 125, 127
Cox, John H. and LaWanda, 25, 30
Cox, Samuel S., 67
Crook, William H., 167
Cullom, Shelby M., 144
Cummings v. *Missouri*, 122
Curtis, Benjamin R., 150, 153, 154, 155, 166

Davis, Henry Winter, 8, 20, 61
Davis, Jefferson, 19, 57, 70, 74, 162
Dawes, Henry L., 110, 120, 157
Defense: Johnson's, 150, 153, 154–55, 163, 166, 167, 222 n. 46
Democratic party: and southern problem, 3; and Johnson, 21, 30, 31–32, 68, 116, 143, 145, 182, 221 n. 17; and 1867 elections, 87 ff., 95; and Pendleton Plan, 104–105; and impeachment, 107–108, 109, 114, 166, 178; and 1868 elections, 150, 182; and Chase, 177, 182; 1874 victory of, 189
Dennison, William, 36, 79
DeWitt, David M., ix, 65, 183, 206 n. 65
Dixon, James, 30, 83, 87, 91–92, 98, 161, 168
Donald, David, 218 n. 31
Doolittle, James H., 30, 62, 65, 78, 123, 135, 190
Douglas, Stephen A., 69
Douglass, Frederick, 15
Drake, Charles D., 8, 166
Dunham, Charles A. *See* Conover, Sanford
Dunning, William A., 169
Duval, T. H., 160

Edmunds, George F., 135, 166, 218 n. 28, 226 n. 35, 227 n. 36
Eldridge, Charles A., 70, 72, 106
Elections: 1865, 21; 1866, 24, 38–41; 1867, 85–97, 104, 105, 109, 115, 219 n. 43; 1868, 140–41, 148, 161, 172, 175, 182, 184, 185
Emory, William H., 138, 147, 153, 174
Enforcement Acts, 188
English, James E., 86
Evans, John, 57